DON JUAN
AND OTHER PLAYS

MOLIÈRE, whose real name was Jean-Baptiste Poquelin, was born in Paris in 1622, the son of a wealthy royal upholsterer. When he was 21 he gave up legal studies, resigned the court post obtained for him by his father, and founded, with Madeleine and Joseph Béjart and others, a dramatic company called the 'Illustre Théâtre'. In 1645, after two difficult years failing to establish a theatre in Paris, the company began to tour the provinces, performing the works of others and plays and sketches written by Molière, influenced by the Italian *commedia dell'arte*. In 1658 the troupe returned to Paris where the favour of Louis XIV's brother secured them the *Salle du Petit-Bourbon* (in the Louvre), until the company moved to the Palais Royal in 1660–1. Molière's first great comedy of manners, *Les Précieuses ridicules*, was performed in 1659 and immediately established its author's reputation for topical social satire. In 1662 Molière married Armande Béjart, Madeleine's sister, and in the same year *L'École des femmes*, a five-act verse comedy, was first performed, prompting a series of attacks and counter-attacks between Molière's company and its rivals at the Hôtel de Bourgogne. Over the next 11 years Molière wrote and performed in a number of verse and prose plays (often with interludes of ballet and music), including *Dom Juan* (1665), *Le Misanthrope* and *Le Médecin malgré lui* (1666), *George Dandin* and *L'Avare* (1668), *Le Bourgeois gentilhomme* (1670), *Les Fourberies de Scapin* (1671), and *Les Femmes savantes* (1672). *Tartuffe*, which satirized religious hypocrisy, was performed privately, condemned by ecclesiastical bodies and banned several times from 1664, before it was finally granted a public licence in 1669.

On 17 February 1673, during the fourth performance of *Le Malade imaginaire*, Molière collapsed on stage and died later the same evening.

IAN MACLEAN is a Fellow and Praelector in French at The Queen's College, Oxford. His previous publications include *Woman triumphant: feminism in French Literature 1610–52* (Oxford, 1977).

OXFORD WORLD'S CLASSICS

*For over 100 years Oxford World's Classics have brought
readers closer to the world's great literature. Now with over 700
titles—from the 4,000-year-old myths of Mesopotamia to the
twentieth century's greatest novels—the series makes available
lesser-known as well as celebrated writing.*

*The pocket-sized hardbacks of the early years contained
introductions by Virginia Woolf, T. S. Eliot, Graham Greene,
and other literary figures which enriched the experience of reading.
Today the series is recognized for its fine scholarship and
reliability in texts that span world literature, drama and poetry,
religion, philosophy and politics. Each edition includes perceptive
commentary and essential background information to meet the
changing needs of readers.*

OXFORD WORLD'S CLASSICS

MOLIÈRE

Don Juan
and Other Plays

Translated by
GEORGE GRAVELEY *and* **IAN MACLEAN**

Edited with an Introduction and Notes by
IAN MACLEAN

OXFORD
UNIVERSITY PRESS

OXFORD
UNIVERSITY PRESS

Great Clarendon Street, Oxford OX2 6DP

Oxford University Press is a department of the University of Oxford.
It furthers the University's objective of excellence in research, scholarship,
and education by publishing worldwide in

Oxford New York

Athens Auckland Bangkok Bogotá Buenos Aires Calcutta
Cape Town Chennai Dar es Salaam Delhi Florence Hong Kong Istanbul
Karachi Kuala Lumpur Madrid Melbourne Mexico City Mumbai
Nairobi Paris São Paulo Singapore Taipei Tokyo Toronto Warsaw

with associated companies in Berlin Ibadan

Oxford is a registered trade mark of Oxford University Press
in the UK and in certain other countries

Published in the United States
by Oxford University Press Inc., New York

All translations except *George Dandin* first published in
The World's Classics 1968
First published as a World's Classics paperback 1989
Reissued as an Oxford World's Classics paperback 1998
Reissued 2008

British Library Cataloguing in Publication Data

Data available

Library of Congress Cataloging in Publication Data
Molière, 1622–1673.
Don Juan and other plays / Molière; translated by George Graveley
and Ian Maclean; edited by Ian Maclean.
p. cm.—(Oxford world's classics)
includes bibliographical references.
1. Molière, 1622–1673—Translations, English. 2. Don Juan
(Legendary character)—Drama. I. Maclean, Ian, 1945–
II. Title. III. Series.
PQ1825.E5M3 1989 842'.4—dc19 89–3101

ISBN 978–0–19–954022–8

14

Printed in Great Britain by
Clays Ltd, Elcograf S.p.A.

CONTENTS

ACKNOWLEDGEMENTS

It gives me great pleasure to acknowledge both the invaluable help and encouragement given to me by my friend and colleague Roger Pearson in the preparation of these translations, and the many helpful suggestions made by Catherine Clarke of the OUP.

INTRODUCTION

ON A public holiday in about 1820, so it is reported,[1] a farmer driving a cart piled up with manuscripts and books appeared at the gates of the Bibliothèque Nationale in Paris— the repository of France's cultural heritage—and asked to speak to the Chief Librarian. He was met by a very junior member of staff, the only one left on duty, whom he told that he had on his cart 'the papers of M. de Molière' which he wished to deposit in the Library. The junior official brusquely pointed out that as the Library was closed, there was no one there to take delivery of new donations, and he instructed the farmer to return on another occasion; which he never did.

Practically none of Molière's private papers have come down to us; this anecdote, if it is true, may explain why. But Molière the playwright is known through his works and their reputation to a large part of literate humanity. Does it matter that we have no record of his private thoughts and intentions? Would we have understood his plays better if his own drafts and annotated copies survived? Critical opinion is sharply divided on these questions. On the one side, there are those (and until the Second World War, they were in the great majority) who believe in an authentic, original version of the plays; who believe that they enshrine their creator's moral outlook; who even believe that they constitute some sort of autobiography. On the other side stand those who look upon the written version of his plays as though they were musical scores, and who see performances as the realization of different possibilities in the plays rather than interpretations which diverge to a greater or lesser degree from an original 'correct' version of the play in question. It is obviously of interest to know what the first performances of Molière's plays were like, and how their creator conceived of them; but

[1] By G. Lenotre, *Existences d'artistes* (Paris, 1940), pp. 25–6.

interpretations need not be bound by such considerations, which, according to these latter critics, are neither authoritative nor conclusive. This view can easily be shown to be true at one level, for Molière's plays have sustained widely divergent interpretations. *Le Misanthrope*, for example, has been played as a near-tragedy, and as a farce of high society; *Dom Juan* as a medieval morality play, as an opera buffa, and as a comedy of manners; *Tartuffe* as an attack on religion and as a defence of good devout practices. Nearly all the plays have been acted in seventeenth-century dress, in modern dress, and in various forms of intermediate attire; they have been performed in French and in nearly every other major language; they have been translated into a myriad of cultural settings. We may still want to know how their creator envisaged his plays, but their potential for almost infinite adaptation has encouraged modern critics to speculate less about their original meaning and more about the range of significations they can sustain.

Not that Molière's own life and his relationship to his plays is of only peripheral or antiquarian interest. Their author belongs to a brilliant generation of artists and writers who flourished under the patronage of Louis XIV and others in an age which marks one of the high points of European culture. Nor was Molière just a writer of plays; he was also an actor, almost certainly the great comic character actor of his day, whose performances were characterized by a wide range of facial expressions, expressive gestures and body language, and a slight speech impediment which rendered him unsuitable for tragic parts. He was moreover a theatrical director and manager of a troupe in whom he inspired deep loyalty, with twenty-five years of experience behind him by the time he wrote and performed *Les Fourberies de Scapin*. To realize the potential for meaning his plays possess it is necessary to appreciate how hardened a campaigner their creator was. He began his career in the theatre as a young man of solid bourgeois stock who abandoned potential careers both in his father's trade as tapestry-maker and upholsterer and in the law to enter the socially deprecated and financially risky acting profession; he survived a disastrous attempt to establish a theatre in Paris which ended in debt and voluntary exile from the capital; for fifteen years he toured the French provinces, providing both private performances for rich patrons in their châteaux and public performances in the towns and cities of southern France; his fourteen years in Paris were spent in sometimes violent theatrical and literary feuding, in the pursuit of royal patronage and public favour, and in clashes with legal and ecclesiastical authorities. More than most writers of his glittering generation, this arch-satirist was subjected to vituperative and scurrilous personal satire; nearly all his actions became a matter of public scandal and controversy. Part of this may be blamed on his enemies, notably the actors of the rival theatre, the Hôtel de Bourgogne, who, among other things, managed to sabotage his attempts to equip his theatre at the Palais-Royal for fourteen years; part, perhaps, can be attributed to Molière's own disputatious character (although we cannot be certain of this); but much of it is to do with the nature of the audiences for whom he produced his plays, with his choice of literary form, and his choice of subject matter.

Molière's plays were produced for two very different clients: the King and his Court, and the Parisian public. When Molière returned to the capital in 1658 after his provincial peregrinations, the Court was just coming back to life after the trauma of the civil wars earlier in the decade, and salon society was flourishing. The young king, whose personal reign was to begin in 1661, had a pronounced taste for lavish festivities, with ballet, opera and drama, and encouraged the less austere faction at court to partake with him in such entertainment. Throughout his career, Molière gratified this desire, first in the form of farces and three-act comedies, then increasingly in the form of spectacles which incorporated music and dancing. Of these *Les Fâcheux* of

1661 is the earliest example; *Le Bourgeois gentilhomme* and *George Dandin* are both later instances of the playwright's willingness to satisfy such a demand. The Court clearly enjoyed satire of the bourgeoisie and its traditional vices: meanness, cowardice, drabness, lack of taste, paternal tyranny; these are represented in a series of five-act plays, including *L'École des femmes*, *L'Avare*, and *Tartuffe*. Parisians seem to have enjoyed these plays also, even though the satire was directed against at least part of the audience. Ballet interludes were omitted from plays such as *George Dandin* to adapt them for performance in Molière's theatre, and a number of plays whose target was the aristocracy were produced with varied success: *Le Misanthrope*, *Dom Juan*, *Les Précieuses ridicules*. Molière also paid attention to shifts in social attitudes and the social order: the last-named farce of 1659 established his reputation for topical satire, which he developed in *Les Fâcheux* (a catalogue of court bores), *Le Misanthrope* (a satire of salon life), and *Le Bourgeois gentilhomme*. Molière's appeal to his two publics—the Court and Paris—is thus clearly reflected in his output, though whether he himself represents bourgeois or aristocratic ideology remains a vexed issue.

The age in which Molière was writing is often described as classical; from this it has sometimes been inferred that Molière's drama incorporates timeless aesthetic and moral values, and perhaps also a timeless comic vision of human folly. His five-act verse comedies are often seen as modern versions of Plautus or Terence; and his subjects—the miser, the misanthropist, the hypochondriac, the social climber—seen as human universals. Such a view disguises the great variety of Molière's choice of form, his inventiveness in combining heterogeneous elements to make a single dramatic unit, and his willingness to experiment. Farce, Italian comedy, opera, burlesque, and ballet are all ingredients in his diverse output, and all have distinctive contributions to make to the range of interpretations to which his plays are open. Molière the actor and the producer of plays in the theatre wrote scripts which he knew he could perform; many of the elements that allow them to be enjoyed still today are drawn from the comic repertoire of European drama. Thus, comic routines appear frequently: quid pro quos, misunderstandings, unmaskings, dramatic irony, brusque reversals of fortune by which the trickster becomes the tricked, ingenious scheming and roguery. Very often characters who are obliged to live together are as ill-assorted as possible; the miser has a spendthrift for a cook (*L'Avare*), the man obsessed with honesty a malicious gossip for a mistress (*Le Misanthrope*), the pretentious bourgeois an unaffected and plain-speaking wife (*Le Bourgeois gentilhomme*), the superstitious valet a freethinker for a master (*Dom Juan*). Those who proclaim a certain philosophy of life are shown to be hypocrites or to be unable to match their practice to their theory: the devout counsellor who recommends asceticism is 'big and fat, with a red mouth and a ruddy complexion' (*Tartuffe*); philosophy masters praise temperance and lose their temper (*Le Bourgeois gentilhomme*); plain-speaking men are obliged to descend to meaningless social compliments (*Le Misanthrope*); jealous, repressive guardians are reduced to promising freedom to their wards (*L'École des femmes*). These formal features of comedy are complemented by sophisticated stagecraft: contemporaries remarked on Molière's careful dramatic choreography and his ability to extract visual comedy from the situations which he engineers on stage. If one adds to these ingredients a delight in the comedy of language itself—puns, malapropisms (*avant la lettre*), abuse of jargon, illogicality, neologisms, wit, paradox—one has some idea of the rich storehouse of techniques which Molière exploits, and the vigour of the traditions on which he was drawing. 'Classical' seems too austere and lofty a description for something as lively and vibrant as this.

Nor is it clear that his comedies address universal or timeless human predicaments. Molière may encourage us to believe that such are his subjects by the choice he makes of

titles for his plays, but he also claims in one of his prefaces
that a comic playwright should address himself to the specific
vices and follies of his own age. With a sharp, opportunist
eye and a quick appreciation of the social and literary
divisions of the capital, Molière began his examination of
contemporary society with a savage attack on the pretentious-
ness of the female denizens of bourgeois salons. The *Précieuses ridicules* is an implicit criticism of the vogue for
romances which earned him the opprobrium of one influential literary clique in Paris; the same clique seems to have
been behind the long public debate about the merits of
L'École des femmes of 1662. With *Tartuffe*, Molière's onslaught
on the hypocrisy of his age becomes over-bold: by attacking
implicitly the religious hierarchy of his day, he delighted the
pleasure-seeking section of the Court but infuriated the *bien-
pensants* who succeeded in banning the play from public
performance for five years. When he turned his attention to
the effect of money on social divisions, notably in *Le Bourgeois
gentilhomme* and *George Dandin*, his bourgeois public were
affronted in turn. The topicality of his plays demonstrates
both his willingness to treat controversial subjects and his
own skill and penchant for contemporary satire.

His observation of society took in also the other great
division which lends itself well to comic treatment: that
between the sexes. The upsurge in salon activity and the
feminism of some of their members had brought into public
consciousness the issues of marriage, social freedom and
education for women; demographic changes, which led to a
sharp rise in the number of independent widows free to
dispose of their own hand and their fortune in the course of
the century, and Counter-Reformation teaching on marriage
all contributed to the debate concerning women, on which
Molière comments in *Les Précieuses ridicules*, *L'École des
femmes*, and *Les Femmes savantes*. Marriage had always, of
course, been a subject for comedy; both as its culmination for
the young lovers who are eventually united after overcoming

—

obstacles in the form of parents, guardians or lack of money, and as motif for the portrayal of ill-matched couples: the farmer with the nobleman's daughter eager for the society of the capital (*George Dandin*), the social climber with the down-to-earth spouse (*Le Bourgeois gentilhomme*), the ineffectual bourgeois with traditional views married to a strong-minded bluestocking (*Les Femmes savantes*). In Molière's plays, a wide range of attitudes to matrimony, to women's education, to their rôle in society, to their pretensions to literary creation, are represented; they constitute the pieces of a jigsaw from which successive generations of readers have tried to form a composite coherent picture. Such an undertaking, however, seems doomed to failure: why should an opportunistic play-wright in search of controversial material limit himself to a single view or a consistent line? Education for women is implicitly defended in *L'École des femmes*; its excesses are attacked in *Les Femmes savantes*. Women's literary creativity in the form of romances is satirized in *Les Précieuses ridicules*; the restrictions of women to such domestic activities as needle-work and sewing and their exclusion from education are impugned in *L'École des femmes*. Nowhere in his writings does Molière undertake to propose or condemn unequivocally one or another view; everywhere there is evidence that he sees the comic possibilities of a myriad of attitudes and beliefs.

The question which has most often been asked about Molière the playwright is whether he has a message. After all, it is averred, he begins one of his defences of his play *Le Tartuffe* with the words 'the duty of comedy is to correct men while entertaining them'; this seems proof enough of an underlying moral purpose. But, as proof, it is not without its difficulties. It occurs in a letter defending the play from the accusation of impiety, and as such is special pleading, not disinterested comment. That Molière was well aware of the tricks and rhetorical devices associated with prefaces and apologetic letters is clear from his amusing parody of a literary preface in *Les Précieuses ridicules* (pp. 3–4). Not only this: the word 'correct' is not without its ambiguity. You can 'correct' men by setting them straight with moral advice; but you can also 'correct' them by offering them rules for social survival which have nothing to do with abstract ethical principles. Moreover, you can also 'correct' them by adjusting their vision of social reality or human nature, without any desire to bring about a change in their behaviour. It is worthy of note that none of Molière's central characters reform themselves; and that in an early play, *L'École des maris* (1661), the successful suitor Ariste ('the best man') suggests that social conformism is more important than complete and unbending philosophical rectitude. Clearly, a comic writer presents excessive characters who carry their beliefs too far, and hence he implicitly recommends moderation in all things; but moderation is not funny, whereas excess can be made so. Comic drama has implicit moral recommendations beyond moderation: reciprocal love always defeats the imposition of a relationship which only one party desires; children nearly always get the better of repressive or tyrannical parents; love is naturally associated in most cases with youth. The standard comic plot—young man desires young woman, who desires him; there is an obstacle which after various trials and tribulations is overcome—predisposes comic playwrights to a compensatory view of society, in which, during the course of the performance, youth gets the better of age, servant of master, wife of husband (or hen-pecked husband of domineering wife), child of parent, client of doctor or lawyer. All of these ethical lessons may be extracted from some part or other of Molière's plays; but so may their converse. Age gets the better of (relative) youth in *L'École des maris*; the master gets the better of the servant for most of *Dom Juan*; the scheming wife gets the better of the husband against all justice and equity in *George Dandin*.

It is easier to extract a fairly consistent social message from the corpus of Molière's plays. It seems that those who follow fashion in a moderate way, who embrace current social

practices, but temperately, who are modest in their expecta-
tions of their fellow men, and charitable when able to exercise
charity and restraint, come off best: Ariste in *L'École des
maris*, Cléante in *Tartuffe*, Philinte in *Le Misanthrope*. But
even this argument cannot be pressed too hard, for in
performances over the centuries Ariste has been legitimately
presented as a doddering voluptuary, Cléante as an ineffectual bore, and Philinte as a disloyal friend. The so-called
raisonneur of Molière's drama—the moderate social conformist with humanitarian leanings—is an invention of those
critics who see a moral purpose as a *sine qua non* of serious
literary artefacts. A more bracing and less comforting view
would make of Molière a relativist in ethical matters, for
whom *raisonner* does not mean 'to speak with wisdom' but
rather 'to speak (perhaps at length) in one's own interest'. If
characters who do this are paired, as they are in many plays,
then the substance of the arguments they represent loses all
respectability, and a low, even cynical depiction of human
nature emerges. In *L'École des femmes*, a man obsessed with
female fidelity, who puts forward a violently repressive theory
of how to treat women (Arnolphe), is pitted in conversation
against Chrysalde, a dishonoured cuckold who is in favour of
treating women liberally and overlooking the dishonour they
bring to their husbands. In *Dom Juan*, a free thinker engages
in theological debate with his superstitious valet; in *Le
Misanthrope*, a man who wants to be different from everyone
else is locked in mental combat with the conformist; in *L'École
des maris*, the sexagenarian liberal man of fashion in the form
of narrow-waisted doublets and tight shoes argues with his
repressive forty-year-old brother who is in favour of sensible
and healthy clothes. No 'correct' view may emerge from these
debates, although in nearly all cases one party comes off well
at the end of the play, and the other is the defeated comic
butt; instead, one may discern here a sophisticated and
mature taste for the depiction of human folly, selfishness, and
pretension.

A different view of Molière the playwright would stress not the rehearsal or even recommendation of moral values but rather his comic vision; that particular ability to reproduce configurations of words, actions, and attitudes and an interplay of appearance and reality which provoke laughter on one level and represent on another a sharp, even painful perception of the paradoxes and tensions of human existence. George Dandin, the cuckolded husband against whom appearances always tell, exclaims: 'I'm beside myself with rage to be found wrong when I'm in the right'; Alceste, the misanthropist, declares bitterly on losing his lawsuit that 'Justice is on my side, but I've lost my case'; Arnolphe, the repressive guardian, can do nothing to prevent the success of his rival's schemes even though he has forewarning of them; Sosie, in *Amphitryon*, finds it difficult to come to terms with his crisis of identity when he discovers that he has a double. In one play, *Sganarelle ou le cocu imaginaire*, all four main protagonists are victims of their plausible misperceptions of reality; in many others, substance and shadow, true and false, word and spirit, real and imaginary, commingle in subtle and surprising ways. The very language of the characters can lose fixed or determinate sense: Tartuffe uses truth-telling to establish a lie—the lie of his piety; Alceste, equally wedded (though for different motives) to plain speaking, becomes at times embroiled in the language of social convention; Dom Juan, the seducer and hypocrite, persuades his victims— country girls, nuns of noble birth, merchants, even his father—to accept as sincere sentiments uttered only for the effect they will have on their receivers. It is on such features of the plays that Molière's well-deserved reputation as a profound comic dramatist rests.

Is Molière a moralist? Does he portray his society and human nature faithfully, or does he merely exploit the comic potential of what he saw around him? Is he original? Did he simply pander to royal or public taste or did he attempt to put forward a serious critique of his contemporaries? How exactly did he envisage the performance of his plays? Such questions are inevitably raised when we read his plays or see them performed, and it is a pity that the farmer with his cartload of Molière's intimate reflections did not return to the Bibliothèque Nationale to satisfy our curiosity on these points. But whatever we might have learned from such a glimpse into Molière's mind, we still have a body of eminently performable, funny, adaptable dramatic scripts to enjoy. Their appeal and their humour have not yet dimmed, and it is up to us to supply from our imagination the flesh and detail on Molière's comic skeleton.

A CHRONOLOGY OF MOLIÈRE

1622   Baptism, on 15 January, of Jean-Baptiste Poquelin, son of Jean Poquelin, royal upholsterer and tapestry-maker, at the church of St Eustache in Paris.

1631–9[?]   Jean-Baptiste Poquelin at the Collège de Clermont in Paris; he completes his education in the humanities.

1640[?]   Begins university law studies.

1643   Abandons the law and renounces his association with his father's trade; together with members of the Béjart family, he founds the 'Illustre Théâtre' troupe and hires a theatre in Paris.

1644   Adopts the name 'de Molière' and becomes the head of the troupe.

1645–58   After difficult beginnings, the Illustre Théâtre abandons the attempt to found a theatre in Paris and tours in the provinces, playing mainly in the south of France.

1658   Return to Paris, under the protection of Louis XIV's brother, Monsieur (who promises an annual pension but never pays it). The troupe is now known as the 'Troupe de Monsieur', and performs both comedy and tragedy in the Salle du Petit-Bourbon, which it shares with Italian actors; it also performs in court festivities and private houses.

1659   First performance, on 18 November, of the *Précieuses ridicules*, a topical satire which draws attention to the troupe.

1660   The troupe prepare the move to the Salle du Palais Royal: first performance of *Sganarelle ou le cocu imaginaire*, a successful one-act comedy.

1661   First performances of a heroic comedy *Dom Garcie de Navarre* (a failure), *L'École des maris* (a success), and *Les Fâcheux*, a three-act comedy commissioned for the court by the Chancellor, Fouquet. Molière attracts the attention of the king.

1662   Marriage to Armande Béjart, sister of Madeleine Béjart, Molière's rejected mistress (contemporary gossip claims that Armande is the daughter, not the sister, of Madeleine). First performance of *L'École des femmes*, a highly successful five-act verse comedy.

1663   Long public debate about the merits of *L'École des femmes*, carried on for the most part in the form of short plays produced by Molière's troupe (the *Critique de l'École des femmes* and the *Impromptu de Versailles*) and their rivals at the Hôtel de Bourgogne, who specialize in performing tragedies.

1664   Molière's first child, Louis, is born (he is to die on 10 November in the same year) and is baptized at the church of St Germain l'Auxerrois with the King as one godparent. A number of plays produced for the court, including an incomplete version of *Tartuffe*, which is immediately banned as sacrilegious, but which is commissioned for private peformance by influential members of the nobility.

1665   *Dom Juan* first performed; Molière's troupe is now called the 'Troupe du Roi' and receives a substantial royal pension. Molière's second child, Esprit Magdaleine, is born on 3 August.

1666   First performance of *Le Misanthrope* (a five-act verse comedy), *Le Médecin malgré lui* and *Mélicerte* (a three-act pastoral comedy).

1667   One public performance of *Tartuffe*, followed by its renewed condemnation and banning by legal and ecclesiastical authorities.

1668   First performances of *Amphytrion* (a three-act comedy), *George Dandin* (with an accompanying ballet at Versailles; without a ballet at the Salle du Palais-Royal), and *L'Avare*.

1669   *Tartuffe* finally is granted a licence for public performance; first performance of *Monsieur de Pourceaugnac* (a three-act comedy-ballet).

1670   First performances of *Les Amants magnifiques* (a three-act comedy-ballet) and *Le Bourgeois gentilhomme*.

1671   First performances of *Psyché* (a five-act tragedy-ballet), *Les Fourberies de Scapin* and *La Comtesse d'Escarbagnas* (a one-act comedy).

1672   First performance of *Les Femmes savantes*, a five-act comedy.

1673   Performance of *Le Malade imaginaire*, a three-act comedy-ballet; at the fourth performance, on 17 February, Molière collapses on stage and dies later in the evening.

A NOTE ON THE SELECTION
AND THE TRANSLATION

THE plays in this collection were all written in prose (although there is some evidence that Molière may have intended, if he had had time, to produce *The Miser* [*L'Avare*] in verse). They constitute a cross-section of Molière's output: *Precious provincials* (*Les Précieuses ridicules*, 1659) is a one-act farce; *Dom Juan* of 1665 is a five-act 'machine' play (that is, using special effects such as nodding statues, ghostly apparitions and the gates of hell); *The Would-be Gentleman* (*Le Bourgeois gentilhomme*, 1670) and *George Dandin* of 1668 are comedy-ballets, although *George Dandin* was also produced as a three-act comedy with elements of farce, in which category *The Reluctant Doctor* (*Le Médecin malgré lui*, 1666) and *Scapin the Schemer* (*Les Fourberies de Scapin*, 1671) also fall. *The Miser* of 1666 is a five-act comedy of manners. This collection therefore manifests different facets of Molière's talent as a playwright throughout his Parisian period (1658–73).

The present volume is the result of periodic revision. George Graveley translated *Les Précieuses ridicules*, *Le Médecin malgré lui*, and *Les Fourberies de Scapin* in 1916, and *L'Avare* in 1919; he revised all these versions in 1945. In 1948 he added translations of *Dom Juan* and *Le Bourgeois gentilhomme*. I have undertaken to revise his translations, some of which were written in the style of restoration comedy; I have tried to render these and the others into modern prose, and have adjusted Graveley's choices of expostulations, prepositions, and colloquial idiom to the same end. The translation of *George Dandin* is my own. All these plays are to a large degree self-explanatory: notes have been kept to a minimum. The roman numerals in the margin indicate the numbers of the scenes in the original French version.

PRECIOUS PROVINCIALS

[*Les Précieuses ridicules*]

Les Précieuses ridicules, *comedy in one act, was first produced in Paris at the Théâtre du Petit-Bourbon on 18 November 1659, with Molière in the part of Mascarille.*

PREFACE

What a strange custom it is that you can appear in print against your wishes. Nothing seems to me more unjust, and I look upon this as the least forgivable form of violence against the person.

Not that I want here to act the part of the modest and honourable author and pour scorn on my own play. It would be inappropriate for me to insult Parisian society by accusing it of having applauded a play bereft of qualities. As the public is the absolute judge of such works as these, it would be impertinent of me to contradict it; even if I had held a very low opinion of *Les Précieuses ridicules* before it was performed, I am obliged to confess now that it has some merit because so many people have spoken well of it. But as the qualities which were found in it depend in large part on stage-play and tone of voice, I thought it important that it was not deprived of these features, and I formed the view that its success in the theatre was great enough for it to be left at that. I was determined therefore that it would be only seen by candle-light, so that no-one could quote a certain well-known proverb against me;* I did not want it to pass out of the theatre and into the bookshop. I was, however, not able to prevent this, and have suffered the misfortune of seeing an illicitly obtained copy of my play fall into the hands of publishers, together with a licence to print which also was not obtained in the proper way. In vain I cried 'O tempora! O mores!';* I was persuaded that I myself had to publish or sue, and as litigation is even worse than publication, I have bowed to fate and consented to something that would have happened whether I had liked it or not.

Heavens, what a strange business it is to publish a book: how green an author is the first time he is published! If only I had been given the time, I would have looked to my reputation and taken all those precautions that the writing fraternity (now my colleagues) habitually takes on such occasions. As well as some great nobleman whom I would have designated without his consent as the protector of my book, and whose generosity I would have prompted with an eloquent dedicatory letter, I would have set out to produce a fine, learned preface (I am not short of books which would have supplied me with erudite information about tragedy and comedy, about the etymology of the words, and about their origins, their definition and so on.) I would also have spoken to my friends who, to commend the book to the public, would have been willing to provide me with some lines of French or Latin verse. I have even got acquaintances who would have praised me in Greek; and, as everyone knows, a Greek eulogy at the beginning of a book is quite remarkably effective. But I am being published without being given the opportunity of obtaining due recognition; indeed, I have not even had the chance to say a few words to justify my intentions as the author of the play. I would have liked to have shown that it never oversteps the limits of decent and acceptable satire; that excellent customs are subject to being aped by poor imitators who deserve to be exposed to ridicule; and that comedy has always dealt with bad copies of good and accomplished things. Furthermore, that just as learned doctors and brave soldiers have not taken it into their heads to take umbrage at the quack or the braggard soldier of comedy, any more than judges are affronted by Trivelino* when he appears on stage, or royalty by seeing princes and kings satirized in the theatre, so also genuine ladies of taste and discernment would be wrong to take offence when those who imitate them so poorly are mocked in my play. But as I have said, I have hardly been given the time to breathe, and my publisher M. de Luynes is eager to take these sheets to the binder: so be it, as it is God's will.

CHARACTERS

LA GRANGE }
DU CROISY } *rejected suitors*

GORGIBUS, *a bourgeois*

MADELON, *daughter of Gorgibus*

CATHOS, *niece of Gorgibus*

MAROTTE, *their maid*

ALMANZOR, *their lackey*

THE MARQUIS DE MASCARILLE, *valet of La Grange*

THE VICOMTE DE JODELET, *valet of Du Croisy*

TWO PORTERS

NEIGHBOURS

MUSICIANS

*The scene is set in Paris, in the house
of Gorgibus*

[*Enter* LA GRANGE *and* DU CROISY.

DU CROISY. Seigneur La Grange . . .

LA GRANGE. Yes?

DU CROISY. A word with you; if you can speak without laughing.

LA GRANGE. Well?

DU CROISY. Do you feel flattered by our reception?

LA GRANGE. Have we any reason to be, either of us?

DU CROISY. Not exactly.

LA GRANGE. I confess I am astounded. Did you ever see two jumped-up girls from the provinces give themselves such superior airs; or know of two men more contemptuously received than we were? They scarcely condescended to ask us to sit down. And how they whispered and yawned and rubbed their eyes, and asked one another the time! Their whole conversation was: *Yes* and *No*. If we had been the very scum of the earth they couldn't have treated us worse.

DU CROISY. You seem to take it very much to heart.

LA GRANGE. I certainly do; so much so indeed that I will be revenged for their impertinence. I know why they despise us. These precious mannerisms have not infected only Paris; they have spread into the provinces as well, and these ridiculous misses have caught a dose of them. They are a kind of compound of affectedness and coquetry. I know the sort of man they would admire; and, if you will back me up, we will play them a trick that will show them their mistake, and teach them a little more discrimination for the future.

DU CROISY. What are you going to to?

LA GRANGE. I have a valet named Mascarille, who passes in the eyes of many for a kind of wit; for you know how cheaply that sort of reputation can be got nowadays. He is a fantastical fellow whose ambition is to be taken for a man of rank and fashion, prides himself on his gallant behaviour and his verses, and holds all other lackeys in such contempt that he calls them vulgar oafs.

DU CROISY. Well, and how will you make use of him?

LA GRANGE. I'll tell you. But let's get away from here first.

II   [*Enter* GORGIBUS.

GORGIBUS. Ah, so you have seen my niece and daugher, gentlemen? All goes well, I hope? May something come of your visit?

LA GRANGE. They can answer that question, Sir, better than we can. All that remains for us is to thank you for your kindness, and to wish you a very good day.

DU CROISY. A very good day.

[*They go out*

GORGIBUS. Hm! They don't seem pleased at all. What can have upset them, I wonder? I'd better look into this. Ho, there!

III   [*Enter* MAROTTE.

MAROTTE. Monsieur?

GORGIBUS. Where are your mistresses?

MAROTTE. Upstairs in their room.

GORGIBUS. What are they doing?

MAROTTE. Making face cream.

GORGIBUS. There's too much of this face-creaming. Tell them to come down at once.

[MAROTTE *goes out*

These minxes with their face cream want to ruin me, I think. Everywhere I go I see nothing but white of egg, skin lotion, and a lot more concoctions that I don't know the use of. Since we've been here they have used up the fat of at least a dozen pigs, and four valets could live like kings on the sheep's trotters they require.

[*Enter* MADELON *and* CATHOS.   IV

Of course I don't complain about your squandering a fortune on greasing your snouts! But may I ask what you have said to these gentlemen that made them go off in such dudgeon? Didn't I tell you to receive them as your future husbands?

MADELON. My dear father, how can you expect us to endure the untutored manners of such people?

CATHOS. How, my dear uncle, could a girl with the smallest pretentions to taste put up with them?

GORGIBUS. And what fault can you find with them?

MADELON. So very gallant, to be sure! What? To mention marriage in the very first sentence?

GORGIBUS. And what would you have them begin with? An invitation to be a concubine? Isn't it to your advantage as much as mine for you to be married? Could anything be more satisfactory? And is not their desire for this holy estate a proof that their intentions are honourable?

MADELON. Oh, my dear father, what you say is the last word in bourgeois vulgarity. I am positively ashamed to hear you. You really must try to set your ideas to a more fashionable tune.

GORGIBUS. A curse on your tunes, and your songs too! I say that marriage is a holy and blessed estate; and it is the mark of a gentleman to begin by proposing it.

MADELON. Heavens above! If everyone were like you a novel would soon reach its last page. A nice thing it would be if Cyrus married Mandane in the first chapter, and Aronce was married to Clélie as a matter of course!*

GORGIBUS. What has all that got to do with it?

MADELON. My dear father, my cousin will tell you as well as I that marriage should come only after a series of adventures. A suitor, to be agreeable, must express the finest

sentiments. He should be a master of the delicacy, tenderness, and passion; and his wooing should run on recognized lines. He should first see the object of his affections
in church, or during her afternoon walk, or at some public
function; or Fate, in the shape of a relation or friend, may
lead him to her home, from whence he departs in a
melancholy dream. At first he keeps the loved one in
ignorance of his passion, but visits her frequently, and
never fails to pose some question about the passion of love
to intrigue the wits of the company. At last the day of
declaration arrives, which should usually take place in
some garden walk, at a short but discreet distance from the
rest of the company. Our face instantly blushes scarlet, and
with haughty indignation we banish the suitor from our
presence. Little by little he finds means to make his peace,
accustoms us gradually to the outpourings of his passion,
and at last draws from us that confession which it is such an
agony to make. After that come adventures; rivals who try to
interfere with a settled attachment, the persecution of parents, jealousy caused by mutual misunderstanding, complaints, despair, abduction and what follows. That is how
these things are managed in the best style, and if the affair is
to be refined they are quite indispensable. But to come point
blank to the altar, to reduce one's courtship to the signing of
the marriage contract, and literally to start at the wrong end
of the novel! Positively, my dear father, nothing could be so
vulgar, and the very idea of it nauseates me.

GORGIBUS. Ridiculous new-fangled rubbish!

CATHOS. I assure you, uncle, what my cousin tells you is
quite true. How could one give a favourable reception to
persons entirely devoid of refinement? I'll vow they have
never heard of the *Map of the Tender Passion;* and that
Billets-doux, Delicate Attentions, Sweet Nothings, and *A Pretty
Copy of Verses* are unknown worlds to them*. You can see
that in their very bearing. They have nothing of that

mysterious quality which at once wins one's good opinion. To pay a lover's call in breeches without canons, a hat sporting no feathers at all, a badly combed wig, and a suit wholly deprived of ribbons from top to bottom! Heavens above! What suitors are these? Such mean apparel! Such barren conversation! One can't put up with that. Even their neckbands, I noticed, were of inferior make; and their breeches unfashionably narrow.

GORGIBUS. I think they're both mad. I cannot understand a word of such gibberish. Now, look here, Cathos, and you too, Madelon . . .

MADELON. Oh, for pity's sake, father, do stop using those uncouth names.

GORGIBUS. Uncouth names? Were they not given to you in baptism?

MADELON. Good God, how vulgar you are! It is a perpetual wonder to me how you ever had a daughter of such wit. Has anyone in good society ever uttered such words as *Cathos* and *Madelon*? And will not even you admit that one of them alone would be enough to bring the best novel in the world into disrepute?

CATHOS. Really, my dear uncle, an ear of any delicacy suffers agony at the sound of such words. But the name of Polixena which my cousin has chosen, and that of Aminta which I have myself adopted have a grace which surely even your ears can appreciate.

GORGIBUS. Now listen to me. I have only one word to say, and that is final. I will not hear of your having different names from those which were given you by your godfathers and godmothers. As for the the gentlemen in question, I am acquainted with their families and with their means; and I am fully resolved that you shall submit to having them as your husbands. I am tired of having you on my hands. The welfare of two girls is too heavy a responsibility for a man of my age.

—

CATHOS. Well, uncle, all I can say is that I consider marriage an extremely indelicate state. How can one bear the thought of getting into bed with a naked man?

MADELON. Do allow us a short breathing space among the smart world of Paris. We have only just arrived. Let us unravel at leisure the plot of our novel, and do not hurry us so fast to the conclusion.

GORGIBUS [aside]. They are clearly as mad as hatters. [Aloud]. Now, for the last time, I will hear no more of this nonsense. I intend to be absolute master in my own family; and, to put an end to all further discussion, you will both of you be married within a few months, or I swear you'll find yourselves in a nunnery.

[He goes out

V   CATHOS. Heavens, my dear, how deeply your father's soul is embedded in brute matter! How dull his intelligence! How unenlightened his soul!

MADELON. What can I say, my dear? I own I am quite ashamed of him. I can hardly believe I am really his daughter. I should not be at all surprised if, one day, some lucky chance revealed that I was of more aristocratic birth.

CATHOS. I could well believe it. Yes, it is extremely probable. I, too, when I think of myself . . .

VI   [Enter MAROTTE].

MAROTTE. A lackey has come to know if you are at home. He says his master would like to pay you a visit.

MADELON. Learn, you foolish child, to express yourself less vulgarly. Say: *There is a chattel here who enquires whether it is your pleasure to be visible.*

MAROTTE. Oh, Lud, I don't understand latin; and I never learnt wordology, like you, out of *Cirrus the Great**.

MADELON. Idiot! How insufferable! Who is he, the master of this lackey?

MAROTTE. The Marquis de Mascarille, he said.

MADELON. My dear! A Marquis! Yes. Go and say that we may be seen. No doubt it is some wit who has heard of us by repute.

CATHOS. Quite so, my dear.

MADELON. We must receive him down here rather than in our room; but at least let us give a final touch to our hair, so as not to belie our reputation. Quick, fly, fetch beauty's counsellor.

MAROTTE. 'Pon my soul, I don't know what kind of beast that may be! You'll have to speak Christian if you want me to understand you.

CATHOS. Bring us the mirror, ignoramus that you are! And take care not to contaminate the glass with the reflection of your visage.

> [*They go out. Two* PORTERS *carry in the* MARQUIS DE   VII
> MASCARILLE *in a chair. They stick in the doorway*].

MASCARILLE. Hold, fellows, hold! La, la, la, la, la, la. I think these scoundrels want to break my limbs by bumping against the walls and paving stones.

1ST PORTER. Damn it! It's the doorway that's so narrow, and you told us to carry you inside.

MASCARILLE. I should say so indeed. Would you have me expose the fine fettle of my feathers to the inclemency of this rainy weather, you rogues, and leave the imprint of my shoes in mud? Go, take your chair away.

2ND PORTER. Pay us then, if you please, Sir.

MASCARILLE. Eh? What?

2ND PORTER. I ask you, Sir, to give us our money, if you please.

MASCARILLE [*striking him*]. How, rascal? Demand money from a man of my rank?

2ND PORTER. Are poor men paid with that? Can we dine off your rank?

MASCARILLE. I'll teach you to know your place. These scum would dare to bandy words with me!

1ST PORTER [*taking one of the chair poles*]. Come, pay us at once.

MASCARILLE. What?

1ST PORTER. I say I mean to have my money at once.

MASCARILLE. Well, that is quite reasonable.

1ST PORTER. Be quick about it, then.

MASCARILLE. Ah, now that is the way to talk. But your mate is a rascal who doesn't know how to talk properly. There! Are you satisfied now?

1ST PORTER. No. I'm not. You struck my mate, and ... [*Raising the pole*].

MASCARILLE. Gently! Gently! [*He gives* 2ND PORTER *money*]. Here is to pay for the blow. A man can get anything from me if he goes the right way about it. Go now, and be sure to come back later to carry me to the Louvre in time for the *petit coucher*.*

VIII   [*The* PORTERS *go out.* MAROTTE *enters*.

MAROTTE. My mistresses will be down immediately, sir.

MASCARILLE. Please ask them not to hurry. I can await them very comfortably here.

MAROTTE. Here they come.

IX   [*Enter* MADELON, CATHOS, *and* ALMANZOR. MAR-OTTE *withdraws*.

MASCARILLE [*greeting them*]. Fair ladies, you will no doubt be surprised at the boldness of my visit; but you must blame your reputation for bringing this misfortune on you. True merit has for me such magical power that I pursue it everywhere.

MADELON. If you are in pursuit of merit, sir, our preserves should not be your hunting ground.

CATHOS. If you see any merit at our house, it must be that which you have brought yourself.

MASCARILLE. Ah, now that I most emphatically deny. I see Rumour did not lie when she told us of your brilliance. I vow you will put all the wits in Paris in eclipse; game, set and match.

MADELON. Your courtesy is too lavish in the generosity of its praise. My cousin and I must not take your sweet flattery too seriously.

CATHOS. My dear, we must ask him to be seated.

MADELON. Ho, there! Almanzor!

ALMANZOR. Madame?

MADELON. Quick! Bring forward the props of conversation.

[ALMANZOR *goes out*

MASCARILLE. But tell me now, can I feel safe in this house?

CATHOS. Why, what should you fear?

MASCARILLE. The theft of my heart, the assassination of my liberty. I can see eyes, oh, very wicked eyes, capable of the cruellest assault upon my freedom. They'd have no more mercy on my heart than a Turk would on a Moor. If any dare approach they put themselves on their murderous guard at once. By God, I don't trust 'em and, unless I have good security that they'll do me no harm, I'll run; I vow I will.

MADELON. Isn't he of a lively temper, my dear?

CATHOS. A veritable Amilcar!*

MADELON. You needn't be afraid. Our eyes are guiltless of any evil purpose, and your heart may rest secure in the assurance of their integrity.

CATHOS. But, Sir, for pity do not turn so inexorable a back to this armchair. It has been stretching out its arms to you for the last quarter of an hour. Pray gratify its desire to embrace you.

MASCARILLE [*after combing his peruke and shaking out the lace canons attached to the lower part of his breeches*]. Well now, ladies, what do you think of Paris?

MADELON. Lord, Sir, what can we say? It would be speaking from the antipodes of reason not to admit that Paris is the great emporium of wonders, the centre of all good taste, wit, and gallant behaviour.

MASCARILLE. I maintain that, for people of breeding, there is no salvation outside Paris.

CATHOS. How true that is!

MASCARILLE. The streets are apt to be a trifle muddy; but then one can always take a chair.

MADELON. A chair is certainly a wonderful protection against the insults which we suffer at the hands of mud and foul weather.

MASCARILLE. You receive many visits, I suppose? What wits frequent your house?

MADELON. Alas, we are not known yet! But we have good hope we soon shall be. An intimate friend has promised to bring here all the contributors to the *Poetical Miscellany*.*

CATHOS. And others too who, we are told, are the supreme arbiters of good taste.

MASCARILLE. I can render you that service better than anyone. They all call on me. And I may say that I have never less than half a dozen wits at my levée.

MADELON. Oh, Sir, our obligation to you will know no bounds if you will give us this proof of your friendship; for indeed one must know all these gentlemen if one wishes to move in good society. They are the creators of reputation in Paris; and there are some, you know, whose mere acquaintance alone will establish one as a critic. But for me the greatest advantage of all is that by frequenting these brilliant assemblies one learns a hundred things absolutely indispensable to the armoury of a wit. There you may hear every day the latest scandal, the newest little love-notes in prose or in verse; and you get all the news at the right moment. So-and-so has written a most charming poem on such a subject; another has written words to such and such an air; one poet has composed a madrigal on one lover's bliss; another has written several stanzas on another lover's infidelity. Last night a certain gallant sent a poem to his mistress who sent him the reply at eight o'clock this morning. Such and such an author has a plan to write this or that; another is in the third chapter of his novel; another has his collected works at the printer's. Knowledge like this gives one a status in good society, and without it all the cleverness in the world is not worth a button.

CATHOS. It positively passes the bounds of the ridiculous for a person to set up as a wit, and be unable to recite the newest quatrain, were it but an hour old. For my part, I should be overwhelmed with shame if anyone were to ask my opinion of some new poem, and I had not seen it.

MASCARILLE. True enough, it is a lasting disgrace not to be the first to know what's written. But have no anxiety on that score. I will found an academy of wits at your house, and I promise you that not a line of verse will be composed in Paris but you shall know it by heart before anyone else. I dabble a little in verse myself when I am in the vein, and you will hear two hundred songs of my composition going the rounds of all the most fashionable salons in Paris; as many sonnets, four hundred epigrams, and more than a thousand madrigals, without counting riddles and portraits.

MADELON. I must confess I delight in portraits. Nothing, to my mind, could be more gallant.

MASCARILLE. Portraits are difficult, and demand a depth of brain. You shall see some of mine which will not displease you, I think.

—

CATHOS. I am terribly fond of riddles.

MASCARILLE. Ah, that taxes one's ingenuity. I made as many as four of them this morning, which I will give you to guess.

MADELON. Madrigals are very pleasant too, when cleverly turned.

MASCARILLE. Now they are absolutely my speciality; and I am even now at work setting in madrigals the entire history of Rome.

MADELON. Oh, but that will touch the meridian of beauty. I claim at least one copy if you have it printed.

MASCARILLE. You shall have one each, and in the very best binding. It's beneath my dignity to print; but I do it for the sake of the book-sellers, who plague me past bearing.

MADELON. Why, I think it would be delightful to see oneself in print.

MASCARILLE. Maybe; but, by God, I must recite to you an extempore I composed yesterday when on a visit to the Duchess; one of my set, you know. I am devilish smart at an extempore.

CATHOS. The extempore is the very touchstone of wit.

MASCARILLE. Now, listen.

MADELON. We are all attention.

MASCARILLE. *Oh, oh! My mind was at ease, and its own thoughts pursued:*
When, with no thought of harm, your fair visage I viewed,
Oh, eye, that by stealth hath encompassed my grief,
My heart thou didst ravish! Oh, fie on thee, thief!
After her, after her, after her, thief!

CATHOS. Heavens, how exquisitely gallant!

MASCARILLE. Everything I write, you see, strikes a dashing note. I take care to avoid the pedantic.

MADELON. This is more than two thousand leagues away from that.

MASCARILLE. Did you notice the beginning: *Oh, Oh!?* Uncommon, isn't it? *Oh, Oh!* Just like a man making a sudden discovery. *Oh, Oh!* Surprise. *Oh, Oh!*

MADELON. Yes. I find *Oh, Oh!* admirable.

MASCARILLE. A mere trifle!

CATHOS. Heavens above! What are you saying? Such things are beyond price.

MADELON. They are indeed. I would rather have written that *Oh, Oh!* than an epic poem.

MASCARILLE. You have good taste, by God!

MADELON. I flatter myself it is not entirely undiscriminating.

MASCARILLE. But do you not also admire *My mind was at ease? My mind was at ease.* I was quite happy and contented. Quite a natural phrase, you see. *My mind was at ease, and its own thoughts pursued. When, with no thought of harm,* when innocently, honestly, like a poor silly sheep, *your fair visage I viewed;* that is to say I took pleasure in watching you, I observed you, I contemplated you. *Oh, eye, that by stealth hath encompassed my grief* . . . How does the word *stealth* strike you? Well chosen, don't you think?

CATHOS. Excellently!

MASCARILLE. *Stealth,* behind the door. Like a cat who has just caught a mouse: *Stealth.*

MADELON. It could not be improved on.

MASCARILLE. *My heart thou didst ravish.* Carried it off, robbed me of it. *Oh, fie on thee, thief! After her, after her, after her, thief!* For all the world just like a man raising hue and cry after a thief. *After her, after her, after her, thief!*

MADELON. I never knew anything so brilliantly contrived.

MASCARILLE. I'd like too to sing you the air I've set it to.

CATHOS. You have learnt harmony?

MASCARILLE. I? Not a note.

CATHOS. How did you do it then?

MASCARILLE. Persons of rank never have to learn anything. They know everything already.

MADELON. Surely you knew that, my dear.

MASCARILLE. Now listen if you like the air. Hum, hum, la, la, la, la, la, la, la, la! This brutal weather has positively committed an outrage against my higher register. But what does it matter? I am among friends. [*Sings*]. *Oh, oh! My mind was at ease, and its own thoughts pursued:* etc.

CATHOS. Oh, what a passionate air! It almost makes one swoon.

MADELON. And so exquisitely chromatic!

MASCARILLE. The thought is well expressed in the setting, don't you think? *After her, thief!* And then, as if shouting at the top of one's voice: *After her, after her, after her, after her, after her, thief!* Then suddenly, like a man quite out of breath: *After her, thief!*

MADELON. Oh, this is to touch the very apex of perfection, the topmost apex, the apex of the apex. The whole thing is quite miraculous. I am enchanted with the air and with the words.

CATHOS. I never heard anything to approach it.

MASCARILLE. Everything I do comes naturally. It is entirely without study.

MADELON. Nature has been to you a most indulgent mother. You are her spoiled child.

MASCARILLE. How do you pass your time?

CATHOS. We do nothing at all.

MADELON. Up to now we have been subjected to a positive fast of social pleasures.

MASCARILLE. Would you care to go with me one day to the theatre? There is a new comedy now in rehearsal; and I should be charmed if we might see it together.

MADELON. It would be difficult to refuse an invitation like that.

MASCARILLE. But I must warn you to applaud vigorously, for I have promised to make the thing go. The author came to beg me again this morning. It is the custom here, you know, for authors to read their latest efforts to persons of rank like ourselves, to secure our approbation and gain a reputation for their work; and as you may well surmise, when we give one verdict, the parterre does not dare give another. Personally I am very conscientious; and, when I have once given my word to a poet, I always shout *Excellent!* even before the candles are lit and the play begins.

MADELON. I quite understand. What a wonderful place is Paris! A thousand things happen every day which one never hears of in the provinces, however avant-garde one may be.

CATHOS. You may rely on us. Now that we know, we will do our duty and applaud loudly at every line.

MASCARILLE. I don't know if I am wrong, but it wouldn't surprise me to hear that you had written a play yourself.

MADELON. Perhaps you're not so far out.

MASCARILLE. Ah, we must see it, by God! Between ourselves, I too have written one which I would like to see played.

CATHOS. To which company will you send it?

MASCARILLE. Can you ask? Why, to the Great Comedians of the Hôtel de Bourgogne of course.* They are the only ones capable of doing a play justice. The others are ignorant brutes who speak their lines just as if they were speaking quite naturally. They don't know how to make the verses roll off the tongue, and pause at the best places.

For how on earth are you to tell a fine passage, if the actor doesn't pause and so warn you when to cry *Bravo?*

CATHOS. Certainly that is the only way to make an audience aware of the beauties of a work. Things are only worth what one makes them worth.

MASCARILLE. What do you think of my accessories? Do they match well, do you think, with the suit?

CATHOS. Perfectly.

MASCARILLE. This ribbon is well chosen, eh?

MADELON. Admirably. It is pure Perdrigeon.*

MASCARILLE. What do you think of my canons?

MADELON. In the very best of taste.

MASCARILLE. I can at least claim that they are a quarter of a yard larger than anyone else's.

MADELON. I must confess that I have never seen a more perfect and elegant ensemble.

MASCARILLE. Pray bring the powers of your olfactory senses to bear on these gloves. [*He presents his gloves for them to smell.*

MADELON. They smell most frightfully sweet.

CATHOS. I never breathed a more high class effluvium.

MASCARILLE. And this? [*He presents the powdered curls of his peruke.*

MADELON. Of the very highest quality. It is delicious. It touches the sublime.

MASCARILLE. You don't mention my feathers. How do you like them?

CATHOS. Marvellously fine.

MASCARILLE. Would you believe that each one separately cost me a louis d'or? I never count cost. I have a mania to have everything the finest that can be procured.

—

MADELON. I see we think alike, you and I. I am exquisitely dainty in everything I wear; and, down to my very under-stockings, I will have nothing that is not of the best.

MASCARILLE [*crying out sharply*]. Ahi! Ahi! Ahi! Gently! By God, ladies, you use me very ill! I must complain of your treatment, indeed I must. This is not fair.

CATHOS. Why, what is it? What's the matter?

MASCARILLE. What? Both besiege my heart at once? Attack me on both flanks? 'Tis a breach of right. The sides are not equal. I vow I'll cry *Murder*.

CATHOS. He certainly has a most original way of putting things.

MADELON. An admirable turn of wit!

CATHOS. Your fear outruns your injury, and your heart cries out before it is flayed.

MASCARILLE. What? By God, it is skinned alive from top to bottom!

[*Enter* MAROTTE.   X

MAROTTE. Madame, there is a gentleman to see you.

MADELON. Who is it?

MAROTTE. The Vicomte de Jodelet.

MASCARILLE. The Vicomte de Jodelet?

MAROTTE. Yes, Sir.

CATHOS. Do you know him?

MASCARILLE. Know him? Why, he is my best friend.

MADELON. Admit him instantly.

[MAROTTE *goes out*

MASCARILLE. It is some time since we have seen each other. I am overjoyed at this unexpected meeting.

CATHOS. Here he comes.

[*Enter the* VICOMTE DE JODELET, *preceded by* ALMAN-   XI
ZOR; MAROTTE *following*.

—

MASCARILLE [*as they embrace*]. Vicomte!

JODELET. Marquis!

MASCARILLE. I *am* glad to see you!

JODELET. How delightful to find you here!

MASCARILLE. Embrace me once more, I beg you, my dear fellow.

MADELON. You see, my dear, we are beginning to be known. Society is finding its way here now.

MASCARILLE. Ladies, pray allow me to present this gentleman. On my honour he is worthy of your acquaintance.

JODELET. It is only right to give merit its due, and your charms make all conditions of men your vassals.

MADELON. I vow you urge your civility to the utmost limits of flattery.

CATHOS. To-day should be marked as a red-letter day in our almanack.

MADELON [*to* ALMANZOR]. Have I always to tell you everything twice, you little rogue? Can you not see that the addition of another armchair is imperative?

MASCARILLE. Don't be surprised to see the Vicomte a trifle under the weather. He has just recovered from an illness, which, as you see, has left him a little pale.*

JODELET. The result, I fear, of late nights at Court, and a hard life in the field.

MASCARILLE. Are you aware, ladies, that in the Vicomte you see one of the most valiant men of the age? A doughty blade, I assure you.

JODELET. You owe me nothing there, Marquis. We all know what you can do too.

MASCARILLE. Ah, yes. Many's the time we've seen each other in action.

JODELET. And in damned hot corners too.

MASCARILLE [*looking at* MADELON *and* CATHOS]. Ah, but not so hot as this is. Ha, ha, ha!

JODELET. It was in the army that we made each other's acquaintance. When we first met he was in command of a cavalry regiment in the galleys at Malta.

MASCARILLE. True; but you were in the service before me. I remember I was still only a cornet when you had the command of two thousand horse.

JODELET. Ah, war is a brave game. But, by God, campaigners like ourselves get small advancement at Court nowadays.

MASCARILLE. That's what makes me want to hang up my sword.

CATHOS. I vow I'm quite crazy about swordsmen.

MADELON. I adore them too, but I like to see their valour seasoned with wit.

MASCARILLE. Vicomte, do you remember that half-moon* we carried at the siege of Arras?

JODELET. What do you mean with your half-moon? It was a full moon, by God!

MASCARILLE. By the Lord, I believe you're right!

JODELET. Heavens, I ought to remember it! I was wounded in the leg by a hand grenade, and carry the marks to this day. Feel the place, ladies. You can tell what a terrible wound it was.

CATHOS [*after feeling the place*]. I can feel a big scar.

MASCARILLE. Give me your hand a moment, and feel this. There! At the back of my head. Have you got it?

MADELON. Yes, I can feel something.

MASCARILLE. A musket shot on my last campaign.

JODELET [*uncovering his chest*]. Here's another, where I was shot right through the body in the attack at Gravelines.

MASCARILLE [*putting his hand on the buttons of his breeches*]. I will show you a frightful gash.

MADELON. I beg you not to trouble. We will take your word for it.

MASCARILLE. These are honourable scars which show what a man is worth.

CATHOS. Oh, we know what you are.

MASCARILLE. Is your carriage outside, Vicomte?

JODELET. Yes. Why?

MASCARILLE. Let's take these ladies for a drive, and then to dinner under the trees.

MADELON. We are not going out to-day.

MASCARILLE. We'll send for the fiddles then, and have a dance.

JODELET. By heaven, what a good idea!

MADELON. We shall be delighted. But we must have some addition to the company.

MASCARILLE. Ho, there! Champagne! Picard! Bourguignon! Cascaret! Basque! La Verdure! Lorrain! Provençal! La Violette! The devil take the lackeys! I don't believe there is a gentleman in France worse served than I am. My rogues are always neglecting me.

MADELON. Almanzor! Tell Monsieur's people to go summon the fiddles. And run and invite these ladies and gentlemen [*giving a list she has written out*] to people the solitude of our ball.

[ALMANZOR *goes out*

MASCARILLE. Vicomte! What is your opinion of these eyes?

JODELET. What do you say yourself, Marquis?

MASCARILLE. Why, that we shall be very lucky to get off without a skirmish. I am beginning to feel the most extraordinary sensations. My heart is hanging by a single thread.

MADELON. Everything he says is so natural. His phrases are most exquisitely turned.

CATHOS. He is certainly most lavish of his wit.

MASCARILLE. To prove to you my sincerity, I will write you an extempore on the subject.

CATHOS. Oh, I do beg you to. I am longing to have something composed especially for us.

JODELET. I would like to oblige you too. But I find my poetic vein somewhat drained by the constant blood-letting of the last few days.

MASCARILLE. What is the problem? I can always get an excellent first line straight off. It's the others that are the difficulty. No. The time is really too short. I will write you the best extempore you've ever heard ... when I've had leisure to think it out.

JODELET. He's devilish smart, by God!

MADELON. And so gallant! Such a fund of well-turned conceits!

MASCARILLE. Tell me, Vicomte, is it long since you saw the Comtesse?

JODELET. It's over three weeks since I called.

MASCARILLE. The Duke came to see me this morning. He wants me to go down to his place to hunt deer.

MADELON. Here come our friends.

> [ALMANZOR *enters, followed by* LUCILE, CÉLIMÈNE, XII *and musicians.*

Ah, my dear friends, forgive us. These gentlemen have the fancy to give souls to our feet, and we have sent for you to fill up the gaps of our assembly.

LUCILE. We are charmed, I'm sure.

MASCARILLE. 'Tis but an informal dance. One of these days we'll give you one in real style. Have the fiddles arrived?

ALMANZOR. Yes, Sir. They are ready.

CATHOS. Come then, good friends. Take your places.

[The music plays.

MASCARILLE [*dancing by himself as a preliminary*]. La, la, la, la, la, la, la, la!

MADELON. What a divinely elegant figure!

CATHOS. And he looks as if he can dance.

MASCARILLE [*having taken* MADELON *as a partner*]. My liberty will dance the coranto as well as my feet. Keep time now, fiddles, keep time! Oh, the ignorant slaves! It's impossible to dance with them. Devil take you, can't you play in time? La, la, la, la, la, la, la! Keep time, you loutish musicians!

JODELET [*dancing too*]. Hey! Don't go so fast. I'm only just out of hospital.

XIII   [LA GRANGE *and* DU CROISY *rush in with sticks in their hands*.

LA GRANGE. Ah, you rascals, what are you doing here? We have been looking for you for the last three hours.

MASCARILLE [*feeling himself beaten*]. Oh, oh, oh! You never told me there was to be a thrashing into the bargain.

JODELET. Oh, oh, oh!

LA GRANGE. You're a fine one to play the man of rank!

DU CROISY. Here's something will teach you to know your place!

XIV   [LA GRANGE *and* DU CROISY *go out*

MADELON. What is the meaning of this?

JODELET. It was a wager.

CATHOS. What? To let yourselves be thrashed like that?

MASCARILLE. Heavens, I didn't like to notice it. I have a violent temper, and might have lost it.

MADELON. To put up with such an insult in our presence!

MASCARILLE. It's not worth mentioning. Let's go on with the dance. We have known each other for years. Old friends don't call each other out over a little thing like that.

[*Re-enter* LA GRANGE *and* DU CROISY.   XV

LA GRANGE. You shan't make fools of us, you rascals. Come in, there!

[*Enter three or four roysterers.*

MADELON. How dare you make such a disturbance in our house?

DU CROISY. What, ladies? Are we to see our lackeys received with more favour than ourselves? Are they to court you, at our expense; dance with you . . . ?

MADELON. Your lackeys?

LA GRANGE. Yes, our lackeys. It's neither seemly nor honourable to corrupt them in this way.

MADELON. Oh, Heavens, what insolence!

LA GRANGE. But they shan't swagger in our clothes to find favour in your eyes. If you love them it shall be for their good looks alone. Come, strip them at once!

[*The roysterers set upon the valets and divest them of their coats and hats.*

JODELET. Farewell, our finery!

MASCARILLE. Our noble titles have become extinct.

DU CROISY. So you have the impertinence to poach on our preserves, you rascals! If you wish to make yourselves agreeable to these ladies you shall look elsewhere for the means, I promise you.

LA GRANGE. It's too bad to take our places, and in our own clothes too!

MASCARILLE. Oh, Fortune! Oh, inconstant jade!

DU CROISY. Strip them to the last rag.

[*The roysterers complete the spoliation.*

LA GRANGE. Away with this frippery!

[*Roysterers go out with the finery*

Now, ladies, in the state they are in now you are at liberty to dally with them for as long as you please. We give you full permission; and promise you that we shall neither of us feel a single pang of jealousy.

[LA GRANGE *and* DU CROISY *go out, followed by* LUCILE, CÉLIMÈNE, *and* MAROTTE.

CATHOS. Oh! the shame of it all!

MADELON. I shall die of confusion.

1ST MUSICIAN [*to* MASCARILLE]. What does this mean? Who will pay us our fee?

MASCARILLE. Ask the Vicomte.

1ST MUSICIAN [*to* JODELET]. Who will give us our money?

JODELET. Ask the Marquis.

[*Enter* GORGIBUS.

XVI GORGIBUS. Ah, so there you are, you stupid minxes! You have brought us to a pretty pass, from what I can see! A fine story I have just heard from these gentlemen!

MADELON. Oh, father, they have acted out a bloody tragedy.

GORGIBUS. Yes, bloody tragedy indeed; but only the result of your ridiculous behaviour. They naturally resented your impertinence; and I, your wretched father, must swallow the insult.

MADELON. I swear we'll be revenged on them, or I shall die of disgrace. [*Turning to the valets*]. You odious rascals! Do you dare to stay here after your insolence?

MASCARILLE. Is that the way to speak to a Marquis? This is the way of the world. At the first touch of misfortune love turns to contempt. Come, my friend, let us seek our fortune in another place. Here, I see, they only love vain show, and naked merit has no place in their regard.

—

*[*MASCARILLE *and* JODELET *go out* XVII

1ST MUSICIAN. Sir, we've played our fiddles here, and you will have to pay us in their stead.

GORGIBUS. Very well, I'll pay you; and here is the money!

[He beats the musicians, who run out

As for you, you silly creatures, I don't know what holds me back from treating you the same. Your absurdities have made us a public laughing stock. Go and hide yourselves, poor fools, go and hide yourselves for ever.

*[*MADELON *and* CATHOS *go out*

And as for that vile trash which is the cause of their foolishness, that pernicious amusement for idle minds; those rubbishy novels, rhymes, songs, sonnets and sonnet-tesses, the devil take the lot of them!

DON JUAN

[*Dom Juan ou Le Festin de Pierre*]

Dom Juan ou Le Festin de Pierre, *comedy in five acts, was first produced at the Théâtre du Palais-Royal, Paris, on 15 February 1665, with Molière in the part of Sganarelle.*

CHARACTERS

DON JUAN, *son of Don Louis*

SGANARELLE

DONA ELVIRA, *wife of Don Juan*

GUSMAN, *Equerry of Dona Elvira*

DON CARLOS ⎫
DON ALONSO ⎭ *brothers of Dona Elvira*

DON LOUIS, *father of Don Juan*

FRANCISQUE, *a poor man*

CHARLOTTE ⎫
MATHURINE ⎭ *peasant girls*

PIERROT, *a peasant*

THE STATUE OF THE COMMANDER

LA VIOLETTE ⎫
RAGOTIN ⎭ *lackeys of Don Juan*

M. DIMANCHE, *a shopkeeper*

LA RAMÉE, *a ruffian*

A SPECTRE

Attendants of Don Juan

Attendants of Don Carlos and Don Alonso

The scene is set in Sicily

ACT ONE

A palace

[*Enter* SGANARELLE *and* GUSMAN.

SGANARELLE [*holding a snuffbox in his hand*]. I don't care what Aristotle and the philosophers say: there's nothing in this world like snuff. All right-minded people adore it; and anyone who is able to live without it is unworthy to draw breath. It not only clears and delights the brain; but it also inclines the heart towards virtue, and helps one to become a gentleman. Haven't you noticed how, as soon as one begins to take it, one becomes uncommonly generous to everybody, ready to present one's box right and left wherever one goes? You don't even wait to be asked, but anticipate the desires of others; and it can even be truly said that snuff inspires all its devotees with the principles of honour and virtue. But enough of that! To go back to what we were saying. You tell me, my dear Gusman, that Dona Elvira, your mistress, was so taken aback by our sudden departure that she has set off after us; and her heart, which my master has won only too completely, will stop beating, you say, unless she comes here to look for him. Well, shall I tell you what I think? In strict confidence of course. I'm afraid her devotion may meet with rather a poor return, her journey here be productive of very little good, and that you would both have done just as well to stay were you were.

GUSMAN. But why? Do tell me, Sganarelle, I beg of you, what grounds you have for such an ill-omened suspicion. Has your master opened his heart to you at all? Has he told you that any sudden coldness towards us was the cause of his departure?

—

SGANARELLE. No. But I can give a pretty shrewd guess how things are going by the way the land lies; and, though he hasn't said anything to me about it, I'd be ready to wager that that's how it is. I may be mistaken, of course. But experience has given me a pretty clear insight into such matters.

GUSMAN. What! You mean that this sudden departure is an infidelity of Don Juan? He would do such a wrong to the chaste and devoted Don Elvira?

SGANARELLE. Oh, no. It's only that he's still young, and he hasn't the strength . . .

GUSMAN. A man of his rank to be guilty of such disgraceful behaviour!

SGANARELLE. Ho! His rank! That's good. Do you suppose that would stop him?

GUSMAN. But he is tied by the holy bonds of marriage.

SGANARELLE. Oh, my poor Gusman, my dear friend, I'm afraid you don't know what kind of man Don Juan is.

GUSMAN. I certainly don't know what kind of man he can be, if he has deceived us like that. I cannot understand how, after all the love and impetuosity he has shown, the homage, the vows, the sighs, the tears, the passionate letters, the protestations, the oft-repeated oaths, his savage determination in forcing even the sacred doors of a convent to gain possession of Dona Elvira; how, after all that, he can have the heart to go back on his word.

SGANARELLE. I can understand it easily enough; and so would you, if you were as well acquainted with the fellow as I am. I don't say that his feelings *are* changed towards Dona Elvira. I have no sure knowledge of that yet.—You know that, by his orders, I set off before him; and since his arrival he has not spoken to me on the subject.—But I ought to warn you, strictly between the pair of us, that in Don Juan my master you see the greatest scoundrel that

ever walked the earth. He is a madman, a dog, a devil, a
Turk. He is a heretic who believes in neither Heaven, nor
saint, nor God, nor the bogeyman. He lives the life an an
absolute brute beast. He is an Epicurean hog, a regular
Sardanapalus* who is deaf to every Christian remon-
strance, and looks on all that we others believe as nothing
but old wives' tales. You say he has married your mistress.
He would have done far more than that to gratify his
desires. He would have married you, and her dog and cat
as well. It costs him nothing to marry. That is the best
baited trap he has. He marries right and left. Fine lady,
ward, town dweller or country girl, none are too hot or too
cold for him. And if I were to give you the names of all the
women he has married, in this place and that, it would be
sundown before I had done. You seem surprised and upset
at what I say. But this is only the merest sketch. To finish
the picture I should have to paint with a broader brush
still. One day the wrath of Heaven will strike him; that's
for certain. I might as well wait on the devil as wait on him;
and he makes me live with such horrors that I wish he was
already I don't know where. A great gentleman who is
really wicked is a terrible thing. But I must be faithful to
him, however I feel. Fear makes me his accomplice. It
stifles my feelings; and I often find myself applauding what
I loathe with my very soul. Here he comes now to take a
walk in the palace. We mustn't be seen together. I have
taken you into my confidence quite frankly, rather too
frankly perhaps; but I warn you that, if any of this ever
comes to his ears, I shall swear black and blue that you're
lying.

[GUSMAN *goes out. Enter* DON JUAN   II

DON JUAN. What fellow was that speaking to you? He looked
to me like old Gusman, Dona Elvira's man.

SGANARELLE. It was him, or his spitting image.

DON JUAN. What! It was he?

SGANARELLE. The very man himself.

DON JUAN. How long has he been in this town?

SGANARELLE. Since yesterday evening.

DON JUAN. What has he come for?

SGANARELLE. Can't you guess what it is that's worrying him?

DON JUAN. Our coming away, I suppose.

SGANARELLE. Yes. The poor fellow is quite heartbroken, and asked me why we had left.

DON JUAN. Well, what did you say?

SGANARELLE. That you hadn't told me.

DON JUAN. But what do you think yourself? What's your own idea?

SGANARELLE. Me? Well, with no disrespect to you, I think that you have some new affair on hand.

DON JUAN. Ah, so that's what you think, is it?

SGANARELLE. Yes.

DON JUAN. Then, by God! you think right. I freely admit that a new object has driven Dona Elvira's image quite out of my heart.

SGANARELLE. There now! What did I say? I know my Don Juan like the palm of my hand. Your heart is the greatest nomad that ever was. It likes to be always on the move. It hates to stay in one place for long together.

DON JUAN. Am I not right then to let it follow its bent?

SGANARELLE. Well, Sir . . .

DON JUAN. Answer me.

SGANARELLE. Certainly your Honour' right, if that's your Honour's will. That can't be denied. But, if it wasn't your Honour's will, perhaps it would be a different story.

DON JUAN. Come now. I give you free rein to say exactly what you think.

SGANARELLE. Very well then, Sir, I'll tell you quite frankly that I don't think you behave in the right way at all. I think it's very wicked to go loving right and left as you do.

DON JUAN. So you think we should be tied for ever to the first object that takes our fancy, forswear the rest of the world, and have no eyes for anyone else? A nice thing indeed to take seriously to heart such a false point of honour as fidelity; to bury myself for ever in one passionate affair, and to be dead from henceforth to everything that my eyes tell me is worthy of devotion! No, no. Constancy is only fit for idiots. Every pretty woman has the right to attract us, and the mere accident of being seen first should not rob the others of their privilege of subjugating our hearts. Beauty delights me wherever I find it, and I fall a willing slave to the sweet force with which it seeks to bind me. However my heart may be engaged, the love I have for one woman has no power to make me unfair to the rest. My eyes see the merits of each, and pay homage and tribute wherever it is due. If I see an attractive woman, my heart is hers; and, had I ten thousand hearts, I would give them all to a face that was worthy of them. After all, the growth of a passion has infinite charm, and the true pleasure of love is its variety. How deliciously sweet to lay siege to a young heart; to watch one's progress day by day; to overcome by means of vows, tears and groans, the delicate modesty of a soul which sighs in surrender; to break down little by little the weakening resistance, the maidenly scruples that her honour dictates, and bring her at last where we would have her be. But once we have had our way with her, there is no more to wish for. The best is behind us. And so we slumber on, lulled by our love, until a new object appears to reawaken our desire, and lure us on with the charms of a new conquest. There is nothing so sweet as to overcome the resistance of a beautiful woman; and, where they are concerned, I have the ambition of a conqueror, who goes from triumph to triumph, and can never be satisfied. Nothing shall stand in the way of my desire. My heart is big enough to love the whole world; and I could wish, with Alexander,* that there were more worlds still, so that I might carry yet further my prowess in love.

SGANARELLE. Heavens above! How you do run on! Just as if you'd learnt it all by heart out of a book.

DON JUAN. Well, what answer can you make to that?

SGANARELLE. Heavens, I say . . . I don't know what to say. You twist everything so that I could almost say you were right, if I didn't know very well that you are wrong. I had the most uplifting things to say, and now you've put them all out of my head. But never mind. Another time I'll have it all written down on paper, so that I can meet you on more equal terms.

DON JUAN. A very good idea!

SGANARELLE. But, Sir, will it be included in the permission you have given me, if I say that I am really rather scandalized by the sort of life you lead?

DON JUAN. Why, what sort of life do I lead?

SGANARELLE. Oh, a very good sort of life. But, for instance, this trick you have of getting married every month or so.

DON JUAN. Could anything be more delightful?

SGANARELLE. Oh, no. I admit that it's very delightful and very amusing; and it would suit me well enough, if there were no harm in it. But, Sir, to trifle like that with a sacred mystery, and . . .

DON JUAN. Pshaw! The matter is entirely between Heaven and myself. We shall settle it quite well together, without you losing your sleep over it.

SGANARELLE. Heavens! Sir, I've always heard that it's rather risky to mock God, and that unbelievers come to a bad end.

—

DON JUAN. I've told you already, my prize fool, that I am not fond of moralizers.

SGANARELLE. Oh, I'm not speaking of you. Far be it from me. You know your own business best. If you believe in nothing, you have good reasons for it. But there are a set of little know-alls in this world, who live a heathen life without in the least knowing why; who set up for free thinkers out of sheer self-conceit; and, if I had a master of that kind, I'd tell him straight out to his face: 'Aren't you afraid', I'd say, 'to set yourself up against God; and sneer, as you do, at the most sacred mysteries? It well becomes you, a mere worm, a pygmy'—I'm speaking to this imaginary master of mine—'to affect to make light of what everybody else in the world holds in reverence! Do you think that, because you have rank, a fashionable wig, feathers in your hat, a coat all over gold, and ribbons the colour of hell-fire'—I'm not speaking to you, you know, but the other—'do you think, I say, that for that you are wiser than everyone else; that you can do exactly as you like; and that no one will dare to tell you the truth about yourself? Let me tell you, though I am only your valet, that sooner or later God punishes the wicked. A bad life comes to a bad end, and . . .'

DON JUAN. That's enough now.

SGANARELLE. Why, what's the matter?

DON JUAN. The matter is that a new beauty has possession of my heart, and her charms have led me to follow her to this town.

SGANARELLE. But aren't you afraid, Sir? Don't you remember that it was here you killed the Commander in a duel six months ago?

DON JUAN. What should I be afraid of? Didn't I kill him stone dead?

SGANARELLE. Oh, yes, Sir; as dead as mutton. He has no complaint against you on that score.

DON JUAN. Besides, I had my pardon for that affair.

SGANARELLE. Granted. But that hasn't done away the resentment of his family and friends.

DON JUAN. Oh, don't let us bother about all the ills that might happen. Let us think rather of how we can enjoy ourselves. The lady in question is a charming young girl, who came here in the company of the man she is going to marry. I saw her by pure chance, with her fiancé, three or four days before they set out. Never have I seen two people so happily in love. Their obvious tenderness for each other went straight to my heart, and my love found its first inspiration in jealousy. It was torture to me to see them so happy together. I was consumed with envy; and I could imagine no greater pleasure than to come between them, and break an attachment so offensive to my dearest susceptibilities. But so far, all my attempts have been unavailing; and as a last resort I have decided to take desperate measures. Her intended is to take her to-day for a little outing on the water. Without saying anything to you, I have already made all my preparations. I have a boat and a crew, and I don't anticipate any difficulty in carrying her off.

SGANARELLE. Oh, Sir!

DON JUAN. What is it?

SGANARELLE. You've done absolutely right. The only important thing in this world is to have what you want.

DON JUAN. Then get ready to come with me. And don't forget to bring my weapons, in case ... [catching sight of DONA ELVIRA]. Of all the unlucky meetings! You treacherous rascal, you didn't tell me she was here herself.

SGANARELLE. You never asked me, Sir.

DON JUAN. At least she might have changed her clothes! She must be off her head to come here dressed in those old country things.

III

[*Enter* DONA ELVIRA.]

DONA ELVIRA. Don Juan, won't you condescend to recognize your wife? For pity's sake, look at me.

DON JUAN. I confess that I am surprised, Madame. I did not expect to see you here.

DONA ELVIRA. No. That's plain enough. It is certainly a surprise to you, and a very different one to what I'd hoped. Your manner shows me only too clearly what I have tried hard not to believe. I was a poor weak fool to doubt of your desertion, when so many proofs confirmed it. I confess I have been so easy-going, or rather so silly, as to try to deceive myself; to give the lie to what my eyes and my own good sense have shown me but too clearly. In my love for you, I have found excuses for your growing coldness. I have invented a hundred good reasons for your precipitate departure, to absolve you from a crime of which my reason accused you. I resolutely shut my ears against the just suspicions which cried aloud that you were false, and encouraged a thousand silly fancies to make you innocent in my heart. But the way you have now received me leaves no more room for doubt. It has shown me far more than I need to know. But may I not hear from your own lips why you have left me? What can you say, Don Juan, to justify your behaviour?

DON JUAN. Ask Sganarelle, Madame. He knows why I came away.

SGANARELLE [*aside, to* DON JUAN]. Me, Sir? I know nothing about it, thank you very much.

DONA ELVIRA. Very well then, you tell me, Sganarelle. It is of no real consequence from whose lips I hear it.

DON JUAN [*beckoning to* SGANARELLE *to come closer*]. Come along now. Tell Madame the reason.

SGANARELLE [*aside, to* DON JUAN]. What do you want me to say?

DONA ELVIRA. Tell me, since he wishes it, Sganarelle. Tell me why he went away so suddenly.

DON JUAN. You won't speak?

SGANARELLE [*aside, to* DON JUAN]. I haven't anything to say. You're trying to make a fool of me.

DON JUAN. Will you answer?

SGANARELLE. Madame . . .

DONA ELVIRA. Yes.

SGANARELLE [*turning towards his master*]. Sir . . .

DON JUAN [*threatening him*]. If . . .

SGANARELLE. Madame, we went away because . . . because of Alexander and other worlds to conquer. There, Sir, that's all I can say about it!

DONA ELVIRA. Then, Don Juan, will you please clear up this wonderful mystery.

DON JUAN. To tell you the truth, Madame . . .

DONA ELVIRA. How poorly you defend yourself! A courtier should be more accustomed to such situations. I pity your confusion. Where is your armour of majestic shamelessness? Why don't you swear that your heart is unchanged, that you adore me as much as ever, and that nothing but death can tear you from my side? You should say that you were called away by business so urgent that you had no time to give me even a minute's warning; that, much to your regret, you will be detained here for some time; but that, if I will only go home quietly, I may rest assured that you will follow me as soon as ever your affairs will let you. That you only live in the thought of returning to me, and away from my side you suffer the torments of a body divorced from its soul. That is the defence you ought to make, and not be so tongue-tied as you are.

DON JUAN. I own to you, Madame, I have no talents for lying. It is my nature to be open and sincere. I won't tell you that I feel the same towards you as I did, and that I long to be with you again, because it is evident that I came away with the express purpose of escaping from you. Not for the reasons you suppose, but from a scruple of pure conscience; and because I believe that I cannot continue to live with you without mortal sin. I have scruples, Madame. My soul's eyes are opened at last to what I have done. I have meditated on the fact that, in order to marry you, I stole you from the cloister; that you have broken vows which committed you to another life, and that Heaven is a jealous rival. Fearful of divine wrath, I have repented of my sin. I have recognized that our marriage was nothing but adultery in disguise, which would bring on us some dreadful punishment; and that it was my duty to try to forget you, and allow you to return to your lawful obligations. Will you dare to oppose such a holy purpose, Madame? Would you have me, for your sake, take issue with Heaven? Would you . . . ?

DONA ELVIRA. Oh, you scoundrel! At last I see you as you really are. But, unhappily, the knowledge comes too late; and can only serve to drive me to desperation. But, be sure, your villainy will not remain unpunished. The Heaven you mock will avenge me for your faithlessness.

DON JUAN. Heaven! Fancy that, Sganarelle!

SGANARELLE. Ho! We snap our fingers at it.

DON JUAN. Madame . . .

DONA ELVIRA. No. I won't hear another word. I blame myself for listening so long already. Only cowards will stay to hear the story of their shame. For a noble heart, to know is to act. Don't expect me to break out into reproaches. My anger has no breath to waste in empty words. It needs it all for its revenge. I say again, Heaven will punish you, you faithless villain; and, if you are not afraid of Heaven, at least beware the anger of the wife you have betrayed.

[She goes out

SGANARELLE [*aside*]. If only he could feel remorse!

DON JUAN [*after a moment's thought*]. Come, let us start on our new amorous adventure.

[*He goes out*

SGANARELLE. Oh, what a wicked master I'm forced to serve!

ACT TWO

A country place by the sea

I   [*Enter* CHARLOTTE *and* PIERROT.

CHARLOTTE. Marcy, Piarrot, it be a good thing you was on the spot!

PIERROT. 'Tweren't by more'n the thickness of a pin they wasn't both drownded.

CHARLOTTE. Is'pose it was that squall this morning as tumbled 'em in the sea.

PIERROT. Look here, Charlotte, I'll tell 'ee word for word just how it fell out; for I was the first to see 'em, as you might say. The first to see 'em was I. Us was just at the edge of the tide, me and fat Lucas, larking about and chucking bits of mud at each other's heads; for you know fat Lucas do love a lark, and so does I too, if it come to that. As us was larking about then, as larking about us was, I sees afar off some' at moving in the water, and coming towards us by jerks. I sees that as plain as plain; and then all at once I sees as I don't see nothing at all. 'Lucas,' I sez, 'seem to me that's folks swimming out there.' 'Bah,' sez he, 'you've been squinting at the sun, you're seeing crooked.' 'I bean't seeing crooked,' I sez, 'that's folks,' I sez. 'Nary a bit,' sez he, 'you've got happaritions.' 'Will you bet', sez I, 'that I ain't been seeing things', sez I, 'and that it be two men', sez I, 'a swimming towards us?' sez I. 'I bet it bean't', sez he. 'Oh!' sez I, 'will you bet ten sous on it?'

sez I. 'Right,' sez he, 'and there be the money,' sez he. Well, I keeps my head and I plonks down the sum in small change, as bold as though I waz drinking a glass of wine; for I be a venturesome lad and don't stay to look behind me. I knew what I was doing though. 'What a fool!' thinks I. And there! Us had no sooner made the bet than I sees the two men as plain as I sees 'ee now, making signs to we to go and help 'em. So I sweeps up the cash, and 'Come Lucas,' sez I, 'you see as they'm a calling to we. Let's in quick and help 'em.' 'Not likely,' sez he, 'it's becoz of them I've lost.' Well, to cut a long story short, I gives him such a slice of my jaw that at last there us was in a boat, and somehow us manages to drag 'em out of the water. And then us gets 'em home, and puts 'em before the fire. And then they strips theirselves stark naked to get dry. And then two more of the same party turns up what have managed to save theirselves. And then Mathurine comes along, and the genelman makes sheep's eyes at her. And that Charlotte, be the very way as it all fell out.

CHARLOTTE. Didn't you say, Piarrot, as there was one of 'em was handsomer than the rest?

PIERROT. Ay, that be the maister. He must be some very great genelman; for his coat be all over gold from the top to the bottom, and them that serves him be genelmen theirselves. But for all that, great genelman though he be, he'd have been drownded all right, if I hadn't been by.

CHARLOTTE. Well! Just think of that now!

PIERROT. Oh, ay, his number would've been up sure enough, if it hadn't been for we.

CHARLOTTE. Be he still at your place naked, Piarrot?

PIERROT. No, no. They dressed him up again before us all. Marcy, I've never seen anyone dressed like that before! What a rigmarole of frippery these court folks does put on! I'd never find my way in it all. I was quite flabbergasted.

Why, Charlotte, they've hair that bean't fixed to their heads, and they claps it on at the last like a great bonnet. Their shirts have sleeves big enough for 'ee and me to walk about in. Instead of breeches, they wears a great apron as large as from here to Easter. Instead of waistcoat, a little vest that hardly reaches to the belly; and instead of neckband, a large neckerchief with four huge linen tassels a hanging down in front. They've other little neckbands at the ends of their arms; and great funnels of lace round their legs; and among it all be such a lot of ribbons, such a lot of ribbons that it be like as they was quilted all over. Why even their shoes are so bebowed and beribboned, that I'm sure I should trip up in 'em and break my neck.

CHARLOTTE. Lord, Piarrot, I must go and see all this!

PIERROT. Not so fast, Charlotte. I've summat else to say to 'ee.

CHARLOTTE. Well? What be it then?

PIERROT. I must say what's on my mind, as the saying goes. I loves 'ee, Charlotte, as you knows very well, and I wants us to get married. But I'm not at all satisfied with 'ee.

CHARLOTTE. Why, what be the matter?

PIERROT. The matter be that you're just breaking my heart.

CHARLOTTE. How then?

PIERROT. You don't love me.

CHARLOTTE [*laughing*]. Oh, be that all?

PIERROT. Ay, that it be, and enough too.

CHARLOTTE. Lord sakes, Piarrot, you're allus telling me the same thing.

PIERROT. I allus tells 'ee the same thing, because it allus be the same thing; and if it wasn't allus the same thing, I shouldn't tell 'ee allus the same thing.

CHARLOTTE. But what be it you want? What be I to do?

PIERROT. Marcy, I wants 'ee to love me!

CHARLOTTE. But don't I love 'ee then?

PIERROT. No, you don't love me. And yet I does all I can to make 'ee. I buys 'ee ribbons from every pedlar that comes along, without one word of complaint. I breaks my neck to get blackbirds for 'ee out of the nest. I gets the hurdy-gurdy man to play for 'ee on your birthday. And all the time I'm butting my head against a stone wall. It bean't neither good nor honest not to love folks as love we.

CHARLOTTE. But Lord sakes, Piarrot, I *do* love 'ee.

PIERROT. Oh, ay, you loves me in a fine fashion.

CHARLOTTE. But what do you want me to do?

PIERROT. I wants 'ee to do what one does when one loves properly.

CHARLOTTE. But don't I love 'ee properly?

PIERROT. No. When that be so, it be easily seen. One plays a thousand little monkey tricks on folks, when one loves from the bottom of one's heart. Look at fat Thomasse, how mad she be after young Robin. She be for ever about him and annoying him, and never gives him a minute's peace. She be allus playing some trick on him or giving him a thump as she passes. Why, t'other day, when he was sitting on a stool, she pulled it from under him, and he fell all his length on the floor. That's how folks does when they love. But you! You never says a word to me. You stands there just like a block of wood. If I was to pass before 'ee twenty times, you'd never move to give me that least little thump, or say the least little thing to me. Marcy, it bean't nice. It be treating folks too cold.

CHARLOTTE. Well, what can I do about it? That be my way. I can't make myself any different.

PIERROT. Way or no, when one has a friendship for folks, one allus shows it a little.

CHARLOTTE. Well, I can't say more'n I loves 'ee as much as I can. And if that doesn't please 'ee, you can take your love somewhere else.

PIERROT. There! You see? Darn it, if you loved me, would you say a thing like that?

CHARLOTTE. Well, why do you want to come and plague me so?

PIERROT. What harm have I done to 'ee? I only ask 'ee for a little affection.

CHARLOTTE. Very well then, leave me alone; and don't pester me so. P'raps it will come all of a sudden of itself.

PIERROT. Will 'ee shake 'ands on that then, Charlotte?

CHARLOTTE. Very well.

PIERROT. Promise me as you'll try to love me better.

CHARLOTTE. I'll do what I can. But it must come of itself. Oh, Piarrot, be that the genelman?

PIERROT. Ay, that be he.

CHARLOTTE. Lord sakes, he be a proper man! It'd have been a great pity if he'd been drownded.

PIERROT. I'll be back in a jiffy. I only wants to wet my whistle, to set me up again after the hexertions I've had.

II   [*He goes · out. Enter* DON JUAN *and* SGANARELLE. CHARLOTTE *remains in the background.*

DON JUAN. We have failed in our plan, Sganarelle. The sudden squall has upset our project with our boat. But this peasant girl I have just parted from makes up for all. Her charms have made me forget all my disappointment at our failure. A heart like hers must not escape me; and I have already prepared the ground in such a way, that I think I shall not sigh long in vain.

SGANARELLE. Sir, I'm simply dumbfounded. Here we are having narrowly escaped from death; and, instead of giving thanks to Heaven for the care It has deigned to take of us, you are starting afresh to call down Its anger by your usual crimin . . . [*seeing that* DON JUAN *is angry*]. Have done with your nonsense, you silly fellow. The Master knows his own business best. Get along with you.

DON JUAN [*perceiving* CHARLOTTE]. Hullo! Where has this other peasant girl come from, Sganarelle? Did you ever see anything so charming? Don't you think she's quite as attractive as the other?

SGANARELLE. Oh, quite. [*aside*]. Now for another seduction!

DON JUAN [*to* CHARLOTTE]. To what happy chance do I owe this pleasant meeting, my fair one? Can beings like you be found in this rustic solitude, with only trees and rocks for company?

CHARLOTTE. As you see, Sir.

DON JUAN. Do you belong to this village?

CHARLOTTE. Yes, Sir.

DON JUAN. You live here?

CHARLOTTE. Yes, Sir.

DON JUAN. What is your name?

CHARLOTTE. Charlotte, at your service.

DON JUAN. What a ravishing creature! What sparkling eyes!

CHARLOTTE. Oh, Sir, you make me ashamed!

DON JUAN. You need not be ashamed to hear the truth. What do you say, Sganarelle? Was ever anything more delightful? Would you oblige me by turning round. What a pretty figure! Won't you hold up your head? Oh, what a delicate little face! Let me look right into your eyes. How beautiful! Will you allow me to see your teeth? Oh, they are made for love. And these tempting lips as well. I am quite enchanted. I have never seen so charming a person.

CHARLOTTE. You are pleased to say so, Sir. I think you must be making fun of me.

DON JUAN. Making fun of you? God forbid! I love you too much for that. I speak from the very bottom of my heart.

CHARLOTTE. If that's true, I'm much obliged to you.

DON JUAN. Please don't mention it. There's nothing to be obliged to me for. Your own beauty is the cause.

CHARLOTTE. All this is too grand for me, Sir. I am too simple to know how to answer.

DON JUAN. Look at her hands, Sganarelle.

CHARLOTTE. Oh, Sir, they're as black as I don't know what.

DON JUAN. What are you saying? They are the loveliest in the whole world. I beg you will allow me to kiss them.

CHARLOTTE. You do me too much honour, Sir. If I'd known, I'd have given them a good wash with bran.

DON JUAN. I take it, fair Charlotte, that you are not married?

CHARLOTTE. No, Monsieur, but I'm soon going to be; to Piarrot, the son of our neighbour Simonette.

DON JUAN. What? A girl like you the wife of a simple peasant? Never! It would be profanation. You weren't born to live all your life in a village. You deserve a better fate than that. And Heaven, who knows what you deserve, has sent me here on purpose to prevent this marriage, and to do justice to your charms. I love you, fair Charlotte, with all my heart; and, if you will give me the chance, I will take you away from this miserable place, and put you in a position more worthy of you. My love may appear a trifle sudden. But what of it? It is the effect of your great beauty, Charlotte. What would take six months in the case of another, with you is only the matter of a quarter of an hour.

CHARLOTTE. Truly, Sir, I'm all in a flutter to hear you talk like that. What you say gives me pleasure, and I'd give the world to believe you; but I've allus been told never to believe what gentlemen say. I've heard that you court folk are all dissemblers, who only mean to ruin poor girls.

DON JUAN. I'm not one of that kind.

SGANARELLE [aside]. Oh, no, not at all.

CHARLOTTE. You see, I don't want to be deceived, sir. I am only a poor peasant girl, but I value my good name. I'd rather die than lose my honour.

DON JUAN. Do you think I would be so wicked as to deceive a girl like you? Do you think I would be such a scoundrel as to betray you? No, no, I have too much conscience to do such a thing. I love you, Charlotte, in all true faith and honour; and, to show you that I am in earnest, it is my wish to marry you. Could you have a greater proof than that? I am ready whenever you will. And I call on this man here to witness my promise.

SGANARELLE. Oh, yes, you needn't be afraid. He'll marry you as much as ever you like.

DON JUAN. Ah, Charlotte, I can see that you don't know me yet. You wrong me to judge of me by others. If there are scoundrels in the world, whose only thought is to seduce poor girls, you ought not to count me among the number, or to doubt the sincerity of my proposal. Besides, your beauty makes you quite safe. A girl like you ought to be beyond fears of that sort. Believe me, you haven't at all the look of a person whom one could deceive. Why, I'd rather pierce my heart with a thousand daggers than have the least thought of betraying you.

CHARLOTTE. Faith! I don't know if you're speaking the truth or not. But you somehow make one believe you.

DON JUAN. In believing me you will only do me justice. And I here repeat the promise I have given you. Will you accept? Do you consent to be my wife?

CHARLOTTE. I will, if my aunt agrees.

DON JUAN. Give me your hand on it then, Charlotte, since you are willing.

CHARLOTTE. But I do beg you, Sir, not to deceive me. It wouldn't be right of you, seeing that I am acting in all good faith.

D.J.A.O.S.—4

DON JUAN. What? You seem to doubt me still. Would you have me swear it with a dreadful oath? May Heaven. . . .!

CHARLOTTE. No, no, for the love of God, don't swear! I believe you.

DON JUAN. Then give me a little kiss to seal your promise.

CHARLOTTE. Oh, Sir, please wait until we're married. I'll kiss you as much as you like then.

DON JUAN. Very well then, fair Charlotte. Your wishes shall be mine; but at least give me your hand, and let me by a thousand kisses express the delight I. . . .

III   [*Re-enter* PIERROT.

PIERROT [*pushing* DON JUAN, *who is kissing* CHARLOTTE'S *hand*]. Hey, just a minute, Sir! Hands off, if you please! You'll heat yourself, and catch purisy.

DON JUAN [*pushing* PIERROT *away roughly*]. What's this block-head interfering for?

PIERROT [*putting himself between* DON JUAN *and* CHARLOTTE]. Hands off, I say! You've no right to come here and kiss our sweethearts.

DON JUAN [*pushing* PIERROT *again*]. What a fuss about nothing!

PIERROT. Here! What sort of a way be that to push folks about?

CHARLOTTE [*taking* PIERROT *by the arm*]. Well, you leave him be too, Piarrot.

PIERROT. Leave him be, d'you say? There be two ways to that.

DON JUAN. Ah!

PIERROT. What! 'Cos you're a genelman, are you to come a-kissing our girls before our very faces? Go away and kiss your own.

DON JUAN. Hey?

—

PIERROT. Yes, hey! [DON JUAN *strikes him*]. Here, don't hit me. [DON JUAN *strikes him again*]. Oh, Crimini! [*another blow*]. Zimini! [*another blow*]. Jimini! It bean't right to beat folks like that. That bean't the way to pay me for saving 'ee from being drownded.

CHARLOTTE. Don't be cross, Piarrot.

PIERROT. I will be cross. You're nobbut a hussy to let him fondle 'ee like that.

CHARLOTTE. Oh, Piarrot, it's not what you think at all. This genelman wants to marry me. You've nothing to be cross about.

PIERROT. What's that? But you promised me.

CHARLOTTE. Oh, that doesn't matter. If you love me, Piarrot, you ought to be pleased to see me a fine lady.

PIERROT. Not me. I'd rather see 'ee dead than belong to another.

CHARLOTTE. Come, Piarrot, don't be upset. When I'm a lady, I'll be able to do you a good turn. We'll buy all our cheese and butter from you.

PIERROT. No, you won't; not if you was to pay me double. So that's how you lets him wheedle 'ee? Jimini! If I'd known that before, I'd have thought twice before I lugged him out of the water; and I'd have given him a crack on the head with my oar as well.

DON JUAN [*approaching* PIERROT *to strike him*]. What's that you say?

PIERROT [*hiding behind* CHARLOTTE]. I'm not afraid of nobody.

DON JUAN [*coming after him*]. Wait till I catch you.

PIERROT [*coming round again*]. I don't give a fig for 'ee.

DON JUAN [*running after him again*]. We'll see about that.

PIERROT [*escaping behind* CHARLOTTE *again*]. I've seen too much already.

DON JUAN. Ouf!

SGANARELLE. Leave the poor wretch alone, Sir. It's a shame to strike him. [*To* PIERROT, *putting himself between him and* DON JUAN]. Listen, my poor fellow. Don't say any more, but go away.

PIERROT [*passing in front of* SGANARELLE *and looking scornfully at* DON JUAN]. I have got some more to say.

DON JUAN [*raising his hand to strike* PIERROT]. I'll teach you.

> [PIERROT *ducks his head and* SGANARELLE *receives the blow.*

SGANARELLE [*looking at* PIERROT]. The devil take the bumkin!

DON JUAN [*to* SGANARELLE]. That's what your kind heart gets you.

PIERROT. Jimini! I'll tell her aunt of all these goings on.

> [*He goes out*

DON JUAN [*to* CHARLOTTE]. I shall be the happiest man alive. I wouldn't give my good fortune for anything in the world. What bliss it will be when you are my wife, and. . . .

IV   [*Enter* MATHURINE.

SGANARELLE [*seeing* MATHURINE]. Oho! Oho!

MATHURINE [*to* DON JUAN]. Sir, what are you doing there with Charlotte? Are you courting her as well?

DON JUAN [*aside to* MATHURINE]. No, no. It's *she* who wants to marry *me*. But I've told her I am engaged to you.

CHARLOTTE [*to* DON JUAN]. What's Mathurine got to say to you?

DON JUAN [*aside to* CHARLOTTE]. She's jealous of my speaking to you. She insists that I'm engaged to her. But I've told her that you're the one I want.

MATHURINE. What? Charlotte. . . .

DON JUAN [*aside to* MATHURINE]. Its no use talking to her. She's very obstinate.

CHARLOTTE. What's that? Mathurine. . . .

DON JUAN [*aside to* CHARLOTTE]. Nothing you say will have any effect. You'll never shake her delusion.

MATHURINE. Do you mean to say . . .?

DON JUAN [*aside to* MATHURINE]. It's impossible to make her hear reason.

CHARLOTTE. I'd like. . . .

DON JUAN [*aside to* CHARLOTTE]. She's as obstinate as the devil.

MATHURINE. Really. . . .

DON JUAN [*aside to* MATHURINE]. Don't say anything to her. She's mad.

CHARLOTTE. It seems to me. . . .

DON JUAN [*aside to* CHARLOTTE]. Let her alone. She's quite out of her mind.

MATHURINE. No, no. I must speak to her.

CHARLOTTE. I want to know why she's so cocksure.

MATHURINE. What. . . .?

DON JUAN [*aside to* MATHURINE]. I bet she'll tell you I've promised to marry her.

CHARLOTTE. I. . . .

DON JUAN [*aside to* CHARLOTTE]. What will you bet that she says I've promised to make her my wife?

MATHURINE. It's not fair, Charlotte, to try to cut me out.

CHARLOTTE. You've no right to be jealous, Mathurine, because the genelman is speaking to me.

MATHURINE. The genelman saw me first.

CHARLOTTE. If he saw you first, he saw me second. And he has promised to marry me.

DON JUAN [*aside to* MATHURINE]. There! What did I tell you?

MATHURINE [*to* CHARLOTTE]. I like that. It's me, not you, he has promised to marry.

DON JUAN [*aside to* CHARLOTTE]. There! Wasn't I right?

CHARLOTTE. Pull the other one. It's me, I tell you.

MATHURINE. You're crazy. It's me, me, me.

CHARLOTTE. Ask him himself if I'm not right.

MATHURINE. Let him deny it then, if I am lying.

CHARLOTTE. Have you promised to marry her, Sir?

DON JUAN [*aside to* CHARLOTTE]. Don't be absurd.

MATHURINE. Is it true, Sir, you have promised to be her husband?

DON JUAN [*aside to* MATHURINE]. Is it likely?

CHARLOTTE. You see how cocksure she is.

DON JUAN [*aside to* CHARLOTTE]. Let her think what she likes.

MATHURINE. You see that she won't give in.

DON JUAN [*aside to* MATHURINE]. Let her say what she pleases.

CHARLOTTE. No, no. I must know the truth.

MATHURINE. It must be settled one way or the other.

CHARLOTTE. I want the genelman to show you how simple you have been, Mathurine.

MATHURINE. I want the genelman to show you how silly you are, Charlotte.

CHARLOTTE. Will you please put an end to the argument, Sir.

MATHURINE. Settle it between us, Sir.

CHARLOTTE [*to* MATHURINE]. Now you'll see.

MATHURINE [*to* CHARLOTTE]. It's you who are going to see.

CHARLOTTE [*to* DON JUAN]. Tell her.

MATHURINE [*to* DON JUAN]. Tell her.

DON JUAN. What do you want me to say? You both maintain that I've promised to marry you. Isn't it sufficient that each of you knows the truth, without my having to say anything further? Why make me repeat myself? Surely the one who has my promise can safely ignore the claims of the other; and, if I keep my word, what has she to worry about? Argument leads nowhere. It's deeds that count, not words. And that's how I mean to settle the question between you. When I marry, it will be seen at once which of the two has possession of my heart. [*aside to* MATHURINE]. Let her believe whatever she likes. [*aside to* CHARLOTTE]. Let her go on living in her fool's paradise. [*aside to* MATHURINE]. I adore you. [*aside to* CHARLOTTE]. I am yours for ever. [*aside to* MATHURINE]. All other faces are ugly beside yours. [*aside to* CHARLOTTE]. It would be impossible to love anyone else after you. [*aloud*]. I have a few orders to give. I'll be back directly.

[*He goes out*

CHARLOTTE [*to* MATHURINE]. I am the one he loves.

MATHURINE [*to* CHARLOTTE]. It's me he's going to marry.

SGANARELLE [*interrupting their dispute*]. Poor simple girls! I feel sorry for your innocence. I can't bear to see you rush to your doom. Take my advice, both of you. Don't believe a single word he says, and stay in your village.

[*Re-enter* DON JUAN *at the back.*

DON JUAN [*aside*]. Why isn't Sganarelle following me! What's he up to?

SGANARELLE. My master is a rogue. His only purpose is to seduce you, as he has seduced hundreds of others. He is ready to marry the whole human race, and . . . [*seeing* DON JUAN]. It's a lie; and whoever says so, you can tell him he's a liar. My master is not ready to marry the whole human race. He is not a rogue. He has no intention of seducing you, and he has not seduced hundreds of others. Ah, there he is! He'll tell you the same himself.

DON JUAN [*to* SGANARELLE, *thinking he has spoken*]. Yes? What is it?

SGANARELLE. Monsieur, as the world is full of slanderers, I've taken the bull by the horns, and told them straight out that, if any one speaks ill of you, they are not to believe it, but to tell him he's a liar.

DON JUAN. Sganarelle!

SGANARELLE [*to* CHARLOTTE *and* MATHURINE]. Yes, my master is a man of honour. I vouch for him myself.

DON JUAN. Hm!

SGANARELLE. Only an idiot would say anything else.

V   [*Enter* LA RAMÉE.

LA RAMÉE [*aside to* DON JUAN]. Sir, I come to warn you that you are in danger here.

DON JUAN. How so?

LA RAMÉE. Twelve men on horseback are out looking for you. They may be here at any minute. I don't know how they knew you were here; but I was told by a peasant of whom they asked the way, and to whom they described you in detail. There's not a moment to be lost. The sooner you are away from here the better.

DON JUAN [*to* CHARLOTTE *and* MATHURINE]. Urgent business compels me to leave you. But don't forget my promise. You shall hear from me before to-morrow evening.

[MATHURINE *and* CHARLOTTE *go out*

As these rascals have the advantage in numbers, we must resort to subterfuge to escape the trap they've laid for me. You, Sganarelle, will change clothes with me; and I. . . .

SGANARELLE. Not likely, Sir. What? Run the risk of being killed in your clothes, and. . . .

DON JUAN. Come along. Be quick. I'm doing you a great service. Happy the servant who can aspire to the honour of dying in his master's place.

SGANARELLE. I'm much obliged for the honour.

[DON JUAN *goes out*

Oh, kind Heaven, if death is in the wind, don't let me be mistaken for another!

ACT THREE

A forest

[*Enter* DON JUAN *in country costume and* SGANARELLE   I *dressed as a doctor.*

SGANARELLE. Come, Sir admit that I was right, and that we couldn't be better disguised. Your first idea was no good at all. This will do our business much better than what you suggested.

DON JUAN. It certainly suits you. I can't imagine where you managed to dig out such a ridiculous costume.

SGANARELLE. It's good, isn't it? It's the dress of an old doctor, which was left in pawn at the place where I got it— and it cost me a pretty penny too I can tell you. But, do you know, Sir, it has already given me a certain status. People bow to me in the streets; and some have even asked my advice, as if I was learned in the science.

DON JUAN. How do you mean?

SGANARELLE. Why, five or six country people, who saw me go by, came to consult me about their ailments.

DON JUAN. And of course you told them that you knew nothing about it?

SGANARELLE. Not me. I wasn't going to disgrace my dress. I held forth on their illnesses, and prescribed for them all.

—

DON JUAN. What remedies did you give them then?

SGANARELLE. Heavens, Sir, I put down the first thing that came into my head! I wrote my prescriptions at random. It will be a good joke if they get cured after all, and come to thank me.

DON JUAN. And why shouldn't they? Why shouldn't you enjoy the same advantage as other doctors? They're no more responsible for their cures than you are. Their whole art is sheer humbug. All they do is to take the credit for a bit of luck. You have as much right as they have to profit by the patient's good fortune, and have attributed to your medicine what is really due to natural causes or mere chance.

SGANARELLE. What, Sir, you're a heathen about medicine as well?

DON JUAN. It's one of mankind's greatest delusions.

SGANARELLE. You mean you don't believe in senna or cassia or emetic wine?

DON JUAN. Why should I believe in them?

SGANARELLE. You must have a very unbelieving soul. But look what a reputation emetic wine has got in the last few years. Its wonders have won over the most sceptical. Why, only three weeks ago, I saw a wonderful proof myself.

DON JUAN. What was that?

SGANARELLE. A man was at the point of death for six whole days. They didn't know what to do for him. Nothing had any effect. Then suddenly they decided to give him a dose of emetic wine.

DON JUAN. And he recovered?

SGANARELLE. No. He died.

DON JUAN. An admirable effect, truly.

SGANARELLE. What? For six whole days he couldn't die; and that finished him off at once. Could anything be more effective?

—

DON JUAN. No, I grant you that.

SGANARELLE. But, leaving medicine for the moment, as you don't believe in it, let's discuss something else. This dress has sharpened my wits, and I feel in the vein for debating. You allow me to argue, you know. It's only moralizing that you've forbidden.

DON JUAN. Very well, fire away.

SGANARELLE. I want to get to the bottom of what you really think. Is it possible that you don't believe in Heaven at all?

DON JUAN. Let that question alone.

SGANARELLE. That means you don't. And Hell?

DON JUAN. Enough!

SGANARELLE. Ditto. What about the devil then?

DON JUAN. Oh, of course.

SGANARELLE. As little. Do you believe in an after life?

DON JUAN. Ha! ha! ha!

SGANARELLE. Here's a man I shall have a job to convert. Come now. Father Christmas:* what do you think about him?

DON JUAN. Imbecile!

SGANARELLE. Oh, this is really too much! There's nothing as true as Father Christmas. I'd go to the gallows for him. But everybody must believe in something. What do you believe in?

DON JUAN. What do I believe?

SGANARELLE. Yes.

DON JUAN. I believe that two and two make four, Sganarelle, and four and four make eight.

SGANARELLE. That's a fine thing to believe! What fine articles of faith! Your religion then is nothing but arithmetic. Some people do have queer ideas in their heads, and those that have been educated are often the silliest. I never

studied like you, thank God, and no one can boast he taught me anything. But, to my poor way of thinking, my eyes are better than books. I know very well that this world we see around us is not a mushroom grown up in a single night. Who made those trees, those rocks, this earth, and that sky above there? Did all that make itself? There's yourself now. There you are. Did you come into being just like that? Didn't your father have to get your mother with child to make you? Can you see all the elements which go to make up the machine called man, without marvelling how they all fit in with one another? These nerves, these bones, these veins, these arteries, these . . . these lungs, this heart, this liver, and all the other ingredients there are, which. . . . Oh, do please interrupt me. I can't go on arguing if you don't interrupt. You're holding your tongue on purpose, and letting me run on, just to make a fool of me.

DON JUAN. I was waiting until your argument was finished.

SGANARELLE. My argument is that there's something wonderful in Man, which none of your clever scientists can explain. I don't care what you say. Isn't it wonderful that I am standing here, and that I have something in my head which makes me think a hundred different thoughts at once, and makes my body do whatever it likes? I clap my hands, raise my arms, look up to Heaven, bow my head, move my feet, go to the right, go to the left, go forward, go back, turn round. . . . [*As he turns he falls down*].

DON JUAN. Splendid! There lies your argument with a broken nose.

SGANARELLE. Oh, I'm a fool to waste my time arguing with you. Believe what you like. It's no affair of mine if you're damned.

DON JUAN. While we've been arguing, I believe we've lost our way. Call to that man over there and ask him the road.

[*Enter a poor man.*   II

SGANARELLE. Hola! Ho man! Ho, you there! Ho, friend! One word, if you please. Will you show us the way back to the town?

MAN. You have only to follow this road, gentlemen, and turn to your right when you are out of the forest. But I must warn you to be on your guard. There are robbers about.

DON JUAN. I am much obliged to you, my friend. Many thanks. .

MAN. If you could spare me a little something, Sir.

DON JUAN. Oho! So your advice was prompted merely by self-interest!

MAN. I am a poor man, Sir, and I've lived alone in this wood for ten years. I will pray Heaven to give you every happiness.

DON JUAN. Pray Heaven to give you a new coat. That will do you more good than bothering about other people.

SGANARELLE. You don't know this gentleman, my good fellow. He doesn't believe in anything but two and two make four, and four and four make eight.

DON JUAN. How do you pass your time here among all these trees?

MAN. I pray all day long for the prosperity of the kind people who give me alms.

DON JUAN. You are quite comfortably off then, I suppose?

MAN. Alas, no, Sir! I am in the greatest penury.

DON JUAN. What? A man who prays all day long can't fail to be well off.

MAN. I assure you, Sir, I often haven't even a crust to put in my mouth.

DON JUAN. That's strange. You're not very well rewarded for your trouble. See here. I'll give you a gold louis, if you'll utter a blasphemy.

MAN. Oh, Sir, would you have me commit such a terrible sin?

DON JUAN. The question is, do you want this gold piece or not? I'll give it to you if you blaspheme. Come now.

MAN. Sir. . . .

DON JUAN. You shan't have it unless you do.

SGANARELLE. Come along! Just one little blasphemy. There's no harm in it.

DON JUAN. Here you are; take it! Take it, I say. Blaspheme.

MAN. No, Sir. I would rather die of starvation.

DON JUAN. Oh, very well then. I give it you for the love of . . . humanity. [*looking off into the forest*]. But what's happening over there? A man attacked by three at once! That's too great odds. I can't see such a dastardly action without intervening.

III   [*He draws his sword and rushes into the fray. The poor man goes out.*

SGANARELLE. My master must be mad, to go rushing into a fight that doesn't concern him. But, Jove, he's done the trick! The two have put the three to fight.

[*Re-enter* DON JUAN *with* DON CARLOS: SGANARELLE *remains in the background.*

DON CARLOS [*sheathing his sword*]. The flight of these rascally footpads proves your courage in a fray. Allow me to thank you, Sir, for your noble action; and. . . .

DON JUAN. It's no more than you would have done yourself, my dear Sir. Such adventures are a consequence of our sense of honour. Not to intervene in such a cowardly and one-sided affair would make one an accomplice. But by what misadventure did you fall into their hands?

DON CARLOS. I got separated from my brother and the rest of our company by accident; and, as I was attempting to rejoin them, I met these thieves, who first killed my horse, and, without your courageous intervention, would have done as much for me.

DON JUAN. Are you going in the direction of the town?

DON CARLOS. Yes, but without entering the gates. My brother and I are obliged to keep to the open country, on account of one of those unlucky affairs, through which a gentleman is forced to sacrifice himself and his family to the strict law of honour. For, in such a business, even victory is disastrous. If one comes off with one's life, one has to fly the country. I consider that a gentleman is most unfortunate in these matters. Instead of being able to be answerable for the prudence and honour of his own behaviour only, he is at the mercy of another's villainy, and has to see his life, his peace and his property depend on the whim of the first scoundrel who chooses to do him the sort of injury for which a gentleman is expected to put his life in danger.

DON JUAN. We have at least the consolation that we make those who offend us, out of thoughtless irresponsibility, take the same risks as ourselves and have as bad a time of it. But may I, without indiscretion, ask the particulars of your affair?

DON CARLOS. It won't be a secret much longer; and when once the injury is known, our honour will not be concerned to hide our shame, but to take public revenge; and even publish our intention of doing so. The offence we seek to avenge, Sir, is the seduction of our sister, who was carried off from a convent by a certain Don Juan Tenorio, the son of Don Louis Tenorio. We have been looking for him for several days, and we followed him this morning on the information of a servant, who told us that he had ridden in this direction with four or five others. But all our efforts have been vain. We haven't been able to find him anywhere.

DON JUAN. Are you acquainted with this Don Juan, Sir?

DON CARLOS. I have never seen him personally. I have only heard him described by my brother. But his reputation is none of the best. He is a man whose life. . . .

DON JUAN. I may not listen to this, Sir. He is by way of being one of my friends; and I cannot, without dishonour, hear him ill spoken of.

DON CARLOS. Then out of consideration for you, Sir, I will say no more. I owe you my life. The least I can do is to be silent before you about a gentleman you honour with your friendship, especially as I can say no good of him. But, though you are his friend, I dare to hope that you will not approve his conduct, or think it unnatural that we seek revenge for it.

DON JUAN. On the contrary, Sir, I would like to serve you, and spare you unnecessary trouble. I cannot help being Don Juan's friend; but it is not right that he should offend gentlemen with impunity, and I pledge you my word he shall give you satisfaction.

DON CARLOS. What satisfaction can he give for such an injury?

DON JUAN. The fullest your honour can require. You need search for Don Juan no further. I engage that he shall meet you when and where you will.

DON CARLOS. Your words bring balm to an offended spirit, Sir. But, in view of what I owe you, it would be a matter of deep regret to me if you yourself were to be of the party.

DON JUAN. I am so much his friend that, if he fights, I must do so too. I can answer for him as for myself. You have only to say when you wish him to appear, and offer you satisfaction.

DON CARLOS. What a cruel stroke of ill fortune that I should owe you my life and that you should be a friend of Don Juan!

IV

[*Enter* DON ALONSO.

DON ALONSO [*speaking to his followers without seeing* DON CARLOS *or* DON JUAN]. Give my horses drink, and bring them after us. I will go on on foot. [*perceiving them both*]. Good God, brother, what's this? You are talking with our mortal enemy?

DON CARLOS. Our mortal enemy?

DON JUAN [*putting his hand on his sword*]. Yes, I am Don Juan himself. No disadvantage in numbers shall make me deny my name.

DON ALONSO [*drawing his sword*]. Treacherous villain! You shall die, and. . . .

[SGANARELLE *runs to hide*

DON CARLOS. Stay, brother, on your life! I owe him my very existence. Without his help I should have been killed by robbers.

DON ALONSO. And is that a reason we should forgo our revenge? A service rendered by an enemy has no claim on our gratitude. Weigh but the obligation against the wrong, and all gratitude would be ridiculous. Honour is more precious than life. He that gives life in exchange for stolen honour leaves no debt on our side.

DON CARLOS. I recognize the distinction a gentleman should always make between them, and my sense of gratitude has not wiped out my anger for the injury; but let me pay my debt by delaying our revenge, and leaving him free to enjoy for a few days more the liberty and life I owe him.

DON ALONSO. No, no. We risk losing our revenge altogether by postponing it. Fate has given us this opportunity. Let us take it, or it may not come again. In a case of wounded honour, squeamishness is out of place. If you are reluctant to put your own hand to the work, withdraw; and let me have the fully glory to myself.

DON CARLOS. Brother, I beg you to. . . .

DON ALONSO. All argument is useless. He must die.

DON CARLOS. I warn you I will not stand by and see it done. I swear by Heaven that I will stand to his defence against the world, and make a rampart of this same life he has ransomed. Your sword shall reach him only through my body.

DON ALONSO. So you take our enemy's part against me; and, instead of being roused to fury at the sight of him, as I am, you are moved to show him kindness!

DON CARLOS. My dear brother, we are perfectly justified in avenging our honour; but let us lay all anger aside, and proceed with moderation. Let our temper be under control, our determination free from ferocity; and let us show that we are governed by reason, and not by the heady rashness of blind fury. I do not want to remain in my enemy's debt. My obligation must be discharged before everything. Our revenge will not be less striking for being deferred. On the contrary, it will gain by it. Our letting this opportunity go will justify us still further in the eyes of the world.

DON ALONSO. What blind and lamentable weakness, to risk our honour for the ridiculous scruples of an imaginary debt!

DON CARLOS. Do not say so, my dear brother. If I am wrong, I shall know how to make amends for it. I take the whole charge of our honour upon myself. I know what it requires of us; and this loss of a single day, which my gratitude demands, will only increase my determination to satisfy it. Don Juan, you see how anxious I am to repay the good offices I have received from you, and from that you may judge of what is to come. You will see that I can claim a debt with as much resolution as I pay it, and that I shall be as quick to pay an injury as a benefit. I do not ask you to state your intentions now. You will have time to consider that at your leisure. You are aware of the gravity of the wrong you have done, and will judge of what is fitting to do in reparation. There is a peaceful way to satisfy us, and one that is violent and bloody; but, whichever you choose, you have pledged me your word that Don Juan shall stand to his answer. Do not forget your promise; and remember that, once off this ground, I owe nothing but to my honour.

DON JUAN. I have asked for no favour, and I will keep my promise.

DON CARLOS. Let us go, brother. A moment of courtesy can be no prejudice to our honour.

[DON CARLOS *and* DON ALONSO *go out* V

DON JUAN. Hola, there! Sganarelle!

SGANARELLE [*coming out from his hiding place*]. What's your will, Sir?

DON JUAN. You rascal! When I'm attacked you run away.

SGANARELLE. I beg your pardon, Sir. I only went round the corner. I think this dress must have a purgative effect. It's as good as taking medicine to wear it.

DON JUAN. Enough of this impertinence! At least make a more decent excuse for your cowardice. Do you know who it was whose life I saved?

SGANARELLE. No. Who?

DON JUAN. One of Elvira's brothers.

SGANARELLE. One of. . . .

DON JUAN. He is quite a decent fellow, and has behaved very well. I am sorry to have to fight him.

SGANARELLE. You can easily make it up.

DON JUAN. Yes. But my passion for Dona Elvira is worn out, and it doesn't suit my humour to be tied. For me, freedom in love is everything. I could never endure to immure my heart within four walls. I have told you over and over that I like to follow whatever draws me on. My heart is the prize of all beautiful women. It is theirs to take in turn, and to keep for as long as they can. But what's that magnificent building I see among those trees?

SGANARELLE. Don't you know?

DON JUAN. No.

SGANARELLE. Really? Why, it's the tomb the Commander was having built when you killed him.

DON JUAN. Ah, yes. I didn't know it was in this direction. Everyone has told me what a wonderful piece of work it is; and the Commander's statue too. I should like to see it.

SGANARELLE. Oh, Sir, don't go in there.

DON JUAN. Why not?

SGANARELLE. It wouldn't be good manners to call on a man you've killed.

DON JUAN. On the contrary, I should like to pay him the compliment. He ought to be very pleased, if he has any breeding. Come along. Let's go inside.

[*The tomb opens and the Commander's statue is seen.*

SGANARELLE. Oh, how beautiful! What beautiful statues! And look at the beautiful marble and the beautiful pillars! Isn't it beautiful? What do you think, Sir?

DON JUAN. That the ostentation of a dead man could hardly go further. What astonishes me is that a man, who in his lifetime was content with quite a simple home, should want to build such a grand one for when he no longer has any use for it.

SGANARELLE. There's the Commander's statue.

DON JUAN. God, doesn't he look a figure of fun, dressed up like a Roman emperor?

SGANARELLE. Heavens, Sir, it's a good bit of work! Why, he almost seems alive; as if he was just going to speak. He's looking at us in a way that would frighten me if I was alone. I don't think he likes to see us here.

DON JUAN. He should do. It's a poor return for my compliment else. Ask him if he'd care to have supper with me.

SGANARELLE. He's past that sort of thing now, I believe.

DON JUAN. Ask him.

SGANARELLE. What do you mean? Only a fool would go and talk to a statue.

DON JUAN. Do as I tell you.

SGANARELLE. How ridiculous! My lord Commander. . . . [aside]. I can't help laughing at my silliness, but it's my master that makes me do it. [aloud]. My lord Commander, my master Don Juan asks if you will do him the honour to come and sup with him.

[The statue nods its head.

Oh!

DON JUAN. What is it? What's the matter with you? Answer. Will you speak?

SGANARELLE [nodding his head like the statue]. The statue. . . .

DON JUAN. Well? What, you rascal?

SGANARELLE. I tell you, the statue. . . .

DON JUAN. Well? The statue? I'll break your head open if you don't speak out.

SGANARELLE. The statue nodded.

DON JUAN. Plague take the fool!

SGANARELLE. It nodded its head, I tell you. As true as I stand here. Go and speak to it yourself, and see. Perhaps. . . .

DON JUAN. Come with me, you rascal, come with me. You shall see what a miserable coward you are. Now watch. Will the Lord Commander come and sup with me?

[The statue nods again.

SGANARELLE. I'd have give ten pistoles not to have missed witnessing this scene. Well, Sir?

DON JUAN. Let's get out of here at once.

[*He goes out*

SGANARELLE. Where are your free thinkers now, who believe in nothing at all?

ACT FOUR

Don Juan's apartment

I   [*Enter* DON JUAN, SGANARELLE *and* RAGOTIN.

DON JUAN [*to* SGANARELLE]. Well, whatever it was, say no more about it. It's of no importance. We may have been deceived by the bad light, or a slight swimming in the head may have prevented our seeing properly.

SGANARELLE. Oh, Sir, don't try to explain away what we saw distinctly. As true as I stand here, he nodded his head. There's no doubt that Heaven is scandalized at your way of life; and has brought about this miracle, to convert you, and save you from. . . .

DON JUAN. Now listen. If you annoy me any more with your stupid moralizing, or say another word about it, I'll send for a rawhide whip, have you held by the arms and legs, and thrash you within an inch of your life. Do you understand?

SGANARELLE. Very well indeed, Sir. You couldn't speak plainer. That's one good thing about you. You don't beat about the bush. You say what you mean, without any possibility of mistake.

DON JUAN. Then let me have supper as soon as possible [*to* RAGOTIN]. Bring a chair, boy.

II   [*Enter* LA VIOLETTE.

LA VIOLETTE. Sir, Monsieur Dimanche the shopkeeper is asking to speak with you.

SGANARELLE. That's splendid! All we needed was a creditor to come and dun us for money. What does he mean by coming here asking for money? Why didn't you tell him that the master wasn't at home?

LA VIOLETTE. I have been telling him so for the last three-quarters of an hour, but he won't believe it. He's sitting down there, inside the door, waiting.

SGANARELLE. Then let him wait.

DON JUAN. No, on the contrary, tell him to come up. It's very bad policy to hide oneself from creditors. They must be paid with something. I know the way to send them away satisfied, without giving them a penny.

[*Enter* M. DIMANCHE.   III

Ah, come in, Monsieur Dimanche. I am delighted to see you. My rascals shall smart for not letting you up at once. It's true I had given orders that no one was to be admitted, but that was not meant for you. My door will always be open to you.

M. DIMANCHE. I am most humbly obliged to you, Sir.

DON JUAN [*to* LA VIOLETTE *and* RAGOTIN]. Dammit, you rogues, I'll teach you to leave Monsieur Dimanche to kick his heels in an antechamber! You shall learn a little more discrimination.

M. DIMANCHE. Please say no more about it, Sir.

DON JUAN [*to* M. DIMANCHE]. What! Deny me to you; to Monsieur Dimanche, my best friend?

M. DIMANCHE. Monsieur, I am your most devoted servant. I came to. . . .

DON JUAN. A seat there for Monsieur Dimanche!

M. DIMANCHE. I shall do very well as I am, Sir.

DON JUAN. By no means. I want you to come here and sit by me.

M. DIMANCHE. It's really not necessary, Sir.

DON JUAN. Take this stool away, and bring an armchair.

M. DIMANCHE. You can't be serious, Sir. I. . . .

DON JUAN. No, no, I know what's due to you. I wish there to be no distinction between us.

M. DIMANCHE. Sir. . . .

DON JUAN. Come, sit down.

M. DIMANCHE. There's no occasion at all, Sir. I have very little to say. I was. . . .

DON JUAN. Sit down, I beg of you.

M. DIMANCHE. No, Sir. I am quite all right. I came to. . . .

DON JUAN. I won't listen, unless you sit down.

M. DIMANCHE. Very well then, Sir; if you wish it. I. . . .

DON JUAN. I hope I see you well, Monsieur Dimanche.

M. DIMANCHE. Oh, yes, Sir, thank you kindly. I have come to. . . .

DON JUAN. You have a regular fund of good health; full lips, fresh colour, and bright eyes.

M. DIMANCHE. I would. . . .

DON JUAN. How is Madame Dimanche, your wife?

M. DIMANCHE. In good health, Sir, I thank God.

DON JUAN. A splendid woman!

M. DIMANCHE. She is your very humble servant, Sir. I came. . . .

DON JUAN. And Claudine, your little girl? How is she?

M. DIMANCHE. Quite well.

DON JUAN. What a pretty little girl she is! I adore her.

M. DIMANCHE. You do her too much honour, Sir. I. . . .

DON JUAN. And little Colin? Does he make as much noise as ever with his little drum?

M. DIMANCHE. Just the same, Sir. I. . . .

DON JUAN. And your little dog Brusquet? Does he still growl as fiercely, and bite the legs of everyone who comes to the house?

M. DIMANCHE. Worse and worse, Sir. We're at out wits' end how to stop him.

DON JUAN. You mustn't be surprised at my asking after all your family. I take the greatest interest in them.

M. DIMANCHE. We are most gratified, Sir. I. . . .

DON JUAN [*holding out his hand*]. Your hand, Monsieur Dimanche. I may look on you as one of my friends?

M. DIMANCHE. I am your very humble servant, Sir.

DON JUAN. Dammit, I regard your interests as my own.

M. DIMANCHE. You do me too much honour. I. . . .

DON JUAN. There's nothing I wouldn't do for you.

M. DIMANCHE. Sir, you are too kind.

DON JUAN. With no motives of self interest, I beg you to believe.

M. DIMANCHE. I have not deserved such consideration. But, Sir. . . .

DON JUAN. Come, Monsieur Dimanche, let there be no ceremony between us. Will you sup with me to-night?

M. DIMANCHE Forgive me, Sir, but I am obliged to return home immediately. I. . . .

DON JUAN [*rising*]. A torch there, to go before Monsieur Dimanche! Let four or five of my people take muskets, and accompany him.

M. DIMANCHE [*rising also*]. I beg you will not trouble, Sir. I can go quite well alone. But. . . .

[SGANARELLE *quickly removes the chairs.*

DON JUAN. You must certainly not go unattended. Your safety is too dear to me. I am your servant, and, what's more, your debtor.

M. DIMANCHE. Ah, Sir. . . .

DON JUAN. I make no secret of it. I admit it openly.

M. DIMANCHE. If. . . .

DON JUAN. May I conduct you?

M. DIMANCHE. You cannot be serious, Sir. . . .

DON JUAN. Embrace me, Monsieur Dimanche. And, once more, I beg you to believe that I am entirely at your service. There is nothing in the world I would not do for you.

[*He goes out, followed by* LA VIOLETTE *and* RAGOTIN

SGANARELLE. The master undoubtedly has a very high regard for you.

M. DIMANCHE. Yes. He is so unwearingly kind and considerate, that I shall never have the face to ask him for my money.

SGANARELLE. We are all of us yours to the death, I assure you. I only wish you might meet with some little accident, or that someone would take it into his head to give you a good thrashing, so that we could prove how. . . .

M. DIMANCHE. Oh, I believe you without that. But Sganarelle, can't you manage to slip in a little word about my money?

SGANARELLE. Oh, don't you worry about your money. He'll pay you all right.

M. DIMANCHE. But you, too, Sganarelle. You have a small account with me as well.

SGANARELLE. Ssh! Not a word about that!

M. DIMANCHE. How do you mean? I. . . .

SGANARELLE. Don't I know well enough what I owe you?

M. DIMANCHE. Yes, but. . . .

SGANARELLE. Come, Monsieur Dimanche, I will light you to the door.

M. DIMANCHE. But my money!

SGANARELLE [*taking him by the arm*]. You can't mean it.

M. DIMANCHE. I want. . . .

SGANARELLE [*pulling him*]. Come.

M. DIMANCHE. I intend to. . . .

SGANARELLE [*pushing him towards the door*]. Nonsense!

M. DIMANCHE. But. . . .

DON JUAN [*pushing him*]. For shame!

M. DIMANCHE. I. . . .

SGANARELLE [*pushing him right off the stage*]. For shame, Monsieur Dimanche, for shame!

[DON JUAN *and* LA VIOLETTE *both return.*   IV

LA VIOLETTE [*to* DON JUAN]. Here comes your father, sir.

DON JUAN. The devil! A visit from him was all I needed.

[*Enter* DON LOUIS.

DON LOUIS. It is easy to see that my coming is unwelcome, and causes you more embarrassment than pleasure. Each of us is a thorn in the side of the other; and, if you are weary of me, I am equally weary of your bad behaviour. Alas! We little know what we are doing when, instead of leaving to God the choice of what is good for us, we try to be wiser than He, and pester Him with our blind and ill-considered longings. To have a son was the dearest wish of my heart, for which I never ceased to pray. And this son, granted at last to my unwearying petition, has made my life a misery and a burden, instead of being, as I had hoped, its joy and consolation. Do you think I can see without shame and indignation this continued course of disgraceful actions? They are beyond any possibility of excuse; and are fast exhausting the patience of the King our master, and outweighing in his eyes both my past services and the credit of my friends. What baseness! Are you not ashamed to dishonour your family in this way? You have lost even the right to be proud of your descent, so little is your conduct worthy of a nobleman. Do you think it is enough to bear the name and the escutcheon, or that noble blood can confer honour on a man who lives in infamy? No, no. Birth is of no account unless accompanied by nobility of character. The measure of our share in our ancestors' renown is the measure of our efforts to resemble them; and the very lustre of their achievements, in whose reflected glory we shine, obliges us, by following in the same paths of virtue, to return the honour we have received; or we proclaim ourselves no true descendants of them. You may no longer claim the consideration due to noble birth. Your ancestors cast you out. The fame of their great deeds, which should have brought you credit, is a beacon in whose light your dishonour shows the blacker. A gentleman who lives an evil life is a freak of nature. Virtue is the true title to nobility. I judge of a man, not by who he is, but by what he does; and I would have more respect for the son of a street-porter who was an honest man, than for the son of an emperor who lived like you.

DON JUAN. Won't you take a chair, Sir? You could talk so much more comfortably if you were sitting down.

DON LOUIS. No, rascal, I will not sit down; nor stay to speak to you any more. I know well enough that nothing I can say will ever touch your heart. But listen carefully. Your unworthy conduct has almost extinguished your father's love; and, sooner perhaps than you think, I shall find a way to put a stop to your disorders; forestall the anger of Heaven; and, by your punishment, wash away my dishonour in having been your father.

V   [He goes out

DON JUAN [calling after him]. Make haste and die. The sooner the better. Every dog should have his day. No father ought to go on living after his son is of age. [He throws himself into an armchair].

SGANARELLE. Oh, Sir, you are wrong; indeed you are.

—

DON JUAN [*rising*]. Wrong?

SGANARELLE [*trembling*]. Sir. . . .

DON JUAN. Wrong did you say?

SGANARELLE. Yes, Sir, you were very wrong to let him talk to you like that. You should have taken him by the shoulders, and put him outside. Could there be anything so out of place as for a father to come and complain of his son's conduct, tell him to alter his way of life, to remember his birth, to live as a gentleman ought to live, and other childishness of that sort? I wonder that a man of the world like you would suffer it. I admire your patience. If I'd been in your shoes, I'd soon have sent him packing. [*aside*]. Oh, my damned cowardice! The things it makes me say and do!

DON JUAN. Will supper soon be ready?

[*Enter* RAGOTIN.   VI

RAGOTIN. Sir, there's a lady in a veil who wishes to speak with you.

DON JUAN. Who can this be?

SGANARELLE. It won't be long before we know.

[RAGOTIN *goes out. Then enter* DONA ELVIRA, *veiled.*

DONA ELVIRA. Do not be surprised, Don Juan, to see me again so soon, and in these clothes; but I have urgent reasons for coming, and what I have to say to you will admit of no delay. My anger of this morning is all gone, and I come to you now in a very different frame of mind. I am no longer the Dona Elvira who prayed for your punishment, and whose outraged feelings found an outlet in threats of vengeance. Heaven has banished from my heart all that was unworthy in my love for you; the heady violence of a criminal attachment, the shameful transports of a gross and earthly love. All that remains for you in my heart is a flame purged of sensuality, a holy affection, a pure and disinterested love which, with no thought of self, thinks only of your good.

DON JUAN [*aside to* SGANARELLE]. You appear to be crying.

SGANARELLE. Forgive me.

DONA ELVIRA. Moved by this pure and perfect love, I come to bring you a warning from Heaven; to try to draw you back from the precipice, over which you are rushing to destruction. I know the disorders of your life; and the same Heaven which has touched my heart, and opened my eyes to the irregularities of my own behaviour, has inspired me to seek you out, and deliver Its message. Don Juan, the cup of your offences is full. The terrible wrath of God is ready to fall, and there is no escape but by immediate repentance. Perhaps you have only this one day left, to save yourself from the last and greatest of all calamities. I am no longer bound to you by any earthly ties. By God's grace, I have renounced for ever my mad and unruly passions; and, once more in the convent, I ask for no more of life than time to expiate my sins; and, by a severe penance, win pardon for the crimes into which a shameful passion has plunged me. But, lost to the world though I am, it would be a lasting grief to me if one I had loved so dearly became a fearful example of the justice of God; and a joy above all others, if I might only prevail on you to turn aside the deadly blow which threatens you. For pity's sake, Don Juan, as my last request, grant me this sweet satisfaction. With tears I beg you to look to your salvation. If your own self-interest carries no weight with you, at least let my prayers; and spare me the agony of seeing you condemned to everlasting punishment.

SGANARELLE [*aside*]. Poor woman!

DONA ELVIRA. I had for you a love past telling. You were dearer to me than anything in the world. There was nothing I would not have done for you. For you I forgot my vows. All I ask in return is that you will live a better life, and save yourself from destruction. Save yourself, Don Juan, I beseech you; if not for your own sake, then for love of me. With my tears I implore you. And if the tears of one you have loved are of no avail, then I conjure you by anything which has the power to move you.

SGANARELLE [*aside, looking at* DON JUAN]. Oh, heart of stone!

DONA ELVIRA. I am going now, Don Juan. I have given my warning. I have no more to say.

DON JUAN. It is getting late, Madame. Won't you stay here? We will do our best to make you comfortable.

DONA ELVIRA. No, Don Juan. Do not try to detain me.

DON JUAN. I assure you, Madame, it would make me most happy if you would stay.

DONA ELVIRA. No, no. Let us waste no time in idle argument. Think only of my warning, and let me go on my way, alone.

[*She goes out*   VII

DON JUAN. Do you know, I still have some slight feeling for her. There is something rather charming about this strange new fancy. Her simplicity of dress, her sorrow and her tears have reawakened some few sparks of a fire I had thought quite burnt out.

SGANARELLE. That's as much as to say that her words have made no impression on you at all.

DON JUAN. Supper! Quick!

SGANARELLE. Very good, Sir.

[*Enter* LA VIOLETTE *and* RAGOTIN.

DON JUAN [*sitting down to table*]. For all that, Sganarelle, we must begin to think about reforming ourselves.

SGANARELLE [*earnestly*]. Oh, Sir, will you really?

DON JUAN. Yes, indeed, we must reform ourselves! Another twenty or thirty years of this kind of life, and then we'll have to look to our style of life.

SGANARELLE. Oh!

DON JUAN. What's your own opinion?

SGANARELLE. I haven't any. Here's supper.

[*He takes a morsel from one of the dishes which are brought in, and puts in his mouth.*

DON JUAN. Your cheek appears to be swollen. What is it? Tell me. What have you got there?

SGANARELLE. Nothing.

DON JUAN. Show me. Good God, you've got an abscess in your cheek! Quick! It must be slit with a lancet. The poor fellow is quite overcome. He may be suffocated. There now, it has broken of itself! Ah, you rogue!

SGANARELLE. Heavens, Sir, I only wanted to make sure that the cook hadn't put in too much salt and pepper.

DON JUAN. Come now, sit down and eat. I shall want you after supper. You seem hungry.

SGANARELLE [*sitting at table*]. I believe you, Sir. I've had nothing since breakfast. I'll have some of that. It looks delicious. [*To* RAGOTIN, *who, as soon as* SGANARELLE *puts something on his plate, takes it from him while his head is turned*]. My plate! my plate! Just a minute, if you please. By God, you're very quick at bringing clean plates, my young friend! Aha, young La Violette, I see you know when to hand the wine!

[*While* LA VIOLETTE *pours out for* SGANARELLE, RAGOTIN *takes his plate away again.*

DON JUAN. Who's that knocking so loud?

SGANARELLE. Who the devil's this, coming to disturb our supper?

DON JUAN. I want to sup in peace. Don't admit anybody.

SGANARELLE. Leave it to me. I'll see to it.

DON JUAN [*seeing* SGANARELLE *return terrified*]. What is it then? What's the matter?

SGANARELLE [*nodding his head like the statue*]. The ... is there.

DON JUAN. I'll go myself. I'll show you that nothing can frighten me.

SGANARELLE. Oh, poor Sganarelle, what hole can you find to creep into?

[*Enter the* STATUE OF THE COMMANDER.   VIII

DON JUAN [*to the lackeys*]. A chair and place setting, quick!

[DON JUAN *and the* STATUE *sit down to table*.

[*to* SGANARELLE]. Come on now. Sit down.

SGANARELLE. I'm not hungry any more, Sir.

DON JUAN. Sit down, I say. Bring wine. To the health of the Commander! Come along, Sganarelle. Give him some wine.

SGANARELLE. I'm not thirsty, Sir.

DON JUAN. Have some wine; then sing your song, to entertain the Commander.

SGANARELLE. I've got a cold, Sir.

DON JUAN. Never mind. Come along. [*to the lackeys*]. You there, come and sing with him.

THE STATUE. Enough, Don Juan! Tomorrow I invite you to sup with me. Have you the courage to come?

DON JUAN. Yes, certainly I'll come; and I'll bring Sganarelle.

SGANARELLE. Thank you very much, but it's a fast day for me tomorrow.

DON JUAN [*to* SGANARELLE]. Take this torch, and light the Commander.

THE STATUE. There is no need of light when Heaven is our guide.

ACT FIVE

A place in the country near the city

I   [*Enter* DON JUAN, DON LOUIS *and* SGANARELLE.

DON LOUIS. Oh, my son, has God really been so merciful as to hear my prayers? Is what you tell me really true? Don't buoy me up with false hopes. Am I to believe that this miraculous change of heart will last?

DON JUAN. Yes, I have renounced my wicked way of life. I have become a different person since last night. Heaven has changed me in a moment so completely, that it will astound the world. My soul has been touched, my eyes opened, and I look back with horror on the long night of blindness in which I have walked; and on the criminal debauchery of the life I have led. When I think of my crimes, I am astounded that Heaven has borne with them so long, and has not stricken me to the earth with righteous indignation. I am keenly aware of Its goodness in sparing me my punishment; and, that I may profit by it as I ought, I mean to show the world a sudden reformation, which shall make amends for the scandal of my past life, and win for me a full pardon from Heaven. That is my wish, Sir; and I beg you will help me by pointing out to me a fit person to act as my mentor, under whose guidance I may walk straight in the way I have laid down for myself.

DON LOUIS. Ah, my dear son, a father's love is easily regained. At the first word of repentance, a child's offences vanish like smoke. I have forgotten already the misery you have caused me. All is wiped out by the assurance I have just heard. I am beside myself with delight. I weep for joy. My dearest wish is granted, and I have nothing further to ask for. Kiss me, my son. Let nothing induce you to go

back on your praiseworthy determination. I myself will
hasten to carry the good news to your mother, who will
share in my joy; and to give thanks to God for inspiring
you with such a holy resolution.

[*He goes out* II

SGANARELLE. Oh, Sir, I am so glad that you are converted.
It's what I have long been waiting for; and now, God be
thanked, my wish is granted!

DON JUAN. What on earth is the fool talking about?

SGANARELLE. Why *fool*, Sir?

DON JUAN. What? Did you really take what I said just now
for genuine currency? You thought I spoke what was really
in my heart?

SGANARELLE. You mean it wasn't . . . you didn't . . . you. . . .
[*aside*]. Oh, what a man! What a man! What a man!

DON JUAN. Of course not. I haven't changed in the least. My
opinions are the same as they always were.

SGANARELLE. You're not affected by the wonderful miracle
of a statue that moves and speaks?

DON JUAN. True, there is something in that I can't quite
make out. But, whatever the explanation, it shall neither
shake my courage, nor influence my judgement. When I
said that I meant to change my way of life for one more
exemplary, I was moved purely by considerations of the
best tactics and most useful policy to adopt. I am forced
into this unavoidable deception by the necessity of
humouring my father, who may still be useful to me, to
protect myself from certain men, and to escape various
unpleasant contingencies which might arise. I take you into
my confidence, Sganarelle, because it pleases me to have a
witness of my true state of mind, and of my reasons for
acting as I do.

SGANARELLE. What? You believe in absolutely nothing, and
yet you propose to pass yourself off as a good man?

DON JUAN. Why not? There are many others who do the same; who use this same mask to deceive the world.

SGANARELLE. What a man! What a man!

DON JUAN. There's no longer any disgrace in it. Hypocrisy has become a fashionable vice, and all such vices pass for virtues. The mask of a good man is the best mask to wear. At no time could the profession of a hypocrite be carried on more advantageously than today. That sort of imposture is always respected; and, even if it is found out, no one dare say anything against it. All other vices come under censure, and everyone is free to rail against them; but hypocrisy is privileged and enjoys special immunity. No one dare open his mouth. By this kind of deceit, one forms a solid pact with all others of the same persuasion. If one is attacked, the rest rush to his defence at once; and even those who act in good faith, and are known to be genuinely religious, are always the dupes of the others. They fall head foremost into the hypocrites' trap, and blindly back them up in everything they do. Do you think I don't know hundreds of others who have glossed over in this way the debauchery of their youth; made themselves a shield out of the cloak of religion; and, under its cover, have continued to be the greatest scoundrels living? Even if you see through them, and know them for what they are, they still enjoy credit in the eyes of the world; and whatever ill they do is easily put right by hanging their head, groaning deeply and casting a pious glance up to heaven. It is in this safe harbour that I mean to take refuge, and set my affairs in order. I shall not give up my favourite sins, but I shall engage in them in secret; and take my pleasures without making such a noise about it. Then, if I am found out, the whole cabal will take up the cudgels without my stirring a limb, and defend me against all and sundry. That is the only way I can do whatever I like with no risk of being called to account for it. I shall set up as a censor of other people's actions, think the worst of everybody, and have no good opinion of anyone but myself. If anyone offends me, be it ever so slightly, I shall never forgive him, and have a secret grudge against him for ever after. I shall appoint myself the avenger of Heaven; and, under this convenient pretext, I shall harass my enemies, accuse them of impiety, and let loose upon them a whole horde of crazy zealots, who, without the least knowledge of the matter, will preach against them in public, cover them with abuse, and consign them to perdition by their own private authority. It's only commonsense to take advantage of the weaknesses of mankind, and adjust one's behaviour to fit in with the vices of one's age.

SGANARELLE. God in Heaven, I can hardly believe my ears! You only needed hypocrisy to be complete; and that's the worst sin of all. It's no use, Sir; I must speak. This last is more than I can stomach. Do to me whatever you like. Strike me. Beat me black and blue. Kill me, if you will. But I must say what is in my heart. It's only my duty as your faithful servant. It's the last straw that breaks the camel's back, Sir. As that author, whose name I've forgotten, said very wisely: Man in this world is like a bird on a bough. The bough is attached to the tree. Whoever keeps hold of the tree is guided by good principles. Good principles are better than fine words. Fine words are spoken at Court. At Court there are courtiers. Courtiers follow the fashion. The fashion is a product of fancy. Fancy is a faculty of the spirit. The spirit is the source of life. Life ends in death. Death makes us think of heaven. Heaven is above the earth. The earth is not the sea. The sea is subject to storms. Storms are dangerous to ships. Ships need a good pilot. A good pilot is prudent. Prudence is not found in the young. The young owe obedience to the old. The old love riches. Riches make rich men. Rich men are not poor. The poor know necessity. Necessity knows no

law. Whoever knows no law lives like a brute beast. Q.E.D.:
you'll be damned for ever.

DON JUAN. An excellent chain of reasoning!

SGANARELLE. If you won't give in after that, so much the
worse for you!

III   [*Enter* DON CARLOS.

DON CARLOS. Well met, Don Juan. This is a fitter place for
our discussion than your own apartment. What have you
decided to do? You know that at our last meeting I made
myself responsible for the affair, and that I am determined
to obtain satisfaction; but I admit that I should prefer the
matter to be settled quietly. It is my earnest hope that I
may be able to persuade you to take this course, and
publicly to acknowledge my sister as your wife.

DON JUAN [*hypocritically*]. Alas! I would most willingly give
you the satisfaction you require; but Heaven commands
the contrary. A holy influence has inspired me to change
my way of life; and, from now on, I have no thoughts but
to renounce all earthly ties, abandon all the vanities of the
world, and atone by the strictest piety for the criminal
profligacy into which my blind and headstrong youth has
plunged me.

DON CARLOS. But, Don Juan, there is nothing in this
incompatible with what I wish. The companionship of your
lawful wife will be no hindrance to the praiseworthy resolve
that Heaven has put into your heart.

DON JUAN. Alas, yes! Your sister's own design forbids it. She
is returning to the convent. We both saw the light at the
same moment.

DON CARLOS. This must not be. Her retreat will be attributed to your contempt for her, and for our family. Our
honour demands that she live with you.

DON JUAN. I assure you it is impossible. If I were to consult
my own inclination, there is nothing I should like better;

but I have even now been asking Heaven for guidance, and a voice replied that I must think of your sister no longer, as with her I could never gain salvation.

DON CARLOS. Do you think you can put us off with excuses like these, Don Juan?

DON JUAN. I am obeying the voice from on high.

DON CARLOS. And you think I'll be content with that?

DON JUAN. It is the will of Heaven.

DON CARLOS. You take my sister from a convent, and then leave her!

DON JUAN. Heaven bids me do so.

DON CARLOS. Do you imagine that we will tolerate such a blot on our escutcheon?

DON JUAN. You must lay the blame on Heaven.

DON CARLOS. Heaven again! Always Heaven!

DON JUAN. Heaven wills it so.

DON CARLOS. Enough, Don Juan. I understand your meaning. This is no fit place for further action; but, before long, you shall hear from me.

DON JUAN. You must do as you please. You know I don't lack courage, and that I know how to use my sword. I am going to walk now in the little side street, which leads to the big convent. I have no wish to fight you. Heaven forbid the thought! But, if you attack me, we shall see what will come of it.

DON CARLOS. Yes, we shall see. Have no fear of that.

[*He goes out*   IV

SGANARELLE. What the devil is this new style of talking, Sir? It's worse than anything. I liked you better as you were before. I've always had some faint hope of your salvation; but now I quite despair of it. Up to now you've been let alone, but Heaven will never put up with this latest abomination.

—

DON JUAN. Nonsense! Heaven is not so particular as you think. Why, if every time a man. . . .

V   [*A* SPECTRE *enters in the form of a veiled woman.*

SGANARELLE [*seeing the* SPECTRE]. Oh, Sir, Heaven is speaking to you. It is sending you a warning.

DON JUAN. If Heaven wishes to warn me, It must speak a little plainer, if It wants me to understand.

THE SPECTRE. Don Juan has no more than a minute left, to make his peace with Heaven. Unless he repents at once, he is lost for ever.

SGANARELLE. Oh, Sir, do you hear?

DON JUAN. Who dares say such a thing? I think I recognize that voice.

SGANARELLE. Oh, Sir, it's a ghost. I can tell by the way it walks.

DON JUAN. Spook, ghost or devil, I'll see what it is.

          [*The* SPECTRE *changes into the figure of Time, with his scythe in his hand.*

SGANARELLE. Heavens, Sir! Do you see? It's changed its shape.

DON JUAN. Nothing that was ever made can frighten me. I will soon prove with my sword whether it's a body or a spirit.

          [*The* SPECTRE *vanishes as* DON JUAN *makes to strike it.*

SGANARELLE. Oh, Sir, don't stand out against all these portents. Repent while there's still time.

DON JUAN. No. It shall never be said that I was capable of repenting, happen what may. Come, follow me.

VI   [*Enter the* STATUE OF THE COMMANDER.

THE STATUE. Stay, Don Juan! Yesterday you promised that you would sup with me.

DON JUAN. I did. Where am I to go?

—

THE STATUE. Give me your hand.

DON JUAN. There it is.

THE STATUE. Don Juan, the wages of sin is death. He who rejects God's mercy stands defenceless before His wrath.

DON JUAN. Oh, God! I can go on no longer. An invisible flame is burning me. Through all my body runs a white hot fire.

> [*A loud clap of thunder. Flashes of lightning play upon* DON JUAN. *The earth opens and engulfs him. Flames issue from the place into which he has fallen.*

SGANARELLE. Oh, my wages, my wages! By his death everyone else is satisfied; Heaven he offended, laws he set at defiance, girls he seduced, families he disgraced, parents he outraged, wives he ruined, husbands he drove to distraction. Everyone is content. I am the only one to suffer, I who after so many years' service have no other reward than that of seeing with my own eyes my master's impious behaviour punished by the most horrible punishment imaginable. But who will pay my wages?

THE RELUCTANT DOCTOR
[*Le Médecin malgré lui*]

Le Médecin malgré lui, *comedy in three acts, was first produced at the Théâtre du Palais-Royal, Paris, on 6 August 1666, with Molière in the part of Sganarelle.*

CHARACTERS

GÉRONTE, *father of Lucinde*

LUCINDE, *daughter of Géronte*

LÉANDRE, *in love with Lucinde*

SGANARELLE, *husband of Martine*

MARTINE, *wife of Sganarelle*

MONSIEUR ROBERT, *neighbour of Sganarelle*

VALÈRE, *steward to Géronte*

LUCAS, *husband of Jacqueline*

JACQUELINE, *wet nurse in Géronte's house, and wife of Lucas*

THIBAUT, *a peasant*

PERRIN, *his son*

ACT ONE

[*Enter* SGANARELLE *and* MARTINE, *in the middle of an argument.*

SGANARELLE. No, no; I refuse to do anything about it. I am the one to give orders. I mean to be master in my own house.

MARTINE. And I am determined you shall do what I want. I didn't marry you to put up with your tricks.

SGANARELLE. Oh, how exhausting it is to have a wife! Aristotle was quite right when he said that a wife is worse than a fiend.

MARTINE. Just listen to the learned man, with his silly Aristotle!

SGANARELLE. Yes, I am a learned man. Show me another woodcutter who can reason as well as me, who was six years in the service of an eminent doctor, and who knew his three R's by heart when he was a boy.

MARTINE. You crazy fool!

SGANARELLE. You impudent slut!

MARTINE. A curse on the day and hour when I consented to say 'I will'.

SGANARELLE. Curses on the cuckold of an attorney who made me sign my own ruin!

MARTINE. You've got fine cause to complain! Why, you ought to thank Heaven every day on your knees that you've got me for a wife. You didn't deserve to marry a woman like me.

SGANARELLE. True enough! You did me too much honour, of course; and our wedding night made clear to me just how much honour. Hell! Don't make me go on. I should end up saying something. . . .

MARTINE. Well? What would you say?

SGANARELLE. Enough said. Let us stop there. It is sufficient that we know what we know, and that you were very lucky to get me.

MARTINE. Lucky to get you, do you call it? A man who has nearly reduced me to penury; an unfaithful rake who devours all my property!

SGANARELLE. That's a lie. I drink part of it.

MARTINE. Who sells everything in my house, bit by bit!

SGANARELLE. That's known as home economics.

MARTINE. Who has robbed me of my very bed!

SGANARELLE. It will be easier for you to get up earlier in the morning.

MARTINE. Who hasn't left a stick of furniture in the whole place!

SGANARELLE. So there'll be less trouble when we want to move.

MARTINE. And who, from morning till night, does nothing but gamble and get drunk!

SGANARELLE. It keeps me from getting bored.

MARTINE. And what do you expect me to do with my family all this while?

SGANARELLE. Do exactly what you like.

MARTINE. I have four poor little children on my hands.

SGANARELLE. Put them down for a bit.

MARTINE. They cry to me for bread.

SGANARELLE. Give them a taste of the whip. When I have had my bellyful, I like everyone else to get theirs too.

MARTINE. And do you think things are going on like this for ever, you drunken rogue?

—

SGANARELLE. Now, wife, don't let's get worked up.

MARTINE. Do you think I shall put up with your rudeness and debauchery for ever?

SGANARELLE. Let's keep our temper, wife.

MARTINE. I'll soon find a way to teach you your duty.

SGANARELLE. You know I'm not very patient, wife; and that my strong arm is strong.

MARTINE. A fig for your threats!

SGANARELLE. Ah, my darling, my little love, you're just itching to be beaten, as usual.

MARTINE. I'll soon show you I'm not afraid of you.

SGANARELLE. My beloved half, you're asking for something.

MARTINE. Do you think you can frighten me?

SGANARELLE. My precious one, I'll box your ears.

MARTINE. Drunken beast!

SGANARELLE. I'll take a stick to you.

MARTINE. Drunkard!

SGANARELLE. I'll thrash you.

MARTINE. Brute!

SGANARELLE. I'll flay you alive.

MARTINE. Cheat! Upstart! Deceiver! Coward! Knave! Criminal! Beggar! Ragamuffin! Swindler! Scoundrel! Thief!

SGANARELLE. So you will have it then?

[SGANARELLE *takes a stick and beats his wife.*

MARTINE. Oh, oh, oh, oh!

SGANARELLE. That's the only way to calm you down.

[*Enter* MONSIEUR ROBERT.   II

ROBERT. Hola! Hola! Ho, there! What's this? What a shocking sight! Devil take the fellow to beat his wife like that!

MARTINE [*Hands on hips, making him back away as she speaks to him, eventually slapping him*]. And what if I like him to beat me?

ROBERT. Oh, in that case I have no more to say.

MARTINE. What are you interfering for?

ROBERT. I have no right to at all.

MARTINE. Is it any business of yours?

ROBERT. No; none.

MARTINE. Did you ever hear such impertinence? To try to stop husbands beating their wives!

ROBERT. I take it all back.

MARTINE. What has it got to do with you?

ROBERT. Nothing.

MARTINE. Is there any call for you to poke your nose in?

ROBERT. None in the world.

MARTINE. Mind your own business then.

ROBERT. I won't say another word.

MARTINE. I like being beaten.

ROBERT. Very well.

MARTINE. It doesn't hurt *you*.

ROBERT. No.

MARTINE. Then you're a fool to meddle in what isn't your business.

ROBERT [*moves across to* SGANARELLE *who also makes him back away, and beats him with his stick*]. My friend, I humbly ask your pardon. Thrash away! Beat your wife as much as you please. I'll help if you like.

SGANARELLE. I don't like.

ROBERT. Ah! Then in that case we'll say no more about it.

SGANARELLE. I'll beat her when I feel like it; and I won't when I don't.

ROBERT. Very good.

SGANARELLE. She's my wife, not yours.

ROBERT. Certainly.

SGANARELLE. You have no right to give me orders.

ROBERT. None at all.

SGANARELLE. I don't need your help.

ROBERT. No. I. . . .

SGANARELLE. Then you're an impertinent fellow to interfere in other folks' business. Remember what Cicero says: *One mustn't put the bark between the tree and the finger.*

> [*He beats* MONSIEUR ROBERT *and drives him away. Then he goes over to his wife and says, pressing her hand*:

Come, now. Let's be friends. Give me your hand.

MARTINE. What! After a beating like that?

SGANARELLE. It was a mere trifle. Give me your hand.

MARTINE. I don't want to.

SGANARELLE. You won't?

MARTINE. No.

SGANARELLE. My darling!

MARTINE. No. I won't.

SGANARELLE. Make it up.

MARTINE. No, I tell you.

SGANARELLE. Come on, now.

MARTINE. No. I'm still angry.

SGANARELLE. Come now! It's not worth thinking about. Come now, do.

MARTINE. Leave me alone.

SGANARELLE. Give me your hand.

MARTINE. No. You have gone too far.

SGANARELLE. Very well then, I'm sorry. Now, will you shake?

MARTINE. Oh, all right then; I'll forgive you. [*aside*]. But just you wait.

SGANARELLE. You are a fool to make such a fuss. These little things are bound to happen now and then between people who are close to one another. When two people love each other, a blow or two only makes their hearts grow fonder. Well, I'm off to the wood now. And I'm going to bring you home more than a hundred faggots as a peace offering.

III   MARTINE. For all that, you've not heard the last of this, my man. I'm determined to find a way to pay you back for that beating. I know it's easy enough for a woman in some ways to get back at her husband; but that kind of revenge is too subtle for the scoundrel I'm married to. I need to find a sharper means of vengeance to make up for the injuries I have suffered.

IV   [*Enter* VALÈRE *and* LUCAS. *They do not see* MARTINE.

LUCAS. Here be the devil of a job us has got to do; I don't see how us'll ever get through with 'un.

VALÈRE. Cheer up, Lucas! We must obey our master. And it's to our advantage too that his daughter, our mistress, should recover. For sure her marriage, which this illness is postponing, will put something in our pockets. Monsieur Horace is an open-handed gentleman, and he is like to be the lucky one; for, though she has shown some partiality for young Léandre, her father, you know, has up to now refused to entertain him as his son-in-law.

MARTINE [*aside*]. Isn't there *something* I could do to pay him back?

LUCAS. What maggot has he got into his head now then, since all they doctors have done nowt but waste their Latin?

VALÈRE. A remedy is sometimes found, if one looks long enough; and often in the unlikeliest places.

MARTINE [*aside*]. I must be revenged at all costs. That beating rankles in my mind. I won't put up with that, and ... [*running into* VALÈRE *and* LUCAS]. Ah, Gentlemen, I beg your pardon. I did not see you. I was trying to think out something which is puzzling me.

VALÈRE. We all have our troubles in this world. We too are in search of something we would gladly find.

MARTINE. Is it anything I can help you in?

VALÈRE. Possibly. We are looking for a clever doctor, a brilliant specialist, to cure our master's daughter of a sudden affliction which has deprived her of the use of her tongue. Several doctors have exhausted all their knowledge in her case already; but sometimes one hears of people with wonderful secrets, special remedies, which often succeed where everything else has failed; and this is what we are looking for.

MARTINE [*aside*]. Ah, here's a perfect way of being revenged on my good-for-nothing husband. [*aloud*]. You could not meet anyone better able to help you than I am. We have a doctor here, who is the most wonderful man in the world for such desperate cases.

VALÈRE. Oh, for pity's sake, tell us where we can find him.

MARTINE. He is now in that little clearing over there, cutting wood.

LUCAS. A doctor cutting wood!

VALÈRE. Gathering herbs, you mean, surely!

MARTINE. No, I don't. That's how he chooses to pass his time. He is a most eccentric man, an absolute oddity; a whimsical fellow if ever there was one. You'd never take him for what he is. He goes about dressed in the queerest way; often pretends complete ignorance, hides his knowledge from the world, and hates nothing so much as making use of his Heaven-sent gift for medicine.

VALÈRE. It's a curious thing that all great men seem to have some small eccentricity, some little grain of madness in their genius.

MARTINE. His madness is almost past belief. Sometimes he will even submit to a thrashing rather than admit his knowledge; and I warn you that, if he is in one of his moods, you will never get him to admit that he is a doctor, unless each of you take a thick stick, and by a good beating force his secret from him. That's what we do when we have need of him.

VALÈRE. A strange form of madness!

MARTINE. Yes. But, after that, you'll see he'll do wonders.

VALÈRE. What is his name?

MARTINE. Sganarelle. But you can't mistake him. He has a big black moustache, and wears a ruff and a green and yellow suit.

LUCAS. A green and yellow suit? Be he a parrot doctor then?

VALÈRE. But is he really as clever as you say?

MARTINE. What! Why, the man has worked miracles. Only six months ago, a woman was given up as hopeless by every doctor in the area. She had lain to all appearance dead for six hours; and they were laying her out for burial, when someone thought of Sganarelle, and forced him to come and see her. He poured a tiny drop of something or other in her mouth; and she got out of bed at once, and began to walk about the room as if there'd been nothing the matter with her.

LUCAS. Goodness!

VALÈRE. It must have been a drop of liquid gold elixir.

MARTINE. I wouldn't be surprised. Again, not three weeks ago, a child of twelve fell from the top of the clock tower, and broke his skull, arms and legs on the paving stones. They no sooner brought our man on the scene, than he rubbed the body all over with some special ointment of which he had the recipe; and the child immediately jumped up, and ran off to play hopscotch.

LUCAS. Heavens above!

VALÈRE. Why, the man must have discovered the universal panacea!

MARTINE. There's not a doubt of it.

LUCAS. By Gor! He be the man for we, and no mistake! Let's go to him at once.

VALÈRE. We cannot thank you enough for your invaluable information.

MARTINE. Be sure you don't forget the advice I gave you.

LUCAS. Oh, by Gor, leave that to we! If a thrashing be all he wants, the beast be our'n.

[*She goes out*

VALÈRE. We are very lucky to have met this woman. I feel most hopeful.

SGANARELLE [*singing off stage*]. La, la, la.   V

VALÈRE. I can hear someone now, singing and cutting wood.

[SGANARELLE *enters with a bottle in his hand. He does not see* VALÈRE *and* LUCAS.

SGANARELLE [*singing*]. La, la, la . . . I've worked long enough for a drink, by God! Let's have a breather! [*he drinks*]. This woodcutting makes one as dry as Hell. [*sings*].

> *Oh, 'tis music in mine ear*
> *When the gurgling I hear*
> *Of the liquor from the bottle running free;*
> *But, if the bottle's always full*
> *When I want to take a pull,*
> *All my comrades full of jealousy will be;*
> *But if the cork goes 'pop',*
> *And it don't contain a drop,*
> *What the devil is the good of it to me?*

It's not a bit of good moping.

VALÈRE [*aside to* LUCAS]. It's the very man himself.

LUCAS. Right you be. I'd nosed him out too.

VALÈRE. Let's wait a bit, and see what he does.

SGANARELLE [*hugging his bottle*]. Ah, you little rogue, how I love thee! My little darling! [*sings: then, seeing the others observing him, he lowers his voice*]. All my comrades full of jealousy will be. But. . . . [*seeing they are watching him more closely*]. The devil! What do these people want?

VALÈRE. It's him right enough.

LUCAS. It be the dead spit of him, by Gor! Just as he was miscribed to we.

> [SGANARELLE *puts the bottle on the ground; but, seeing* VALÈRE *bowing to him by way of salutation, thinks he is going to take it. He puts it on the other side of him; but,* LUCAS *doing the same as* VALÈRE, SGANARELLE *takes up the bottle and holds it against his chest, with by-play and other amusing gestures.*

SGANARELLE [*aside*]. I believe they're talking about me. What's their game, I wonder?

VALÈRE. Sir, is not your name Sganarelle?

SGANARELLE. Eh? What?

VALÈRE. I ask if you are not called Sganarelle.

SGANARELLE [*turning towards* VALÈRE; *then towards* LUCAS]. Yes and no; according to what you want with him.

VALÈRE. We wish him nothing but good, I assure you.

SGANARELLE. In that case, my name is Sganarelle.

VALÈRE. We are delighted to meet you, my dear Sir. We are in great trouble. Your name has been mentioned to us, and we have come to beg you to give us the benefit of your advice.

SGANARELLE. If it is anything in my line, Gentlemen, I am ready to do my best for you.

VALÈRE. You are too kind, Sir. But, my dear Sir, I beg you will put on your hat. You will get sunstroke.

LUCAS. Cover yerself up, Sir.

SGANARELLE [*aside*]. These people are extraordinarily polite.
[*He puts on his hat.*

VALÈRE. My dear Sir, please do not think it strange that we have come to you. Exceptional men are always in request, and we have heard of your great ability.

SGANARELLE. I am certainly the best man in the country for cutting faggots.

VALÈRE. Oh, Sir!

SGANARELLE. I'm a conscientious workman, and never give any cause for complaint.

VALÈRE. Sir, we are not concerned with that at present.

SGANARELLE. But my price is a hundred and ten sols the hundred.

VALÈRE. We won't discuss that now.

SGANARELLE. You shan't have them for less.

VALÈRE. Sir, we know everything.

SGANARELLE. If you know everything, then you know that that's my price.

VALÈRE. This is no time for joking, Sir.

SGANARELLE. Joking? I was never more in earnest. I won't come down in price.

VALÈRE. Oh, for Heaven's sake, talk sense!

SGANARELLE. You can get them cheaper in some places. There are faggots and faggots. But if you want mine. . . .

VALÈRE. My dear Sir, that's enough of that, I beg of you.

SGANARELLE. I swear you shan't have them for a penny less.

VALÈRE. This is really too bad.

SGANARELLE. No. You shall pay the fair price. I am too honest to overcharge.

VALÈRE. Sir, how can a man of your eminence descend to this ridiculous subterfuge? How can a brilliant man like you, a famous doctor, try to hide his knowledge from the world, and bury his talents in the ground?

SGANARELLE [*aside*]. He's off his head.

VALÈRE. For pity's sake, Sir, be open with us.

SGANARELLE. Open with you?

LUCAS. All this hedging about be no good. Us knows what us knows.

SGANARELLE. What on earth do you mean. Who do you take me for?

VALÈRE. For what you are, a great doctor.

SGANARELLE. Doctor yourself. I'm not one, and never have been.

VALÈRE [*aside*]. He's obviously in the grips of his madness. [*aloud*]. Sir, don't deny it any more, I beg you. Don't force us to go to work another way.

SGANARELLE. What way?

VALÈRE. One we should be very sorry to have to take.

SGANARELLE. Dammit! Go to work any way you like. I am not a doctor, and I don't know what you are talking about.

VALÈRE [*aside*]. We shall have to administer the cure after all. [*aloud*]. For the last time, Sir, will you admit to being who you are?

LUCAS. Ay, don't talk no more nonsense. Own up at once that you be a doctor.

SGANARELLE. I shall lose my temper in a minute.

VALÈRE. What's the use of denying what we know already?

LUCAS. Why all this to-do? What good do it do 'ee?

SGANARELLE. Gentlemen, once and for all, I tell you I am not a doctor.

VALÈRE. You're not a doctor?

SGANARELLE. No.

LUCAS. You bean't a doctor?

SGANARELLE. No, I tell you.

VALÈRE. Very well then. If you will have it, here goes.

[*They each take a stick and thrash him.*]

SGANARELLE. Oh, oh, oh, Gentlemen! I'll be anything you like.

VALÈRE. Why, Sir, do you oblige us to use violence?

LUCAS. Why give we the trouble of beating 'ee?

VALÈRE. I assure you I'm extremely sorry for it.

LUCAS. So be I, honest.

SGANARELLE. What the devil does it all mean, Gentlemen? Is it a joke, or are you both mad, to want to make a doctor of me?

VALÈRE. What! You still hold out? You still deny you are a doctor?

SGANARELLE. The devil take me if I am!

LUCAS. It bean't true you be a doctor?

SGANARELLE. No, plague take me!

[*They begin again to beat him.*]

Oh, oh, oh, very well, Gentlemen. Yes, if you insist, I am a doctor, I am a doctor. An apothecary too, if you like. I'll admit anything rather than be beaten.

VALÈRE. Ah, that's better, Sir. I am glad you have come to your senses.

LUCAS. It do my heart good to hear 'ee talk like that.

VALÈRE. I sincerely hope you'll forgive us.

LUCAS. I hope as ye'll pardon the liberty us have took.

SGANARELLE [*aside*]. Phew! Could I have been wrong after all? Can I have become a doctor without knowing it?

VALÈRE. My dear Sir, you will never regret confiding in us. You will have every reason to be satisfied.

SGANARELLE. But, tell me, Gentlemen, you're sure you're not making a mistake? You're quite sure I am a doctor?

LUCAS. Ay, by Gor!

SGANARELLE. Really and truly?

VALÈRE. There's no doubt at all.

SGANARELLE. Devil take me if I was aware of it!

VALÈRE. What? You are the cleverest doctor in the world.

SGANARELLE. Well, well!

LUCAS. A doctor as has cured I dunno how many diseases.

SGANARELLE. Indeed?

VALÈRE. A woman had been given up for dead six hours, and was being laid out for burial; when, with a drop of something or other, you brought her back to life, and she began to walk about the room.

SGANARELLE. Good Lord!

LUCAS. A child of twelve fell from the top of the clock tower, and broke his skull, arms and legs. You come along, smeared him over with some ointment; and up he jumped, and run off to play hopscotch.

SGANARELLE. Heavens above!

VALÈRE. So, if you'll come along with us, Sir, I can guarantee you satisfaction; and you may name your own price.

SGANARELLE. I may name my own price?

VALÈRE. Most certainly.

SGANARELLE. Well then, I'm most certainly a doctor. It's true I had forgotten it. But I remember well enough now. What kind of case is it? Where am I to go?

VALÈRE. We will take you along with us. It is a young girl who has lost her power of speech.

SGANARELLE. I haven't found it, I give you my word.

VALÈRE [*aside to* LUCAS]. He must have his joke. [*aloud*]. Let us go, Sir.

SGANARELLE. What? Without a doctor's robe?

VALÈRE. We'll find you one.

SGANARELLE [*giving his bottle to* VALÈRE]. Carry that then, will you? I keep my decoctions in it.

> [*turning to* LUCAS *and spitting on the ground.*]

Here, you, tread on that. [LUCAS *hesitates*]. Doctor's orders!

LUCAS. By Gor, here be a doctor after my own heart! He be such a merry fellow that I b'lieve he'll do the trick.

ACT TWO

> [*Enter* GÉRONTE, VALÈRE, LUCAS *and* JACQUELINE.   I

VALÈRE. Yes, Sir, I think you will be pleased. We have brought you the greatest doctor in the world.

LUCAS. By Gor, his better bean't to be found! None of the others be fit to pull off his boots.

VALÈRE. He has performed some most miraculous cures.

LUCAS. Cured dead folk he has.

VALÈRE. He is a little eccentric, as I told you; and every now and then he loses his wits, and he seems not quite to be what he is.

LUCAS. Ay, he do love to play the fool; and, begging your pardon, Sir, you'd sometimes think he'd got a screw loose.

VALÈRE. But, at bottom, he's fantastically learned; and will frequently make use of the most recondite terms.

LUCAS. He can talk like a book when he be so minded.

VALÈRE. He has won a great reputation in these parts already. Everyone goes to him.

GÉRONTE. I'm all impatience to see him. Bring him in at once.

VALÈRE. I'll go and fetch him.

[*He goes out*

JACQUELINE. Faith, maister, I bet he'll do no better than all they others! It'll only be the same old story. If you ask me, the best medicine for your darter would be a good and handsome husband, and one as she be in love with.

GÉRONTE. Yes, yes, my dear nurse; but no one is asking your opinion.

LUCAS. Hold your tongue, housekeeper; it bean't for you to poke your nose in.

JACQUELINE. I tell you all the doctors in the world will never do her any good. It bean't rhubarb and senna she needs, but a husband. That be ever the surest treatment when there be a young girl to be cured.

GÉRONTE. But who would want her as a wife, with an affliction like that? And besides, has she not always opposed every suggestion for getting her a husband?

JACQUELINE. Ay, because you'd force on her a man that she don't like. If you'd give her that young Monsieur Léandre she be so fond of, she'd be obedient enough then. And what's more, I'll bet he'd take her as she be now, if only you'd agree.

GÉRONTE. Young Léandre is not a suitable match for her. He is not so well off as the other.

JACQUELINE. He've got a very rich uncle, I'm told, that he be heir to.

GÉRONTE. A bird in the hand is worth two in the bush, my good woman. There's nothing like possession; and it's taking a great risk to count on a fortune that someone else is keeping for you. Death does not always lend a ready ear to the wishes of legatees. You can get very long in the tooth while you're waiting for someone to die.

JACQUELINE. Well, I've allus heard it said that in marriage, as in other things, 'appiness be more than money. Feythers and mothers all have this wretched habit of asking: *What be his means?* and: *How big be her dowry?* There's old Peter now has married his darter Simonette to fat Tom, only becos he's got a corner of a vineyard more'n pore young Robin, that had won the girl's heart; and there be the poor craytur as yellow as a quince, and pining away ever since. It be a warning to you, maister. One has only one's happiness in this world; and I would rather give my darter a good husband that she loved than all the money in the bank.

GÉRONTE. Dammit, nurse, how you do chatter! Be quiet, for Heaven's sake! You take too much on yourself. You'll spoil your milk.

LUCAS [*thumping* GÉRONTE *on the shoulder at each sentence*]. Be quiet now, you impartinent woman. Maister has no time to listen to your babble. He knows what to do. You give suck to your babby, and leave argifying to your betters. Maister be the feyther of his own darter, and he be quite wise enough to know what be right.

GÉRONTE. That's enough now, that's enough.

LUCAS [*still thumping* GÉRONTE *on the shoulder*]. I only want to keep her in order, maister, and teach her a bit more respect.

GÉRONTE. Yes, but you needn't thump so hard.

[VALÈRE *comes back*.

VALÈRE. Here is the doctor, Sir.

[SGANARELLE *enters, wearing a doctor's robe and a very high, pointed hat.*

GÉRONTE. Sir, I am delighted to welcome you to my house. Your skill is most urgently required.

SGANARELLE. Hippocrates says ... that we must keep our hats on.

GÉRONTE. Hippocrates says so?

SGANARELLE. Certainly.

GÉRONTE. In what chapter, pray?

SGANARELLE. In his chapter . . . on hats.

GÉRONTE. Then, if Hippocrates says so, we must.

SGANARELLE. Doctor, after hearing the extraordinary circumstances. . . .

GÉRONTE. To whom are you speaking?

SGANARELLE. You.

GÉRONTE. But I am not a doctor.

SGANARELLE. You're not a doctor?

GÉRONTE. No.

SGANARELLE. Really and truly.

[SGANARELLE *takes a stick and beats him.*

Oh, ooh, ooh!

SGANARELLE. You're a doctor now, all right. That's the only training I ever had.

GÉRONTE [*to* VALÈRE]. What crazy sort of a fellow have you brought here?

VALÈRE. I warned you he was a bit of a joker.

GÉRONTE. If he tries any of his jokes here, I'll soon send him packing.

LUCAS. Don't take no notice of that, maister. It be only a bit of fun.

GÉRONTE. It's a kind of fun I don't like.

SGANARELLE. I ask your pardon, Sir, for taking such a liberty.

GÉRONTE. It's quite alright, Sir.

SGANARELLE. I sincerely apologize. . . .

GÉRONTE. It's of no consequence.

SGANARELLE. For the beating. . . .

GÉRONTE. There's no harm done.

SGANARELLE. Which I have had the honour to give you.

GÉRONTE. I beg you'll say no more about it. I have a daughter who is suffering from a strange malady, Doctor.

SGANARELLE. I am delighted, Sir, that your daughter has need of me; and I wish with all my heart that you and all your family had need of me too, that you might see how eager I am to be of service to you.

GÉRONTE. I'm sure I am very much obliged to you.

SGANARELLE. I'm perfectly sincere in what I say.

GÉRONTE. You are too kind, Doctor.

SGANARELLE. What is your daughter's name?

GÉRONTE. Lucinde.

SGANARELLE. Lucinde? Ah, a most excellent name for a patient! Lucinde!

GÉRONTE. I'll go and see what she is doing.

SGANARELLE. Who is that fine-looking woman over there?

GÉRONTE. That is my baby's wetnurse.

[GÉRONTE *and* VALÈRE *go out*

SGANARELLE [*aside*]. A very juicy bit of goods! [*aloud*]. Ah, my dear Nurse, my doctorship is the very humble slave of your nurseship! I would I were the lucky little tot who sips the milk of your good graces. [*putting his hand on her breast*]. All my knowledge, all my skill is at your service, and. . .

LUCAS. I'll thank 'ee, Maister Doctor, to leave my wife alone.

SGANARELLE. What! Is she your wife?

LUCAS. Ay, that she be.

SGANARELLE. Oh, I didn't know that. I rejoice in your mutual affection. [*He pretends to be going to embrace* LUCAS, *but embraces* JACQUELINE *instead*].

LUCAS [*drawing* SGANARELLE *away, and placing himself between them*]. That will do, maister, if you please.

SGANARELLE. I assure you I am delighted to see such a well-matched couple. I congratulate her on having a husband like you, and I congratulate you on having such a beautiful, modest and well-developed wife.

> [*He again pretends to be going to embrace* LUCAS, *who holds out his arms. Then he passes underneath, and embraces* JACQUELINE.

LUCAS [*drawing him way*]. Eh, by Gor, not so many compliments now!

SGANARELLE. Surely I may rejoice with you over such a perfect union?

LUCAS. With me as much as you like. But hands off my wife.

SGANARELLE. I share equally in the happiness of both. And, if I embrace you to show my pleasure, I embrace her too for the same reason. [*Same business*].

LUCAS [*dragging him away*]. Come now, Maister Doctor, have done with your nonsense.

> [GÉRONTE *re-enters*.

III   GÉRONTE. My daughter will be here directly, Doctor.

SGANARELLE. I await her, Sir, with all my medical equipment.

GÉRONTE. But where is it?

SGANARELLE [*touching his forehead*]. In here.

GÉRONTE. Ah, yes, I see.

SGANARELLE. But, as I take an interest in your whole family . . . I must first sample Nurse's milk.

> [*He approaches* JACQUELINE.

LUCAS [*drawing him away and spinning him round*]. No, no, no; I won't have that.

SGANARELLE. But it's the doctor's business to examine the nurse's breasts.

LUCAS. Not if I know it, maister.

SGANARELLE. How dare you bandy words with the doctor?
Be off with you, my man.

LUCAS. Fiddle-de-dee!

SGANARELLE [*looking askance at him*]. I'll infect you with a
nasty fever.

JACQUELINE [*taking* LUCAS *by the arm and spinning him round
too*]. Yes, be off with you, do. Do you think I bean't old
enough to look after myself, if he does anything he
shouldn't?

LUCAS. I won't have him fiddling about with 'ee.

SGANARELLE. Shame on the rascal! Jealous of his wife!

GÉRONTE. Here is my daughter.

[*Enter* VALÈRE *with* LUCINDE.   IV

SGANARELLE. Is this the invalid?

GÉRONTE. Yes. She is my only daughter. And if she were to
die, my heart would break.

SGANARELLE. Oh, she must be careful not to do that. She
mustn't die except on doctor's orders.

GÉRONTE. A chair there!

SGANARELLE [*sitting between* GÉRONTE *and* LUCINDE]. Ha!
Not a very repulsive invalid! Many a healthy man would
get along with her very well.

GÉRONTE. You've made her laugh, Doctor.

SGANARELLE. So much the better. When the doctor makes
the patient laugh, it is an excellent sign. [*to* LUCINDE].
Well, what's the trouble? What's the matter with you? How
do you feel?

LUCINDE [*touching her lips, her head and under her chin*]. Han,
hi, hon, han.

SGANARELLE. What's that?

LUCINDE [*with the same gestures*]. Han, hi, hon, han, han, hi, hon.

SGANARELLE. What?

LUCINDE. Han, hi, hon.

SGANARELLE. Han, hi, hon, han, ha. I don't understand you. What sort of jargon is that?

GÉRONTE. That is her affliction, Doctor. She has become dumb; and up to now we have been unable to find the reason. Her marriage has had to be postponed.

SGANARELLE. What on earth for?

GÉRONTE. Her intended husband wished to see her cured before agreeing to the wedding.

SGANARELLE. And who is the fool who objects to his wife being dumb? I would to God mine were! I'd think twice before I had her cured.

GÉRONTE. Still, we beg you'll do your best to cure her, Doctor.

SGANARELLE. Don't you worry. Tell me now. Does this trouble affect her much?

GÉRONTE. Yes, Doctor.

SGANARELLE. So much the better. Does she feel much pain?

GÉRONTE. A great deal, Doctor.

SGANARELLE. That's splendid. Does she go to the ... you know?

GÉRONTE. Oh, yes.

SGANARELLE. Successfully?

GÉRONTE. I've no idea.

SGANARELLE. Does it look healthy?

GÉRONTE. I really can't say.

SGANARELLE [*to* LUCINDE]. Give me your arm. [*to* GÉRONTE]. I can tell by this pulse that your daughter is dumb.

GÉRONTE. Yes, Doctor, that is her affliction. You have discovered it at once.

SGANARELLE. Ha!

JACQUELINE. Just see how quickly he's found out her complaint!

SGANARELLE. We great doctors diagnose correctly at once. An ignoramus would have hummed and hawed. He would have said: *It's this* or: *It's that*. But I put my finger on the trouble straight away, and tell you that your daughter is dumb.

GÉRONTE. Yes, but I want you to tell me the cause.

SGANARELLE. Nothing easier. The cause of her dumbess is the loss of her powers of speech.

GÉRONTE. Quite so. But why has she lost her powers of speech?

SGANARELLE. All our best authors will tell you it is an impediment in the action of her tongue.

GÉRONTE. Yes, but what in your opinion has caused this impediment in the action of her tongue?

SGANARELLE. Ah, on that point Aristotle says ... some very fine things indeed.

GÉRONTE. I am sure he does.

SGANARELLE. Ah, there was a great man!

GÉRONTE. No doubt!

SGANARELLE. A very great man; [*raising his arm from the elbow*] greater than me by all that. But to return to what we were saying. In my opinion this impediment in the action of her tongue is caused by certain humours, which we savants call unhealthy humours, that is to say ... unhealthy humours; seeing that the vapours formed by the exhalation of the influences which take rise in the seat of maladies, coming ... so to speak ... from ... er ... Do you understand Latin?

GÉRONTE. Not a word.

SGANARELLE [*rising abruptly*]. You don't know a word of Latin?

GÉRONTE. No.

SGANARELLE [*with enthusiasm*]. Cabricias arci thuram, catalamus, singulariter, nominativo, haec musa, the muse, bonus bona bonum. Deus sanctus, est-ne oratio latinas? Etiam, yes. Quare, why? Quia substantivo, et adjectivum, concordat in generi, numerum et casus.

GÉRONTE. Oh, why didn't I study the arts?

JACQUELINE. There be a clever man for you!

LUCAS. Ay, by Gor, it be so fine I can't understand a word!

SGANARELLE. So these vapours, of which I am speaking, passing from the region of the liver on the left side to the region of the heart on the right, it happens that the lungs, which in Latin we call *armyan*, have communication with the brain, which in Greek we call *nasmus*, by means of the main artery, which in Hebrew we call *cubile*, meet on their way the said vapours which fill the ventricles of the shoulder blade; and because the said vapours. . . . Follow this closely if you please. , . . And because the said vapours have a certain malign influence. . . . Pay great attention to this, I beg of you.

GÉRONTE. Yes.

SGANARELLE. Have a certain malign influence, which is caused . . . Pay close attention, please.

GÉRONTE. I am.

SGANARELLE. Which is caused by the acridity of the humours engendered in the concavity of the diaphragm, it happens that these vapours . . . ossabandus, nequeis, nequer, potarinum, quipsa milus. There, that's the reason why your daughter is dumb!

JACQUELINE. Our doctor knows his business all right.

LUCAS. Would my tongue was as well oiled!

GÉRONTE. A clearer explanation would be impossible. There is only one thing which surprises me. That is the position of the liver and the heart. You seemed to me to place them the wrong way round. I always thought the heart was on the left side, and the liver on the right.

SGANARELLE. Yes, that used to be the case. But we have changed all that. The whole science of medicine is now run on an entirely new system.

GÉRONTE. Oh, I didn't know that. I must ask you to excuse my ignorance.

SGANARELLE. It's quite understandable. You can't be expected to be as clever as we are.

GÉRONTE. Certainly not. But what do you think should be done, Doctor?

SGANARELLE. What do I think should be done?

GÉRONTE. Yes.

SGANARELLE. My advice is this. Put her to bed at once, and administer bread steeped in wine.

GÉRONTE. Why that, Doctor?

SGANARELLE. Because wine and bread mixed together have a sympathetic virtue which causes speech. Don't you know that that's what they give parrots to make them talk?

GÉRONTE. Why, so they do. Ah, what a great man! Quick, a quantity of bread and some wine!

[VALÈRE, LUCAS *and* LUCINDE *go out.* JACQUELINE *is following.*

SGANARELLE. I'll come again in the evening to see how she is. [*to* JACQUELINE]. One moment. [*to* GÉRONTE]. My dear sir, Nurse here would be the better for a little doctoring too.

JACQUELINE. Who? Me? I never felt better in my life.

SGANARELLE. So much the worse, nurse, so much the worse. This rude health is very suspicious. A little gentle bleeding would not be without its advantages, I think; a soothing little injection. . . .

GÉRONTE. I don't understand that at all, Doctor. Why bleed her when she's perfectly well?

SGANARELLE. What has that got to do with it? It's a healthy practice. As one drinks for the thirst to come, so one must be bled for the illness to come.

JACQUELINE [going]. Lorks! How silly! I don't want to make my body into an apothecary's shop.

[She goes out

SGANARELLE. Ah, you're not partial to medicine. But we'll find a way to bring you round. [to GÉRONTE]. I wish you good day.

GÉRONTE. One moment, please.

SGANARELLE. What do you want?

GÉRONTE. To pay you, Doctor.

SGANARELLE [holding out his hand behind his back, while GÉRONTE opens his purse]. I won't take anything, Sir.

GÉRONTE. Doctor!

SGANARELLE [going]. Nothing at all.

GÉRONTE. One moment!

SGANARELLE. No, not one sou.

GÉRONTE [offering money]. Come, come.

SGANARELLE. You're joking.

GÉRONTE. I insist.

SGANARELLE. I won't touch it.

GÉRONTE. Oh, but Doctor!

SGANARELLE. I don't work for money.

GÉRONTE. Of course not.

—

SGANARELLE [*taking it*]. It's not a dud?

GÉRONTE. Certainly not, Doctor.

SGANARELLE. I am not one of your mercenary doctors.

GÉRONTE. I can see that.

SGANARELLE. I never think of my own profit.

GÉRONTE. No. No! I never supposed you did.

SGANARELLE [*looking at the money*]. Things are not going so badly after all; and, if only. . . .

[*Enter* LÉANDRE.

V

LÉANDRE. Doctor, I have been waiting a long time for an opportunity to speak to you. I beg you to help me.

SGANARELLE [*feeling his pulse*]. Your pulse is very weak.

LÉANDRE. I am not ill, Doctor. I haven't come to you for that.

SGANARELLE. If you're not ill, why the devil didn't you say so at once?

LÉANDRE. No. Here is the situation in two words. My name is Léandre, and I am desperately in love with your patient Lucinde. Her father has been cruel enough to forbid me to see her; but, as my happiness and even my life depend on my being able to have a chance to speak to her, I have ventured to ask you to help us, and to give me the opportunity of carrying out a little plan of my own.

SGANARELLE. What do you take me for? What! You dare to ask me to help you in a love affair? Would you compromise the dignity of a doctor by involving him in intrigues of that sort?

LÉANDRE. Please don't speak so loud, Doctor.

SGANARELLE [*pushing him away*]. I will speak loud. You are an impertinent scoundrel.

LÉANDRE. Sh! sh! Doctor!

SGANARELLE. You've made a big mistake, my friend.

LÉANDRE. Hush! For pity's sake!

SGANARELLE. I'll soon show you I am not that kind of man. It's positively insulting. . . .

LÉANDRE. Doctor. . . . [*He draws out his purse*].

SGANARELLE. To try to make me. . . . [*He takes the purse, and immediately his manner changes*]. I'm not referring to you of course. You are an honourable young man, and I should be delighted to help you; but some impertinent fellows misjudge people altogether, and quite frankly, it makes my blood boil.

LÉANDRE. I hope, doctor, you'll excuse the liberty.

SGANARELLE. Nonsense! Tell me what you want me to do.

LÉANDRE. You must know, then, Doctor, that this illness is feigned. The doctors have argued about it in the usual way; some saying it proceeds from the brain, some from the intestines, some from the spleen, some from the liver. But I can assure you that the real cause is love; and Lucinde has only feigned this affliction to avoid an unhappy marriage. But we mustn't be seen talking together. Come with me, and I will tell you what I want you to do, as we go along.

SGANARELLE. Come along then, Sir. I feel the tenderest interest in your love affair already; and I'll stake my doctor's reputation that the patient shall be yours, or die.

ACT THREE

I   [*Enter* LÉANDRE *and* SGANARELLE.

LÉANDRE. I think this dress will do well enough for an apothecary. As her father has hardly ever seen me, the change of coat and wig should be enough disguise.

SGANARELLE. Quite enough.

LÉANDRE. All I need now are five or six long medical words to lard my discourse, and make me seem a knowledgeable man.

SGANARELLE. Oh, that's not at all necessary. The clothes are all you want. I know no more than you do.

LÉANDRE. What?

SGANARELLE. Devil take me if I know anything about medicine. You're a good fellow, and I'll trust you just as you've trusted me.

LÉANDRE. What? You're not really. . . . ?

SGANARELLE. No, I give you my word. They forced me to be a doctor willy nilly. I never set up to be as clever as that. Why, I got no higher than the second form at school. I can't imagine where they got such an idea. But, when I saw that they were determined to make a doctor of me, I decided to play the part at their own expense. You'd never believe how the news has spread, and everyone is possessed of the idea that I'm a learned man. They come to ask my advice for miles around; and, if things go on as well as they've begun, I have a good mind to stick to doctoring for the rest of my life. It's the best trade of all, I find. You get your fee just the same, whether you succeed or fail. A bad job of work never reflects on us, and we cut our cloth into any patterns we please. If a shoemaker, when he is making his shoes, happens to spoil a piece of leather, he has to pay the bill; but we can spoil a man for nothing. We never make mistakes. It's always the corpse's fault. And the best of it is, dead men are very decent discreet sort of folk. You never hear them complain of the doctors who killed them.

LÉANDRE. No; the dead are very decent in this respect.

SGANARELLE [*seeing two men approaching in the distance*]. Those fellows look as though they were coming to consult me now. Go and wait for me near your mistress's house.

II   [LÉANDRE *goes out. Enter* THIBAUT *and* PERRIN.

THIBAUT. Doctor, my son Perrin and I be come to ask your advice.

SGANARELLE. What's the matter?

THIBAUT. His poor mother, my Parette, has been lying ill in bed these six months.

SGANARELLE [*holding out his hand for a fee*]. What do you want me to do?

THIBAUT. Why, Doctor, us was hoping you could give we some little pick-me-up to make her well.

SGANARELLE. We must see what is the matter with her first.

THIBAUT. It be the hypocrisy, Doctor.

SGANARELLE. Hypocrisy?

THIBAUT. Ay, she be all puffed out. They say it be the seriosity in her body that be the cause; and that her liver, or her tummy, or her spleen, as you call it, do make nowt but water instead of blood. Every other day she had a quotidian fever, with lassitude and pains in the cows of her legs. Her phlegm do seem to choke her; and at times she be seized with such syncolies and conversions that I be feared she be gone dead. There be an apothecary in our village, saving your Honour's presence, who've given her I dunno how many histories; and it have cost me mor'n a dozen good pounds in enemies, an it please ye, and imposthumes that they made her take; infections of hyacinth juice and cordial portions. But all that ointment, as he said, be only for a caution, as you might say. He wanted to give her a drug he called hermetic wine. But I daredna let her take un, for fear it ud send her to sleep with her feythers. I've heard tell they big doctors have killed a power of men with that invention.

SGANARELLE [*still holding out his hand*]. Come to the point, my friend, come to the point.

THIBAUT. The point be, Doctor, that I come to beg you to tell we what us must do.

SGANARELLE. I can't make head or tail of what you say.

PERRIN. Doctor, my mother be ill, and here be two pounds to give we some medicine. [*giving money*].

SGANARELLE. Ah, now you I can understand. Here's a lad who speaks plainly, and expresses himself properly. You say your mother is ill with the dropsy, that she is terribly swollen, has fever with pains in the legs, and is sometimes seized with syncopes and convulsions; that is to say she is subject to fainting fits.

PERRIN. Ay, Doctor, that be right!

SGANARELLE. I understood you at once. But your father is quite unintelligible. Now you want me to give you something.

PERRIN. If you please, Doctor.

SGANARELLE. Something to make her well?

PERRIN. That be what us wants, Doctor.

SGANARELLE. Then give her this piece of cheese.

PERRIN. Cheese, Doctor?

SGANARELLE. Yes. It is a special kind of cheese, containing gold, coral, pearls, and a number of other precious ingredients.

PERRIN. Us be main grateful to ee', Doctor. I'll go and give her this at once.

SGANARELLE. Off you go. And, if she dies, be sure you give her the grandest funeral you can afford.

The scene changes to a room in Géronte's house. III

[JACQUELINE *discovered. Enter* SGANARELLE; *then enter* LUCAS *behind.*

SGANARELLE. Here's that lovely nurse. Ah, Nurse of my heart, I'm delighted to see you! The sight of you is as good as rhubarb, senna and cassia to purge my soul of melancholy.

JACQUELINE. Oh, la, Maister Doctor, that be much too fine for me! I don't understand a word of your Latin.

SGANARELLE. Be ill, sweet nurse, do be ill, for love of me. It would be such bliss to make you well.

JACQUELINE. Thank you, Doctor; but I would reyther not have to be made well.

SGANARELLE. Oh, my beauteous one, how I pity you, forced to live with such a jealous tiresome husband!

JACQUELINE. It can't be helped, Doctor. It be a penance for my sins. Where the goat be tied, there she must browse.

SGANARELLE. What! A lout like that; a fellow who is for ever spying on you, and is green with jealousy if you speak to anyone else!

JACQUELINE. Oh, what you've seen be nothing. That be only a very mild specimen of his ill-humour.

SGANARELLE. Is it possible? Can there be a man with soul so base as to ill-treat a wife like you? Ah, sweet nurse, I know some people, not so very far from here, who would be happy only to kiss the tips of your tiny toes. Why must so rare a jewel fall into the hands of such an animal; a stupid, brutish, foolish. . . . ? Forgive me, nurse, for speaking so of your husband.

JACQUELINE. La, Doctor, he desarves all these names, I know.

SGANARELLE. There's not a doubt that he deserves them, nurse; and he deserves too that you should really give him something to complain about to punish him for his suspicions. [*He makes a sign of horns with his hands*].

JACQUELINE. Truly, if I weren't allus thinking of his good, I might be tempted to do something of that kind.

SGANARELLE. It would only serve him right, if you took a lover in revenge. He richly deserves it; and, if I, my dear nurse, were lucky enough to be chosen for. . . .

[*At this point both notice* LUCAS *behind them, listening to their conversation; they retreat to opposite sides of the stage,* SGANARELLE *in a very amusing way. Then* GÉRONTE *enters.*   IV

GÉRONTE. Ah, Lucas! Have you seen our doctor?

LUCAS. Ay, the devil take him! I've seen him, and my wife too.

GÉRONTE. Where is he now then?

LUCAS. I dunno. But I know where I wish he was. In Hell.

GÉRONTE. See what my daughter is doing.

[LUCAS *goes out. Then re-enter* SGANARELLE *with*   V
LÉANDRE.

Ah, Doctor, I was asking for you.

SGANARELLE. I only went into the garden, Sir, to pluck a rose. How's the patient?

GÉRONTE. Rather worse since taking your medicine.

SGANARELLE. Ah, that's splendid. It's a sign that it's working.

GÉRONTE. That may be. But I'm afraid it may choke her in the process.

SGANARELLE. Oh, don't be afraid of that. My remedies are a match for anything. I expected to find her at her last gasp.

GÉRONTE. Who is this you have brought with you?

SGANARELLE [*making signs with his hands to show he is an apothecary*]. He is. . . .

GÉRONTE. What?

SGANARELLE. The man. . . .

GÉRONTE. Eh?

SGANARELLE. Who. . . .

—

GÉRONTE. Ah, I understand.

SGANARELLE. He will be most helpful to your daughter.

VI   [*Enter* JACQUELINE *with* LUCINDE.

JACQUELINE. Here's your daughter, maister. She wants to go for a walk.

SGANARELLE. It will do her all the good in the world. Go with her, Mister Apothecary. Feel her pulse. I shall want to consult with you later on about her complaint.

[*He draws* GÉRONTE *into a corner, throwing his arm over his shoulder and putting his hand under his chin, turning his head forcibly towards him whenever* GÉRONTE *tries to see what his daughter and the apothecary are up to, and speaking throughout to distract his attention.*

It is an important and rather nice question among us doctors, Sir, whether women are easier to cure than men. Pray give me your attention on this point. Some say no; others say yes. But I say yes and no. In as much as the incongruity of the opaque humours, which intermingle in the natural temperament of women, is the cause why the animal spirits always predominate over the spiritual, we can see that the instability of their opinions depends on the oblique motion of the orb of the moon; and as the sun, which darts its rays on the concavity of the earth, finds. . . .

LUCINDE [*to* LÉANDRE]. No. I will never love anyone but you.

GÉRONTE. My daughter is speaking. Oh, marvellous remedy! Oh, wonderful doctor! I cannot sufficiently thank you, Doctor, for this miraculous recovery. What can I do for you to show my gratitude?

SGANARELLE [*walking about the stage and fanning himself with his hat*]. It has certainly given me a great deal of trouble.

LUCINDE. Yes, father, I have recovered my speech; but it is only to tell you that I will never have any other husband but Léandre. It will be quite useless to try to make me marry Horace.

GÉRONTE. But. . . .

LUCINDE. Nothing will make me change my mind.

GÉRONTE. What?

LUCINDE. It's no use trying to persuade me.

GÉRONTE. If. . . .

LUCINDE. Nothing you say will have any effect.

GÉRONTE. I. . . .

LUCINDE. No. I am quite determined.

GÉRONTE. But. . . .

LUCINDE. Though you are my father, you shall never force me to marry against my will.

GÉRONTE. I have. . . .

LUCINDE. It's not a bit of good.

GÉRONTE. He. . . .

LUCINDE. My heart will never submit to such injustice.

GÉRONTE. The. . . .

LUCINDE. I would rather go into a convent than marry a man I do not love.

GÉRONTE. But. . . .

LUCINDE [*with vivacity*]. No. No. No. You are only wasting time. I will never give in. Never. Never. Never.

GÉRONTE. What a torrent of words! There's no standing against it. Oh, Doctor, do make her dumb again!

SGANARELLE. Quite impossible. The best I can do for you is to make you deaf.

GÉRONTE. Thank you very much. [*to* LUCINDE]. Do you really imagine. . . . ?

LUCINDE. No. No arguments will make the smallest impression on me.

—

GÉRONTE. You shall marry Horace this very night.

LUCINDE. I will marry sooner Death.

SGANARELLE. One moment, if you please, Sir. Allow me to prescribe in this affair. She is suffering from an illness, and I know the very way to cure it.

GÉRONTE. What, Doctor? Can you cure this mental illness as well?

SGANARELLE. Most certainly I can. I have a remedy for everything. But I shall want our apothecary's help in this. [to LÉANDRE]. A word with you, Sir. You see that the passion she has for this Léandre is absolutely contrary to her father's wishes. There is not a minute to be lost. The humours are most persistent, and delay will only make matters worse. In the circumstances I see only one possible remedy; and that is a purgative dose of Flight, properly compounded with two drams of Matrimonium Pills. She may make some little difficulty about swallowing this medicine; but you are an experienced young man, and will know the best way to persuade her. Take her for a short walk in the garden to prepare the humours, [lowering his voice] while I keep her father engaged in the house. [aloud]. And above all, lose no time. The remedy, quick! [lowering his voice]. The remedy you know of.

[LUCINDE, JACQUELINE and LÉANDRE go out

VII GÉRONTE. What drugs were those you mentioned just now, Doctor? I don't think I have ever heard of them.

SGANARELLE. We only use them in the most desperate cases.

GÉRONTE. Did you ever hear such impertinence?

SGANARELLE. Girls are sometimes a little wilful.

GÉRONTE. You would never believe how infatuated she is with this Léandre.

SGANARELLE. The hot blood of youth, Sir.

—

GÉRONTE. The moment I discovered how strong this passion was, I took care to keep my daughter locked up.

SGANARELLE. That was very wise of you.

GÉRONTE. And I put a stop to all communication between them.

SGANARELLE. Quite right.

GÉRONTE. They would have been up to some trick, if I'd allowed them to see each other.

SGANARELLE. Very likely.

GÉRONTE. She is just the kind of girl who would have run away with him.

SGANARELLE. I cannot sufficiently praise your foresight.

GÉRONTE. They tell me he is trying all ways to get a chance to speak to her.

SGANARELLE. Aha, the young rascal!

GÉRONTE. But he will only waste his time.

SGANARELLE. Ha, ha!

GÉRONTE. I shall take good care he doesn't see her.

SGANARELLE. He's clearly not dealing with a fool. You know a trick worth two of his. He'll have to be a clever man to get the better of you.

[*Enter* LUCAS.   VIII

LUCAS. Maister! Maister! Here be a fine kettle of fish! Your darter has eloped with her Léandre. It be he as was the apothecary, and there be the doctor who performed the operation.

GÉRONTE. What! So you have been betraying me, you rascal? Lay hold of him, and send for an officer at once. I'll have the law on you, you treacherous villain!

[*He goes out*

LUCAS. You'll be hanged now, Maister Doctor; that be sure. You just stay where you be.

IX   [*Enter* MARTINE.

MARTINE [*to* LUCAS]. Lord, what a job I've had to find this place! How did you like the doctor I sent you?

LUCAS. There he be; and going to be hanged!

MARTINE. What! My husband hanged? Alas! What has he done to deserve that?

LUCAS. He helped a man to run off with our maister's darter.

MARTINE. Oh, my dear husband, is it really true they are going to hang you?

SGANARELLE. It looks like it.

MARTINE. Will you be given a public execution?

SGANARELLE. How can I prevent it?

MARTINE. If only you'd finished cutting the wood, it wouldn't be so bad.

SGANARELLE. Be off with you, woman. You are breaking my heart.

MARTINE. No. I shall stay and encourage you to the very end. I'll never leave you till I've seen you hanged.

SGANARELLE. Oh!

X   [GÉRONTE *re-enters*.

GÉRONTE [*to* SGANARELLE]. The officer will be here immediately, and will put you where he will be responsible for keeping you under lock and key.

SGANARELLE [*falling on his knees*]. Mercy! Mercy! Couldn't you give me a good beating instead?

GÉRONTE. No. The law shall take its course. But what's this?

XI   [*Enter* LÉANDRE *and* LUCINDE.

LÉANDRE. Sir, Léandre has returned to throw off his disguise, and to give Lucinde back into your keeping. We had intended to be married and fly the country; but we have now decided to take a more honest way. I will not steal your daughter, and will marry her only with your consent.

But I should like you to know that I have just received letters, which tell me that my uncle is dead, and has left me heir to all his estates.

GÉRONTE. Sir, I am now persuaded of the true value of your person; and I give you my daughter with the greatest of pleasure!

SGANARELLE [*aside*]. The medical faculty has had a lucky escape.

MARTINE. Then, as you are not going to be hanged after all, you can thank me for your doctor's degree. For it was I who got you that honour.

SGANARELLE. Oh, did you? then you got me a sound beating into the bargain.

LÉANDRE. Come now, be friends. All has ended too happily for you to bear malice.

SGANARELLE. Very well then. [*to* MARTINE]. I forgive you the beating for the sake of my newly acquired dignity. But, from now on, I shall expect you to show the greatest respect towards a man of my importance. And remember that a doctor's wrath is more formidable than you might think.

GEORGE DANDIN

[George Dandin ou le mari confondu]

George Dandin, *comedy in three acts, was first produced as part of the Grand Divertissement royal de Versailles, a court festivity to celebrate the conquest of the Franche-Comté on 18 July 1668; its first performance in Paris was on 9 November 1668 at the Théâtre du Palais-Royal. The July performance was accompanied by a pastoral ballet, the last interlude of which consists of pastoral figures inviting George Dandin to drown his sorrows in wine, followed by a contest between adherents of Bacchus and supporters of Cupid. The Parisian performance consisted only in the text given here.*

CHARACTERS

GEORGE DANDIN, *rich yeoman farmer, husband of Angélique*

ANGÉLIQUE, *his wife, daughter of M. de Sotenville*

M. DE SOTENVILLE, *impoverished country nobleman*

MME DE SOTENVILLE, *his wife*

CLITANDRE, *in love with Angélique*

CLAUDINE, *Angélique's maid*

LUBIN, *a peasant, servant to Clitandre*

COLIN, *George Dandin's valet*

The scene is set outside George Dandin's house

ACT ONE

I

[*Enter* GEORGE DANDIN.]

GEORGE DANDIN. Ah! It's a proper business and no mistake to wed a member of the nobility; my marriage is a clear warning to all those of farming stock who want to rise above themselves and marry into a noble family as I have done. Not that there's anything wrong with the nobility in itself; it's a fine institution; but it's got so many unfortunate aspects that it's a good thing not to rub up against it. I've become all too knowledgeable on this subject to my own cost, and know how the nobility treat the likes of us when they receive us into the families. They hardly marry themselves to us as persons at all; it's only our money they marry, and I would've done much better, rich as I am, to find a match in good and decent yeoman stock than to take a wife who believes herself to be my social superior, who takes umbrage at having to bear my name, and thinks that with all my money I still haven't paid out enough to deserve the rank of husband. Geroge Dandin, my old fellow, it's the stupidest thing in the world that you've done! Your own house has lost its charm for you, and whenever you go home, you find some cause or other for complaint.

[GEORGE DANDIN *sees* LUBIN *coming out of his house.*

What on earth has that chap been up to in my house?

LUBIN [*aside*]. That man's staring at me.

GEORGE DANDIN [*aside*]. He doesn't know me.

LUBIN [*aside*]. He's suspicious about something.

GEORGE DANDIN. Well, well! He doesn't seem keen to say hello.

LUBIN [*aside*]. I'm afraid that he might go round saying that he saw me come out of here.

—

GEORGE DANDIN. Good day.

LUBIN. Your servant.

GEORGE DANDIN. You're not from these parts, are you?

LUBIN. No, I only came for tomorrow's fair.

GEORGE DANDIN. Am I right in thinking you've just come out of there?

LUBIN. Shh!

GEORGE DANDIN. What?

LUBIN. Quiet!

GEORGE DANDIN. What's the matter?

LUBIN. Not a word. You mustn't say that you've seen me coming out of there.

GEORGE DANDIN. Why not?

LUBIN. Heavens above! because ...

GEORGE DANDIN. Because what?

LUBIN. Keep you voice down. I'm afraid that we may be overheard.

GEORGE DANDIN. Not here.

LUBIN. It's just that I have been speaking to the mistress of the house on behalf of a certain gentleman who is courting her and no one must know of it. Do you understand?

GEORGE DANDIN. Yes.

LUBIN. It's because I've been told not to let myself be seen, and I beg you specially not to say that you've seen me.

GEORGE DANDIN. Of course I shan't.

LUBIN. I'm very keen to keep this affair secret, as I've been asked.

GEORGE DANDIN. Quite right.

LUBIN. They say that the husband is jealous and doesn't like people flirting with his wife; he'd make no end of a fuss if this affair came to his ears. Do you understand?

—

GEORGE DANDIN. Indeed.

LUBIN. He mustn't know anything at all about it.

GEORGE DANDIN. Certainly.

LUBIN. The intention is to deceive him quietly. Do you catch my meaning?

GEORGE DANDIN. Perfectly.

LUBIN. If you were to say that you saw me coming out of her house, you'd spoil everything: is that clear?

GEORGE DANDIN. Very clear. By the way, what's the name of the person who sent you in there?

LUBIN. It's a gentleman from my part of the country. Monsieur le Vicomte de . . . Darn it! I can never remember how the heck they gabble his name. Monsieur Cli . . . Clitandre.

GEORGE DANDIN. Is it that young courtier who lives . . .

LUBIN. Yes: just over by those trees.

GEORGE DANDIN [*aside*]. So that's the reason why that fop with his fine manners has come to live on top of me. I thought I could smell trouble, and his being so close had already made me suspicious.

LUBIN. Blow me if he isn't the best gentleman you've ever laid eyes on. He gave me three gold pieces just to go and tell the lady that he was in love with her and that he was desirous of the honour of a conversation with her. It's hardly as if there's a great deal of effort involved for me, to be so well paid; what's a hard day's work, for which I earn a mere ten sous, compared to that?

GEORGE DANDIN. Well, did you pass on your message?

LUBIN. Yes, I found someone called Claudine inside who understood immediately what I wanted and let me speak to her mistress.

GEORGE DANDIN [*aside*]. The brazen girl!

LUBIN. By heck! that Claudine is very pretty! She took my
fancy and she's only to say the word and we'll be married.

GEORGE DANDIN. But what reply did the mistress of the
house give to the fine gentleman?

LUBIN. She told me to say ... hang on, I'm not sure I can
remember it all that well ... Yes, that she is much obliged
to him for the love he bears her but that he should be
careful not to let it be seen because her husband is so
suspicious, and that some scheme would have to be devised
to give them some time in each other's company.

GEORGE DANDIN [*aside*]. What a hussy!

LUBIN. By heck! it's going to be very amusing, for the
husband won't suspect a thing, which is all to the good;
and he'll still be as jealous as he was before: isn't that so?

GEORGE DANDIN. Yes, indeed.

LUBIN. Goodbye. Don't breathe a word about all this. Keep
mum, so that the husband doesn't find out.

GEORGE DANDIN. Of course.

LUBIN. As for me, I'm going to act the innocent; I'm a sly
fellow, no one is able to guess what I'm up to.

III   [LUBIN *goes out*

GEORGE DANDIN. Well, George Dandin, my old friend, you
see how your wife treats you. That's what comes of having
wanted to marry above yourself: you're done down and
beaten without being able to get your revenge; the gentry
have got you in a strait-jacket. Marrying someone from
your own class at least leaves you free to look after your
honour as a husband, and if a farmer's daughter had been
up to such tricks, you would have been at liberty to settle
the matter to your satisfaction by giving her a sound
beating. But you had to get involved with gentry, and you
were tired of being master in your own house. Oh! I'm
beside myself with fury, and I'd give myself a thrashing if I
could. To think that she shamelessly entertained the

advances of a fop, and let him know that she felt the same way about him! By heavens! I'll not let this chance slip away. I'll go at once to complain to her father and mother and make them witnesses to the distress and anger their daughter is causing me, as a wise precaution. But here they are, as luck would have it.

[*Enter* M. *and* MME DE SOTENVILLE.   IV

M. DE SOTENVILLE. What's the matter, son-in-law? You look very upset.

GEORGE DANDIN. And I've got excellent reason to be, for . . .

MME DE SOTENVILLE. Good God, son-in-law, what a lack of manners you display in not greeting people properly when you accost them!

GEORGE DANDIN. Well, mother-in-law, it's because I've got other things on my mind, and . . .

MME DE SOTENVILLE. Really! Can it be that you know so little about polite society son-in-law, that there is no way of teaching you how to live with gentlefolk?

GEORGE DANDIN. What?

MME DE SOTENVILLE. Will you never rid yourself of such a familiar greeting as 'mother-in-law'? Can't you get used to calling me 'Madame'?

GEORGE DANDIN. Hell! If you call me son-in-law, it seems to me that I can call you mother-in-law.

MME DE SOTENVILLE. There's a great deal to be said against it: things are not equal between us. Please take note that it is not for you to use such a form of address with a person of my rank; and that though you may be our son-in-law, there is a great gulf fixed between us, and you should know your place.

M. DE SOTENVILLE. That's enough for now, my dear; let the matter drop.

MME DE SOTENVILLE. Good God, Monsieur de Sotenville, what you are prepared to put up with is your own affair; you simply don't know how to make others treat you with the respect which is your due.

M. DE SOTENVILLE. Forgive me, dammit,. but no one can teach me lessons on that account, and in my life I have shown by a score of resolute acts that I am not a man to abandon any of my rightful claims to respect. But it wasn't necessary to give him more than a little warning on the matter. Let us know, son-in-law, what is on your mind.

GEORGE DANDIN. Since it is necessary to speak bluntly, let me tell you, Monsieur de Sotenville, that I have reason to . . .

M. DE SOTENVILLE. One moment, son-in-law. Take note that it is not respectful to call people by their surname; one must say 'Monsieur' by itself to those who are set above us.

GEORGE DANDIN. Well then, Monsieur by itself, and not Monsieur de Sotenville, what I have to tell you is that my wife is giving me . . .

M. DE SOTENVILLE. One moment! Take note also that you must not say 'my wife' when you talk about our daughter.

GEORGE DANDIN [aside]. I think I'll go mad. [aloud] Isn't my wife my wife, then?

MME DE SOTENVILLE. Yes, son-in-law, she is your wife, but you may not call her so; you would only be able to do so if you had married one of your own kind.

GEORGE DANDIN [aside]. Oh! George Dandin, my old friend, just look where have you landed yourself! [aloud] Please, I beg you, set your gentility to one side for a moment and let me speak to you as best I can. A curse on such tyrannical rules and regulations! I say to you again that I am not satisfied with my marriage.

M. DE SOTENVILLE. Why not, son-in-law?

MME DE SOTENVILLE. What! How can you speak in this way about something from which you have derived such great benefits?

GEORGE DANDIN. What benefits, Madame, since I must call you Madame? The business has been all right from your point of view, for without me your affairs, if I may say so, were in a pretty tumbledown state, and my money has plugged a few yawning holes in them; but tell me how I have come off better, except in having my name made longer, now that instead of George Dandin I have received from you the title of 'Monsieur de la Dandinière'?

M. DE SOTENVILLE. Don't you count for anything the advantage of being related by marriage to the de Sotenville family?

MME DE SOTENVILLE. And to that of de la Prudoterie into which I had the honour of being born; a family whose nobility passes through the distaff side, through which your children, by this great privilege, will become gentry?

GEORGE DANDIN. Yes, that's fine enough: my children will become gentry; but I'll become a cuckold, if something isn't done about it.

M. DE SOTENVILLE. What do you mean, son-in-law?

GEORGE DANDIN. It means that your daughter does not live in the way a wife should and that she acts dishonourably.

MME DE SOTENVILLE. Enough! Be careful what you say. My daughter is from a far too virtuous line ever to allow herself to do anything which is an affront to decent manners; and in the de la Prudoterie family, for the last three hundred years, no wife, thank God, has ever been the subject of gossip.

M. DE SOTENVILLE. By God! There's never been a fast woman in the de Sotenville family: and courage is no less hereditary among the males than chastity among the females.

MME DE SOTENVILLE. There was a Jacqueline de la Prudoterie who refused to become the mistress of a royal duke,
even though he was governor of our province.

M. DE SOTENVILLE. And there was a Mathurine de Sotenville who turned down an offer of 2,000 écus from a royal
favourite who only asked for the favour of conversing with
her.

GEORGE DANDIN. Well! Your daughter isn't as scrupulous
as that; she's become more approachable since she's been
in my house.

M. DE SOTENVILLE. Be explicit, son-in-law. We are not the
sort of people to condone her actions if she has done
wrong, and we will be the first, her mother and I, to see
that justice is done.

MME DE SOTENVILLE. We do not trifle with matters of
honour; we brought her up according to the most severe
code of behaviour.

GEORGE DANDIN. All that I can tell you is that there is
hereabouts a certain young courtier whom you have seen,
who is making up to her right under my very nose, and
who has sent her protestations of his love which she has
graciously consented to lend an ear to.

MME DE SOTENVILLE. By God! I'd strangle her with my own
hands if it turned out that she had sullied the good name
of her mother.

M. DE SOTENVILLE. The devil take me if I wouldn't run her
through with my sword, her and her lover, if she had fallen
down on her honour.

GEORGE DANDIN. I've told you what is happening in order
to bring the matter before you, and I ask you now for
satisfaction.

M. DE SOTENVILLE. Don't worry, I'll give you satisfaction
with respect to both of them; I'm not a man to take any

nonsense from anyone. But are you quite sure of your facts?

GEORGE DANDIN. Very sure.

M. DE SOTENVILLE. Be careful what you say; for these are ticklish matters among gentlemen, and there can be no question of making a mistake.

GEORGE DANDIN. I repeat, I've not told you anything which isn't true.

M. DE SOTENVILLE. My dear, go and speak to our daughter, while I'll go with my son-in-law to speak to the man in question.

MME DE SOTENVILLE. Could it be, my dear one, that she has forgotten herself in this way after the excellent example I have set her, as you well know?

M. DE SOTENVILLE. We'll throw some light on this affair.

[MME DE SOTENVILLE *goes out*

Follow me, son-in-law, and don't be downcast. You'll see what my true mettle is when someone attacks those who are seen to be connected with our family.

GEORGE DANDIN. Here he is, coming towards us.

[*Enter* CLITANDRE.   V

M. DE SOTENVILLE. Sir, am I known to you?

CLITANDRE. Not that I know, Sir.

M. DE SOTENVILLE. I am the Baron de Sotenville.

CLITANDRE. I am delighted to hear it.

M. DE SOTENVILLE. My name is known at court, and I had the honour when young of being prominent among the officers of the Nancy regiment.

CLITANDRE. Well, that's good to know.

M. DE SOTENVILLE. My father, Jean-Giles de Sotenville, had the honour of taking part in the great Siege of Montauban.

CLITANDRE. I'm very glad about it.

M. DE SOTENVILLE. I also had an ancestor, Bertrand de Sotenville, who was held in such high esteem in his day that he was allowed to sell his estate in order to take part in the Crusades.

CLITANDRE. I don't doubt it.

M. DE SOTENVILLE. I have been told, Sir, that you are in love with, and are making advances to, a young person, my daughter, whose honour is as dear to me as is my own, as is that of this man who has the good fortune of being my son-in-law.

CLITANDRE. Who? Me?

M. DE SOTENVILLE. Indeed: and I am glad to have this opportunity to speak to you in order to ascertain from you the truth of the matter, if you would be so kind.

CLITANDRE. What an outrageous calumny! Who told you that, Sir?

M. DE SOTENVILLE. Someone who believes it to be true.

CLITANDRE. That someone has lied. I am a gentleman. Do you believe me capable, Sir, of so cowardly an action? Me? In love with a young and beautiful person who has the honour of being the daughter of the Baron de Sotenville? I hold you in too high esteem for that and am too much your servant. Whoever told you this is a fool.

M. DE SOTENVILLE. Well, then, son-in-law.

GEORGE DANDIN. Well, what?

CLITANDRE. He's a scoundrel and a villain.

M. DE SOTENVILLE. Answer him!

GEORGE DANDIN. Answer him yourself!

CLITANDRE. If I knew who it might be, I'd run him through with my sword in your presence.

M. DE SOTENVILLE. Produce evidence of the accusation.

—

GEORGE DANDIN. I have produced it, and it's true.

CLITANDRE. Is it your son-in-law, Sir, who has . . .

M. DE SOTENVILLE. Yes, he it is who has brought this complaint to me.

CLITANDRE. Well, he can thank heaven for the good fortune of being connected with you; but for that, I'd soon teach him to say such things about a person such as myself.

[*Enter* MME DE SOTENVILLE, ANGÉLIQUE *and*   VI
CLAUDINE.

MME DE SOTENVILLE. Jealousy is indeed a very strange thing! I have brought my daughter here to throw light on this matter in the presence of all concerned.

CLITANDRE. Did you, Madame, tell your husband that I am in love with you?

ANGÉLIQUE. Me? How could I have said such a thing? Is it the case? I should be very pleased if you were in love with me. Just try it, and you will soon find out with whom you are dealing. I really advise you to; try all the tricks of suitors just to see what will happen. Try sending me messages, writing me little secret love letters, picking the moments my husband isn't home, or when I'm out and about, to speak of your love. All you have to do is to present yourself in this way and I promise you you'll get the welcome you deserve.

CLITANDRE. Please calm yourself, Madame; it's not necessary to spell things out for me in this way and to look so shocked. Who has told you that I am thinking of making advances to you?

ANGÉLIQUE. What do I know of all this? I've only just heard about it now.

CLITANDRE. Let them say what they like, but *you* know whether I have spoken to you of love when we met.

ANGÉLIQUE. You would only have got the reception you deserved if you had.

CLITANDRE. I assure you that with me you've nothing to fear; I'm not a man to upset the fair sex; I respect you too much, both you and your esteemed parents, even to think of falling in love with you.

MME DE SOTENVILLE. There, you see.

M. DE SOTENVILLE. Now you are satisfied, son-in-law. What do you say to that?

GEORGE DANDIN. What I say is that these are tall stories; that I know what I know; and that, since I'm forced to speak out, she received a short time ago a message from him.

ANGÉLIQUE. I received a message?

CLITANDRE. I sent a message?

ANGÉLIQUE. Claudine!

CLITANDRE Is it true?

CLAUDINE. Heavens, what a blatant lie.

GEORGE DANDIN. Quiet, you slut. I know a bit about you too: you introduced the messenger into the house.

CLAUDINE. Who, me?

GEORGE DANDIN. Yes, you. Don't come the innocent.

CLAUDINE. Dear me! The world is full of evil nowadays, to go suspecting me of this, me, Claudine, whiter than the driven snow!

GEORGE DANDIN. Keep quiet, you hussy. You act the sly one, but I have known all about you for a long time, and you are no innocent.

CLAUDINE. Madame, may I . . .

GEORGE DANDIN. Shut up, I said; you may end up taking the rap for all of them; you haven't got a nobleman for a father.

ANGÉLIQUE. This is such a monstrous lie, and one which is so deeply wounding to me, that I have not even the strength to reply to it. It's horrible to be accused publicly by one's husband when one has done nothing to him one should not have done. Alas! If I'm to blame for anything, it's for being too easygoing with him.

CLAUDINE. Quite right.

ANGÉLIQUE. My whole misfortune is to show him too much respect; if only I *was* able to entertain the advances of someone, I would not be so much an object of pity. Farewell; I shall withdraw. I cannot put up with any more such insults.

[ANGÉLIQUE *goes out*

MME DE SOTENVILLE. There, you do not deserve the virtuous wife we have given you.

CLAUDINE. By heaven, he deserves to be right about her; if I was in her place, I know who I'd choose. [*addressing* CLITANDRE] Yes, Sir, you should make advances to my mistress to punish him. Press your attention on her, it'd be a very good thing, I say; I hereby offer you my services, because I've already been accused by him of providing them.

M. DE SOTENVILLE. Son-in-law, you deserve to hear such things said to you; your behaviour has set the whole world against you.

MME DE SOTENVILLE. Learn to treat a noblewoman better, and make sure in future that you don't make such mistakes again.

GEORGE DANDIN [*aside*]. I'm beside myself with rage to be found wrong when I'm in the right.

CLITANDRE. Sir, you have seen that I have been falsely accused. You are a man who knows the rules which govern matters of honour. I ask for satisfaction for the insult he has offered me.

M. DE SOTENVILLE. That is quite fair, and it is the way things are done. Now, give this gentleman satisfaction, son-in-law.

GEORGE DANDIN. What do you mean, satisfaction?

M. DE SOTENVILLE. I mean satisfaction, which is due, according to the rules of honour for having accused him unjustly.

GEORGE DANDIN. But I don't agree that I accused him unjustly, and I know what *I* still think about the matter.

M. DE SOTENVILLE. That is neither here nor there. Whatever you still think, he has denied it; that is satisfaction, and no-one can proceed against a man who denies the charge.

GEORGE DANDIN. So that if I found him in bed with my wife, he would only have to deny it to get off?

M. DE SOTENVILLE. Stop arguing. Apologize to him as I have told you to.

GEORGE DANDIN. Me apologize to him after . . .?

M. DE SOTENVILLE. Enough, I said. There is nothing more to be settled, and you should not be afraid of saying too much, since I will guide you in this matter.

GEORGE DANDIN. I am not prepared . . .

M. DE SOTENVILLE. By God, son-in-law, don't make me angry, or I'll take his side against you. Come on, let yourself be guided by me.

GEORGE DANDIN [*aside*]. Oh! George Dandin, you fool!

M. DE SOTENVILLE. First, take your hat off: this gentleman is noble, and you are not.

GEORGE DANDIN [*aside*]. My blood is boiling.

M. DE SOTENVILLE. Repeat after me: 'Sir'.

GEORGE DANDIN. 'Sir'.

M. DE SOTENVILLE. 'I apologize . . .' [*seeing his son-in-law unwilling to obey him*] Grrr!

GEORGE DANDIN. 'I apologize . . .'

M. DE SOTENVILLE. '. . . for the bad thoughts I had about you.'

GEORGE DANDIN. '. . .for the bad thoughts I had about you.'

M. DE SOTENVILLE. 'It was because I did not have the honour of knowing you . . .'

GEORGE DANDIN. 'It was because I did not have the honour of knowing you.'

M. DE SOTENVILLE. '. . . and I ask you to believe me when I say . . .'

GEORGE DANDIN. '. . . and I ask you to believe me when I say . . .'

M. DE SOTENVILLE. '. . . that I am your humble servant.'

GEORGE DANDIN. You want me to say that I am the servant of a man who is trying to cuckold me?

M. DE SOTENVILLE [*making a threatening gesture*]. Grrr!

CLITANDRE. He has said enough, Sir.

M. DE SOTENVILLE. No: I want him to finish so that everything goes according to form. '. . . that I am your humble servant.'

GEORGE DANDIN. '. . . that I am your humble servant.'

CLITANDRE. And I am sincerely yours, Sir; I have wiped from my memory all that has happened here. As for you, Sir, I bid you good day, and much regret the trouble to which you have been put.

M. DE SOTENVILLE. My best respects; whenever you fancy a day's hare coursing, I'll be delighted to provide it.

CLITANDRE. You show me too much kindness.

M. DE SOTENVILLE. This is how to settle matters, son-in-law. Farewell. You know now that you have become a member of a family who will support you and not allow you to be insulted in any way.

[*All but* GEORGE DANDIN *go out*   VII

GEORGE DANDIN. Oh, if I could . . . You asked for it, George Dandin, my old friend, you asked for it and it serves you right: just look at the pickle you are in. But cheer up, it's only a matter of setting her father and mother straight, and there may be a way you can find of managing that.

ACT TWO

I   [*Enter* CLAUDINE *and* LUBIN.

CLAUDINE. Yes, I'd guessed that it just had to have come from you, and that it was you who'd told someone who passed it on to my master.

LUBIN. Darn it! I just mentioned it in passing to a man so that he wouldn't say he saw me come out of here. Folks around here must be real blabbermouths.

CLAUDINE. Really, that Monsieur le Vicomte made a fine choice of ambassador when he chose you; he's picked a risky fellow, and no mistake.

LUBIN. Well I'll be cleverer the next time and take more care.

CLAUDINE. About time too.

LUBIN. Enough of that. Listen.

CLAUDINE. What do you want me to listen to?

LUBIN. Turn your face in my direction.

CLAUDINE. Well, what is it?

LUBIN. Claudine . . .

CLAUDINE. What?

LUBIN. Don't you know what I want to say?

CLAUDINE. No.

LUBIN. Darn it, I love you.

CLAUDINE. Really?

LUBIN. Yes really, the devil take me if I don't. You can believe me because I've sworn an oath on it.

CLAUDINE. So what?

LUBIN. My whole heart goes a-flutter when I look at you.

CLAUDINE. That's nice for you.

LUBIN. How do you manage to be so pretty?

CLAUDINE. I only do what all the others do.

LUBIN. Don't you see? There's no need to beat about the bush any more; if you're willing, you'll be my wife, I'll be your husband and we'll be husband and wife, the pair of us.

CLAUDINE. But you might be jealous like my master.

LUBIN. Not at all.

CLAUDINE. As for me, I can't stand suspicious husbands. I want one who isn't easily shocked, and is so trusting and so confident of my good behaviour that he could come upon me in the company of thirty men and still not be worried.

LUBIN. Well then, I'll be just like that.

CLAUDINE. It's the silliest thing in the world not to trust a wife and to pester her with questions. Nothing is to be gained by such ways, and that's the truth of the matter: it makes us women think of misbehaving, and it's often the husbands themselves who make themselves the cuckolds they are by all the fuss they make.

LUBIN. Well then, I'll give you the freedom to do exactly what you want.

CLAUDINE. That's the way to behave if you don't want to be cuckolded. When husbands trust in our discretion, we only take the liberties we have to. It's like those who open up their purse for us and say 'take what you like'. We act decently and are satisfied with a reasonable amount. But as for those who check up on us all the time, we try our best to fleece them and don't spare them anything.

—

LUBIN. Well then, I'll be like those who open up their purse; all you have to do is marry me.

CLAUDINE. We'll see, we'll see.

LUBIN. Come over here.

CLAUDINE. What do you want?

LUBIN. Come over here, I say.

CLAUDINE. Hey! Watch out: I don't like those who take liberties.

LUBIN. Just a little kiss and cuddle.

CLAUDINE. Leave me alone, I tell you: I won't put up with any nonsense.

LUBIN. Claudine . . .

CLAUDINE. Stop!

LUBIN. Ow! you're very rough with us poor fellows. Why, it's hardly proper to say no to people. Aren't you ashamed of being pretty and not wanting to be cuddled? Come on!

CLAUDINE. I'll give you one on the nose.

LUBIN. Ow! What a savage! a wild beast! Why, you're mean and cruel.

CLAUDINE. And you take too many liberties.

LUBIN. What would it cost you to let me take a few liberties?

CLAUDINE. You must be patient.

LUBIN. Just a little kiss, as an advance on our marriage.

CLAUDINE. I'm very obliged, I'm sure, but no.

LUBIN. Claudine, please, just one on account.

CLAUDINE. Certainly not! I've been caught that way already. Goodbye. Off you go, and tell Monsieur le Vicomte that I'll be sure to pass his letter on.

LUBIN. Goodbye, you rough and stubborn beauty.

CLAUDINE. A very loving farewell, I'm sure.

—

LUBIN. Goodbye, you boulder, you rock, you lump of dressed stone, you hardest of all hard things in the world.

[*Goes out*

CLAUDINE. I'll put the letter into my mistress's hands ... but here she comes, with her husband: I'll move away a little and wait for her to be alone.

[*Enter* GEORGE DANDIN, ANGÉLIQUE *and* CLIT-ANDRE, *at first unseen by the others.*

II

GEORGE DANDIN. No! No! No! I'm not as easy to hoodwink as that; I'm only too sure that what I was told is true. I've got better eyesight than you think, and your piece of nonsense didn't fool me.

CLITANDRE [*aside*]. There she is; but her husband is with her.

GEORGE DANDIN. Through all your play-acting I could see the truth of what I was told, and the lack of respect which you have for the sacred bond which unites us. [ANGÉLIQUE *sees* CLITANDRE, *and curtsys to him*] Don't curtsy to me, for God's sake, I'm not talking about that sort of respect. There's no need to make fun of me.

ANGÉLIQUE. Me. make fun of you? Not at all.

GEORGE DANDIN. I know what you think, and I'm aware ... What, curtsying again? That's enough of your mockery! I know full well that because you are of noble birth you look on me as far beneath you. The respect I'm talking about doesn't concern me as a person: I am speaking about the respect which you owe to the holy bonds of matrimony. [ANGÉLIQUE *gestures to* CLITANDRE] There's no need to shrug your shoulders: I'm not talking nonsense.

ANGÉLIQUE. Who's shrugging their shoulders?

GEORGE DANDIN. God! I'm not blind. Let me tell you once again that marriage is a union to which we must show every respect, and that it's quite wrong of you to treat it as you do. [ANGÉLIQUE *gestures again to* CLITANDRE] Yes, quite wrong; you've no business to shake your head and make faces at me.

ANGÉLIQUE. Me? I don't know what you mean.

GEORGE DANDIN. Well, I know very well what I mean, and I know all about your contempt for me. If I wasn't born of noble blood, at least I come from honest stock without a blemish on its name, and the Dandin family . . .

CLITANDRE [*behind* ANGÉLIQUE, *unseen to* GEORGE DANDIN]. A word with you.

GEORGE DANDIN. What was that?

ANGÉLIQUE. What? I didn't say a word.

GEORGE DANDIN [*catching sight of* CLITANDRE *at last*]. There he is, hanging about you again.

ANGÉLIQUE. Well, is that my fault? What do you want me to do about it?

GEORGE DANDIN. I want you to do what a wife does who wishes to please only her husband. Whatever people say, admirers only press their attentions on women who welcome them. There's a certain sweetness of manner which attracts them, just as flies are attracted to honey; and decent womenfolk behave in a way which sees them off from the very beginning.

ANGÉLIQUE. Me? See them off? And why should I do that? I'm not shocked that men find me attractive; it gives me pleasure.

GEORGE DANDIN. No doubt. But how is your husband meant to act while this courting is taking place?

ANGÉLIQUE. He's meant to act like a gentleman who is pleased to see his wife well looked upon.

GEORGE DANDIN. Well, I'm happy to oblige you, but not in this. It's not my way, and the Dandin family are not used to such a fashion.

ANGÉLIQUE. Oh! The Dandin family will get used to it if they put their mind to it. For myself, let me tell you that *I* don't intend to give up polite society and entomb myself alive in a husband. Really! Because a man takes it upon himself to marry us, must it follow that that's the end of everything for us, and that we must break off all relations with the land of the living? Such tyranny in our husbands and masters is an extraordinary thing, and I think them a bit simple-minded to expect us to live only for them and to be dead to all other social pleasures. I care nothing for all that; *I* don't want to die so young.

GEORGE DANDIN. So that's how you live up to the solemn promises which you made to me publicly!

ANGÉLIQUE. Me? I didn't make them to you with all my heart: you dragged them out of me. Did you ask me before our marriage whether I consented to it, and whether I wished to marry *you*? You only asked my parents; so, properly speaking, you've married them, and that's why you would do well to complain to them about the wrongs which may be done to you. As for me, I didn't ask you to marry me; you took me without asking what my feelings about you were; so I don't consider myself to be obliged to submit to your desires like a slave, and I intend to enjoy the brief time while I am young whether you like it or not, and to profit from the sweet liberties open to those of my generation, to mix in polite society and to have the pleasure of hearing others pay me gallant compliments. You must prepare yourself for this, as a punishment, and thank heaven that I am not capable of worse.

GEORGE DANDIN. So that's how you take things to be. Well, I'm your husband, and let me tell you that I don't see things that way at all.

ANGÉLIQUE. Well I'm your wife, and that's how I see them.

GEORGE DANDIN [*aside*]. I feel sorely tempted to reduce her face to pulp, and to leave her in such a state that she'd

never attract fancy admirers again. Grrr! Come on, George
Dandin, my old friend, you won't be able to control
yourself; it's better you should go off and leave her here.

III   [GEORGE DANDIN *goes out. Enter* CLAUDINE.

CLAUDINE. I was brimming over with impatience for him to
go, Madame, so that I could pass on to you this message
from you know who.

ANGÉLIQUE. Let's see.

CLAUDINE [*aside*]. From what I can see, what he's said to her
hasn't upset her unduly.

ANGÉLIQUE. Ah! Claudine, what an elegantly written letter!
What delightful manners courtiers have got! How agreeably
they speak and act! What is our local society beside them?

CLAUDINE. I think that the Dandins and their like don't
please you much since you have got to know them.

ANGÉLIQUE. Wait here; I'll go and write a reply.

[*Goes out*

CLAUDINE. I hardly think that it's necessary to suggest to her
that she should make it an encouraging one . . ., but just
look who's here.

IV   [*Enter* CLITANDRE *and* LUBIN.

CLAUDINE. Really, sir, you chose a discreet messenger and
no mistake in him.

CLITANDRE. I didn't dare send any of my own servants. But,
my dear Claudine, I must repay you for the help you have
given me.

CLAUDINE. Oh, it's not necessary, Sir. No indeed, you
mustn't put yourself to that trouble; I am at your service
because you deserve it and because I feel that I like you.

CLITANDRE [*giving her money*]. I am much obliged to you.

LUBIN. As we are going to be married, let me have that so
that I can put it with my own.

CLAUDINE. I'll keep it myself, if you don't mind, just as I kept the kiss.

CLITANDRE. Tell me, did you give my message to your pretty mistress?

CLAUDINE. Indeed; and she has gone to write an answer to it.

CLITANDRE. Isn't there any way I could speak to her, Claudine?

CLAUDINE. Yes: come with me and I'll make it possible for you to talk to her.

CLITANDRE. But will she think this wise? Isn't it a bit risky?

CLAUDINE. No, not at all; her husband is out, and in any case, it's not him she has to be careful about but her parents. Provided that they are biased in her favour, there's nothing to fear.

CLITANDRE. I'll let you handle these matters for me.

LUBIN. Darn it! What a clever wife I'll have in her! She's got brains enough for four people.

[CLITANDRE *and* CLAUDINE *go out. Enter* GEORGE   V
DANDIN.

GEORGE DANDIN. Here's my informant from before. I hope to heaven that he'll bring himself to agree to be a witness to my wife's parents of what they refuse to believe.

LUBIN. Ah, there you are, Mr Blabbermouth! I advised you to keep your mouth shut and you promised me to. So you're a gossip who goes round telling all and sundry what I told you in secret?

GEORGE DANDIN. Who? Me?

LUBIN. Yes, you. You went and told the husband and it's your fault that he's kicking up a fuss. I'm glad I found out that you have a loose tongue; that'll teach me to confide in you again.

GEORGE DANDIN. Listen, my friend . . .

LUBIN. If you hadn't gossiped, I'd have told you what went on a moment ago; but as a punishment, I'll not tell you anything.

GEORGE DANDIN. Why? What's been happening?

LUBIN. Nothing at all. Now you see what comes of talking; you'll not get a whiff of the news, and I'll leave you wondering.

GEORGE DANDIN. Wait a moment . . .

LUBIN. No.

GEORGE DANDIN. I only want to say a word to you.

LUBIN. No you don't. You want to worm things out of me.

GEORGE DANDIN. Not at all.

LUBIN. Well I may be stupid, but I can see what you're after.

GEORGE DANDIN. No, it's something different. Listen . . .

LUBIN. No I won't. You want me to tell you that Monsieur le Vicomte has just given some money to Claudine and that she has taken him to meet her mistress. But I'm not that stupid.

GEORGE DANDIN. Please . . .

LUBIN. No.

GEORGE DANDIN. I'll give you . . .

LUBIN [*singing to drown* GEORGE DANDIN's *voice*]. La di da di da . . .

VI   [LUBIN *goes out*

GEORGE DANDIN. I wasn't able to use the plan I had for that simpleton. But the latest news which he blurted out will do the trick as well, and if the young fop is in my house, it will do to show her parents that I am right and to convince them fully that their daughter is behaving shamelessly. The trouble with all this is that I don't know how to go about making the best of such news. If I go in, I'll make the fellow run off and no matter what I see with my own eyes

—

to prove that I have been dishonoured, I would not be believed on my oath alone, and I would be told that I was dreaming it all up. But if, on the other hand, I send for my parents-in-law without being sure that the fellow will be in my house, I'd end up in the same mess as just now. Isn't there a way to find out discreetly whether he's still in the house? By God! there's no doubt about it; I've just seen him through the keyhole. I've been given a heaven-sent opportunity to settle my score with him; and to bring matters to a head, heaven has sent me at just the right moment the very judges whose presence I needed.

[*Enter* M. *and* MME DE SOTENVILLE.   VII

GEORGE DANDIN. Well you didn't want to believe me just now, and your daughter got the better of me; but I've my hands on the evidence to make you see how she treats me. My dishonour is so obvious, thank God, that you will not be able to doubt it.

M. DE SOTENVILLE. Surely, son-in-law, you're not still on about that?

GEORGE DANDIN. Yes, I'm still on about it, and I've never had better reason to be.

MME DE SOTENVILLE. You're not bothering our heads about it again?

GEORGE DANDIN [*making the sign of horns on the head*]. Yes, Madame, and my head is suffering much more than yours.

M. DE SOTENVILLE. Don't you get tired of being a bore?

GEORGE DANDIN. No. I just get tired of being taken for a fool.

MME DE SOTENVILLE. Won't you give up your preposterous suspicions?

GEORGE DANDIN. No, Madame; but I'd like to give up a wife who brings dishonour to me.

MME DE SOTENVILLE.. By heavens, son-in-law, watch what you say.

—

M. DE SOTENVILLE. Dammit! You'd do well to find a less offensive way of expressing yourself.

GEORGE DANDIN. Don't expect a loser to laugh about his loss.

MME DE SOTENVILLE. Don't forget that you have married a lady of noble birth.

GEORGE DANDIN. I'm being reminded of it now, and I don't look like being allowed to forget it.

M. DE SOTENVILLE. Well, if you haven't forgotten it, take good care to speak about her in more respectful terms.

GEORGE DANDIN. But why doesn't she take good care to treat me in a more fitting manner? Hell! Because she's of noble birth, does it mean that she is free to do to me what she likes, without my being able to breathe a word about it?

M. DE SOTENVILLE. What's upsetting you now, and what can you tell us? Didn't you see that this morning she denied knowing the person you talked to me about?

GEORGE DANDIN. Yes. But what would you say if I demonstrated to you that her admirer is with her at this very moment?

MME DE SOTENVILLE. With her?

GEORGE DANDIN. Yes, with her, and in my house.

M. DE SOTENVILLE. In your house?

GEORGE DANDIN. Yes in my house.

MME DE SOTENVILLE. If that's the case, we will be on your side and against her.

M. DE SOTENVILLE. Yes, indeed; our family honour is more precious to us than anything else; if you are telling the truth, we will disown her as a member of our family and abandon her to your anger.

GEORGE DANDIN. All you need do is follow me.

MME DE SOTENVILLE. Be sure that you are not making a mistake.

M. DE SOTENVILLE. Don't do again what you did a short time ago.

GEORGE DANDIN. By God, you'll see. There, have I been lying?

> [ANGÉLIQUE, CLITANDRE *and* CLAUDINE *emerge*   VIII
> *from the house.*

ANGÉLIQUE [*not seeing* GEORGE DANDIN *and her parents*]. Farewell. I'm afraid that someone might find you here; I still have to maintain some discretion.

CLITANDRE [*also unaware of* GEORGE DANDIN *and* M. *and* MME DE SOTENVILLE]. Promise me then, Madame, that I may speak to you tonight.

ANGÉLIQUE. I'll try.

GEORGE DANDIN [*to* M. *and* MME DE SOTENVILLE]. Let's get closer up behind them; try not to be seen.

CLAUDINE [*seeing them*]. Ah, Madame, all is lost, there are your parents with your husband.

CLITANDRE. Heavens!

ANGÉLIQUE [*to* CLITANDRE *and* CLAUDINE]. Don't give anything away, and let me deal with this. [*aloud*] What! You dare to behave in this manner after the fuss just now? So this is how you disguise your true feelings! I have just heard you say that you are in love with me and have designs on my honour; let me make it plain to you how angry I am; I'll make myself clear to you in front of everyone. First, you openly deny everything and give me your word that you have had no thought of offending me; and yet the very same day you are so bold as to come here to my own house to tell me that you love me and spin a hundred silly tales to persuade me to respond to your outrageous proposals: as if I were a wife ever to break my solemn marriage vows or to stray from the paths of virtue which my parents taught me to follow. If my father knew about this, he'd soon teach you a lesson about such behaviour; but a well-bred lady avoids all scandal, so I'll take care not to say anything to him. But I want to show you that, woman though I may be, I am resolute enough to avenge myself of any insults I suffer. Your behaviour has not been that of a gentleman, so I refuse to treat you as a gentleman [*she takes a stick and, pretending to beat* CLITANDRE, *beats her husband who has come between them*].

CLITANDRE. Oh! Oh! Oh! hit me less hard!

CLAUDINE. Harder, Madame! Really give it to him!

ANGÉLIQUE. If there's anything else you feel like saying, this will be my reply.

CLAUDINE. That'll teach you to play around with my mistress.

[CLITANDRE *goes out*

ANGÉLIQUE [*pretending to catch sight of* M. DE SOTENVILLE]. Ah, father! You are here!

M. DE SOTENVILLE. Yes, daughter; I see that you are proving yourself to be a worthy scion of the de Sotenville family in virtue and courage. Come here and let me embrace you.

MME DE SOTENVILLE. Embrace me too, daughter: I can see my own blood in your actions, and shed tears of joy.

M. DE SOTENVILLE. Well, son-in-law, you must be delighted! The incident is full of consolation for you. You had indeed found reason to be alarmed; but your suspicions have been dispelled in the most satisfactory way possible.

MME DE SOTENVILLE. Indeed, son-in-law, now you must be the happiest of men.

CLAUDINE. Certainly. What a wife! You are only too lucky to have married her; you should kiss the ground where her feet have trod.

GEORGE DANDIN. Argh! traitress!

M. DE SOTENVILLE. What is it, son-in-law? Why don't you thank your wife for the affection which, as you have seen, she has shown you?

ANGÉLIQUE. No, father, it's not necessary. He has no obligation to me for what he has just seen; what I have done is only for my own self-esteem.   [*Makes as if to go out*

M. DE SOTENVILLE. Where are you going, daughter?

ANGÉLIQUE. I'm withdrawing, father, so as not to have to listen to his compliments.

[*Goes out*

CLAUDINE. She is right to be angry. She's a wife who deserves to be worshipped; you don't treat her as you should.

[*Goes out*

GEORGE DANDIN. You minx!

M. DE SOTENVILLE. I'm sure it's just a little anger about that other business, and it will pass off when you show her how much you love her. Farewell, son-in-law; now you no longer have any cause for further worry. Make your peace together; try to calm her down by apologizing for your impetuous behaviour.

MME DE SOTENVILLE. You must bear in mind that she is a young girl who has been brought up to behave virtuously, and is not used to being suspected of base behaviour. Farewell. I am delighted to see that the fuss is over and that you're overjoyed by the way she has behaved.

[M. *and* MME DE SOTENVILLE *go out*

GEORGE DANDIN. I won't say a word, because I'll not gain anything by talking. Misfortune on this scale has never been seen before. I am struck dumb by my woes, and by the devilish tricks of my hussy of a wife, who always manages to appear to be in the right and to make me appear in the wrong. Will I always come off worse against her, I ask myself? Will appearances always turn against me? Will I never be able to produce evidence against my shameless wife? I pray heaven to look kindly on my plans and to grant that I may show others that I am being dishonoured.

ACT THREE

I   [*Enter* CLITANDRE *and* LUBIN.

CLITANDRE. It's well on into the night, and I'm afraid that it's too late. I can't see where I'm going. Lubin!

LUBIN. Yes, Sir?

CLITANDRE. Is it over here?

LUBIN. I think so. Darn it, it's very silly of night to be as black as this.

CLITANDRE. It's quite wrong of it, certainly; but if, on the one hand, it stops us seeing where we're going, on the other it prevents us from being seen.

LUBIN. You're right, it isn't so wrong after all. I'd really like to know, Sir, from you who are educated, why it isn't light at night.

CLITANDRE. That's a very big question and a difficult one: you have an enquiring mind, Lubin.

LUBIN. Yes; if I'd studied, I would have ended up thinking of things no one's ever thought of.

CLITANDRE. I can well believe it; you look as though you have a fine, incisive intellect.

LUBIN. That's the case. For example, I can translate Latin, even though I've never learnt it. Seeing the word 'collegium' on a great door the other day, I guessed that it meant 'college'.

CLITANDRE. Amazing! So you can read, Lubin?

LUBIN. Yes, I can read printed characters, but I've never been able to manage handwriting.

CLITANDRE. Here we are, right up against the house. Now for the signal which Claudine gave me.

LUBIN. 'Pon my soul! There's a girl worth all the money in the world! I love her with all my heart.

CLITANDRE. That's why I have brought you along to talk to her.

LUBIN. I'm eternally . . .

CLITANDRE. Quiet! I can hear something.

[ANGÉLIQUE *and* CLAUDINE *emerge from the house.*   II

ANGÉLIQUE. Claudine?

CLAUDINE. Yes?

ANGÉLIQUE. Leave the door ajar.

CLAUDINE. I've done it.

CLITANDRE. It's them. Psst!

ANGÉLIQUE. Psst!

LUBIN. Psst!

CLAUDINE. Psst!

CLITANDRE [*to* CLAUDINE]. Madame . . .

ANGÉLIQUE [*to* LUBIN]. What?

LUBIN [*to* ANGÉLIQUE]. Claudine . . .

CLAUDINE [*to* CLITANDRE]. What is it?

CLITANDRE [*to* CLAUDINE]. Ah, Madame! how overjoyed I am . . .

LUBIN [*to* ANGÉLIQUE]. Claudine, my dearest Claudine.

CLAUDINE [*to* CLITANDRE]. That's enough, Sir!

ANGÉLIQUE [*to* LUBIN]. Stop it, Lubin.

CLITANDRE. So it's *you*, Claudine?

CLAUDINE. Yes.

LUBIN. Is that you, Madame?

ANGÉLIQUE. Yes.

CLAUDINE. You mistook one for the other.

LUBIN. 'Pon my soul, you can't see a sausage at night.

ANGÉLIQUE. Is that you, Clitandre?

CLITANDRE. Yes, Madame.

ANGÉLIQUE. My husband is snoring away as he should, and I have taken the opportunity to have a talk with you.

CLITANDRE. Let's find somewhere to sit down.

CLAUDINE. That's a good idea. [*They withdraw to the back of the stage, except for* LUBIN].

LUBIN. Where are you, Claudine?

III   [*Enter* GEORGE DANDIN.

GEORGE DANDIN. I heard my wife come down, so I've got dressed quickly to follow her. Where can she have gone? Has she slipped out?

LUBIN [*taking* GEORGE DANDIN *for* CLAUDINE]. Where are you, Claudine? Ah, there you are. 'Pon my soul, your master has been nicely had; I find this as funny as the story I was told of the beating he was given earlier on. Your mistress says that he is snoring away like a thousand devils, and doesn't realize that she and Monsieur le Vicomte are together while he sleeps away. I'd like to know what he is dreaming at present! It's all so funny! Why has he got it in his head to be so jealous of his wife and to want her exclusively for himself? He's gone too far, and Monsieur le Vicomte has let him off too lightly. You're not saying anything, Claudine. Let's follow their example; give me your little fist to kiss. How sweet it is! I think I'm eating jam [*as he kisses* GEORGE DANDIN's *hand*, GEORGE DANDIN *punches him in the face.*] Heck! You're a one! That's a rough little fist, and no mistake.

GEORGE DANDIN. Who goes there?

LUBIN. No one [*he runs off.*]

GEORGE DANDIN. He's run away, leaving me with news of yet another infidelity committed by my minx of a wife. I must send for her parents without delay, and use this escapade as a means of bringing about our separation. Hey! Colin!

    [COLIN *appears at the window.*   IV

COLIN. Sir?

GEORGE DANDIN. Down here, quickly.

COLIN [*jumping out of the window*]. Here I am. You can't be quicker than that.

GEORGE DANDIN. Are you there?

COLIN. Yes. [*As* GEORGE DANDIN *goes to one side,* COLIN *goes to the other.*

GEORGE DANDIN. Sshh! Whisper. Now listen. Go to my parents-in-law's house, and tell them to come here at once. Do you understand? Colin? Where are you?

COLIN [*from the other side of the stage*]. Sir?

GEORGE DANDIN. Where the hell are you?

COLIN. Here. [*They look for each other, but pass each other by.*

GEORGE DANDIN. A plague on the fool: he's gone off again! I order you to go at once to my parents-in-law and tell them that I summon them to come here at once. Have you got it? Colin! Colin!

COLIN [*from the other side of the stage*]. Over here, Sir.

GEORGE DANDIN. He'll drive me mad, the villain. Come here! [*They bump into each other*] The clumsy idiot! He's crippled me. Where are you? Come here, I'm going to thrash the daylights out of you. Now he's running away, I think.

COLIN. Quite right.

GEORGE DANDIN. Will you come here?

COLIN. Not on your life!

—

GEORGE DANDIN. Come here, I tell you.

COLIN. Certainly not: you are going to beat me.

GEORGE DANDIN. No, I won't. I'll not do anything to you.

COLIN. Really?

GEORGE DANDIN. Yes. Come over here. At last. You're lucky that I need you. Go quickly to ask my parents-in-law from me to come here as soon as they can; tell them it's a matter of the greatest urgency. If they make a fuss about the time, be sure to hurry them up, and make it clear to them that it is very important for them to come in whatever state of dress they are. Now, have you got that?

COLIN. Yes, Sir.

GEORGE DANDIN. Go quickly, now, and come back as fast.

[COLIN *goes out*

As for me, I'll go back into the house to wait for ... But I can hear someone coming. Isn't that my wife? I must listen in to what is said, under the cover of this darkness.

V   [ANGÉLIQUE, CLITANDRE *and* LUBIN *move to the front of the stage*]

ANGÉLIQUE. Goodbye. It's time I went back.

CLITANDRE. What? So soon?

ANGÉLIQUE. We've said enough to each other.

CLITANDRE. Ah, Madame, could I ever say enough to you? Could I in so short a time find all the words I need to express what I want to express? I would need whole days to explain to you all that I feel and I have not even said the half of what I wanted to say.

ANGÉLIQUE. I'll hear more of it on another occasion.

CLITANDRE. Alas! You wound me to the very quick when you speak of going back: you leave me now in a state of such sadness.

ANGÉLIQUE. We'll find a way to see each other again.

CLITANDRE. Yes, but what is preying on my mind is that in leaving me you will be rejoining your husband. This thought is agony to me, for a husband's privileges are cruel indeed to a lover who is deeply in love.

ANGÉLIQUE. Will you be strong enough to put up with such a thought? Do you really think that it's possible to cherish certain husbands? One marries them because one can't avoid it, and because one is dependent on parents whose only concern is money; but one knows how to give them no more than is their due, and one is not the least bit inclined to show them greater consideration than they deserve.

GEORGE DANDIN [aside]. There are our sluts of wives for you!

CLITANDRE. It must be said that the man who was given to you is hardly worthy of the honour he has received and that the union of a person like you with a person like him is an outlandish thing.

GEORGE DANDIN [aside]. Poor husbands! Just see how you're treated!

CLITANDRE. You deserve a much better fate; heaven did not create you to be the wife of a bumpkin.

GEORGE DANDIN. I wish to God she were yours! You'd soon change your tune. I've heard enough.

[GEORGE DANDIN goes into the house and closes the door.

CLAUDINE. If you want to speak ill of your husband, Madame, hurry up, for it's getting late.

CLITANDRE. Ah, Claudine! how cruel you are!

ANGÉLIQUE. She's right. Let's go our separate ways.

CLITANDRE. I suppose I shall have to, since it is your wish. But please feel some pity for me for the hard time I shall endure.

ANGÉLIQUE. Goodbye.

LUBIN. Where are you, Claudine? I'd like to say goodnight to you.

CLAUDINE. Go now; I'll receive your goodnight from a distance and send you one back at the same time.

VI   [CLITANDRE *and* LUBIN *go out*

ANGÉLIQUE. Let's go back in without making a sound.

CLAUDINE. The door's shut.

ANGÉLIQUE. I've got the key.

CLAUDINE. Open it quietly.

ANGÉLIQUE. It's bolted inside: I don't know how we'll get back in.

CLAUDINE. Call the boy who sleeps up there.

ANGÉLIQUE. Colin! Colin! Colin!

GEORGE DANDIN [*putting his head out of the window*]. Colin? Colin? Ah! I've caught you at last, Madame my wife; so you've been a-roaming while I've been sleeping. I'm as pleased as punch to discover this, and to find you out and about at this time of night.

ANGÉLIQUE. Well, what's so wrong with being out in the cool night air?

GEORGE DANDIN. Nothing at all; it's a good time to take the cool night air. But you have been up to something pretty hot, my coquettish wife. We know all about the planned rendezvous with your pretty young man. We've overheard your amorous dalliance together and the fine poetic eulogies for your husband which you exchanged. My only consolation is that I shall have my revenge, and that your parents will be convinced now that my accusations were justified and that your behaviour has been shameful. I've sent for them; they'll be here shortly.

ANGÉLIQUE. Heavens!

CLAUDINE. Oh, Madame!

GEORGE DANDIN. This is no doubt an unexpected turn of events for you. This time I've come out on top; I've finally got my hands on something which will humble your arrogance and expose your trickery. Up to now you have got out of my accusations, bamboozled your parents and covered up your shameful behaviour. Whatever I said or did was in vain; your cunning always got the better of my rightful claims, and you have always found a way to win the case. But this time, heaven be praised, all will be made clear and your barefacedness will be exposed.

ANGÉLIQUE. I beg you to open the door to me.

GEORGE DANDIN. Certainly not; we must await the arrival of those I have summoned. I want them to find you out and about at this hour of the night. While you're waiting for them why don't you try to think up a new twist or turn to get you out of this mess, or find new ways of dressing up your escapade, or light upon some clever trick to escape from your predicament and appear innocent: perhaps some plausible tale of a nocturnal pilgrimage? or a girl friend in labour whom you've just helped?

ANGÉLIQUE. No: I don't intend to hide anything. I won't even try to defend myself and deny everything, since you know about it all.

GEORGE DANDIN. That's because you can see that all other options are closed and that there's no excuse you could think up which it wouldn't be easy for me to prove false.

ANGÉLIQUE. Yes, I confess that I'm in the wrong, and that you have good reason to bring a complaint against me. But I entreat you to take pity on me and not to expose me to the wrath of my parents: please let me in at once.

GEORGE DANDIN. I'd like to oblige you . . . but not this time.

ANGÉLIQUE. I beg you, my dear, my darling husband.

—

GEORGE DANDIN. Ah! My dear, my darling husband? So I am your darling husband now because you sense you're in a trap. Well, I'm delighted to hear it; you've never thought of uttering such endearments to me before.

ANGÉLIQUE. There, I promise that I'll never give you any cause for complaint again, and that I will . . .

GEORGE DANDIN. All that counts for nothing. I don't want to let this business go by, and it's very important to me that your behaviour will be exposed fully once and for all.

ANGÉLIQUE. Please listen to me. All I ask you for is a moment's audience.

GEORGE DANDIN. Well then, what?

ANGÉLIQUE. I've done wrong, it's true; I admit it to you again and I admit also that your anger is justified; I took the opportunity to go out while you slept and the reason for my going out was to meet the person you say. But these are actions which you should forgive in someone of my age; these are the escapades of a young person who knows nothing of life and has only just entered society; the liberties one allows oneself without thinking of the wrong one is doing, ánd which, when all is said and done, are not so . . .

GEORGE DANDIN. Yes, yes, since it's you who are saying these things they have to be piously believed.

ANGÉLIQUE. I am not trying to excuse myself of being guilty towards you; all I ask is for you to forgive an offence for which I apologize sincerely, and to spare me in this matter the distress which the tiresome reproaches of my parents will cause me. If you are generous enough to grant me the favour which I ask, I will be altogether won over by the decent and kind way you will have treated me. I'll be touched to the heart, and inspired with that love which all the authority of my parents and the bonds of marriage had not been able to kindle in me. In a word, I'll be led to renounce all flirtatious behaviour and to be affectionate only towards you. Indeed, I give you my word that you'll find in me from now on the best wife in the world, and that I'll show you such love, such love that you'll be entirely satisfied.

GEORGE DANDIN. You're nothing but a crocodile who weeps but who eats its victims.

ANGÉLIQUE. Please grant me this favour.

GEORGE DANDIN. Never. I'm unyielding.

ANGÉLIQUE. Show yourself to be noble-spirited.

GEORGE DANDIN. No.

ANGÉLIQUE. Please!

GEORGE DANDIN. No.

ANGÉLIQUE. I beg you with all my heart!

GEORGE DANDIN. No, no, no! I want the scales to fall from people's eyes about you, and I want your exposure to be public.

ANGÉLIQUE. Well, then! Since you have reduced me to despair, I warn you that a woman in such a state is capable of anything and that I am about to do something which you will regret.

GEORGE DANDIN. And what will that be, pray?

ANGÉLIQUE. My heart will be forced to adopt extreme measures; I shall kill myself on the spot with this knife.

GEORGE DANDIN. I'll believe that when I see it!

ANGÉLIQUE. You'll see it sooner than you expect. Everyone knows about our differences, and your endless complaints about me. When I'm found dead, no one will doubt that it's you who have killed me; and my parents are certainly not the sort of people to let such a death go unpunished. They'll pursue you by every legal means open to them to ensure that you are punished and their anger is assuaged. That's how I shall take revenge on you; I shall not be the first to have recourse to such means of vengeance; it isn't difficult to kill ourselves to cause the downfall of those whose cruelty has driven us to this last extremity.

GEORGE DANDIN. Your humble servant, Madame, but people don't think of killing themselves these days; the fashion has long since passed.

ANGÉLIQUE. It's something you'd better be very sure of; if you persist in refusing to let me in, I swear that I'll demonstrate to you just how strong the resolve is of a person driven to despair.

GEORGE DANDIN. Poppycock. You're just trying to frighten me.

ANGÉLIQUE. Well, since I have to, this blow will satisfy us both and show whether I'm serious or not. Ah! I'm dying! I pray Heaven that my death will be avenged as I wish it to be, and the one who has caused it will receive his just deserts for the hardness of heart he has shown me.

GEORGE DANDIN. Oh! Would she be so wicked as to kill herself just to get me hanged? I'd better go outside with a candle just to see what has happened.

ANGÉLIQUE [to CLAUDINE]. Psst! Quiet! Get right up to the door: it doesn't matter which side.

GEORGE DANDIN [in the door]. Would a woman's wickedness go that far?

> [He goes out with his candle without seeing them; they slip in and close the door behind them]

There's no one here. It's just as I thought; the hussy has gone off, seeing that she wasn't going to get any joy out of me by threats or entreaties. So much the better! That'll make her behaviour that much worse, and her parents will see all the more clearly that she has done wrong. Oh dear, the door's closed. Hello! Hello, someone! Open up for me at once!

ANGÉLIQUE [*with* CLAUDINE *at the window*]. What? So it's you? And where have you been, you scoundrel? What sort of time is this to come home? It's nearly dawn! Is this the sort of life a decent husband should be leading?

CLAUDINE. A fine thing it is to go boozing all night and to leave your poor young wife all by herself at home!

GEORGE DANDIN. What? You've got . . .

ANGÉLIQUE. Enough, you villain; I'm fed up with your gallivanting, and I intend to complain to my parents as soon as I can about it.

GEORGE DANDIN. What? You mean to say that you've got the nerve to . . .

[*Enter* M. *and* MME DE SOTENVILLE *in their night-clothes, preceded by* COLIN *carrying a lantern.*   VII

ANGÉLIQUE. Come over here please, and take my side against the outrageous insolence of a husband who has become so befuddled by jealousy and by wine that he no longer knows what he's doing or saying, and who has himself sent for you to bear witness to the most bizarre behaviour that has ever been heard of. Here he is, just back, as you can see, having kept us waiting all night; and if you are indulgent enough to listen to him, he'll tell you that he has the gravest complaints to make about me to you, and that while he slept, I slipped out to dally with others, and a hundred other things of the same kind he has dreamt up.

GEORGE DANDIN. What an evil witch!

CLAUDINE. Yes, he tried to persuade us that he's the one who was in the house, and we were outside; there's no way of getting these delusions out of his head.

M. DE SOTENVILLE. What is the meaning of all this?

MME DE SOTENVILLE. What outrageous impudence to send for us!

GEORGE DANDIN. Never . . .

ANGÉLIQUE. No, father, I simply can't put up with such a husband. My patience is at an end; he's just said a hundred insulting things to me.

M. DE SOTENVILLE. By God, you're no gentleman.

CLAUDINE. It's a crying shame to see a young wife treated in this way: her treatment cries out for vengeance from Heaven.

GEORGE DANDIN. May I . . .

MME DE SOTENVILLE. Enough! You should die of shame.

GEORGE DANDIN. Let me have my say.

ANGÉLIQUE. Just listen, and he'll tell you some tall stories.

GEORGE DANDIN. I give up.

CLAUDINE. He's drunk so much that I don't think that he's fit to be with; you can smell from up here the reek of wine on his breath.

GEORGE DANDIN. I swear to you, father-in-law, that . . .

M. DE SOTENVILLE. Stay away from me; your breath stinks of wine.

GEORGE DANDIN. I beg you, Madame, to . . .

MME DE SOTENVILLE. Heavens! Don't come near me; your breath is foul.

GEORGE DANDIN. Let me . . .

M. DE SOTENVILLE. Stay away from me, I say; your company is unbearable.

GEORGE DANDIN. Allow me, please, to . . .

MME DE SOTENVILLE. Ugh! You make me sick. Speak from over there, if you have to.

GEORGE DANDIN. All right then, I'll speak from over here. I swear to you that I have not left my house at all, and that she's the one who went out.

ANGÉLIQUE. What did I say?

CLAUDINE. A likely story.

M. DE SOTENVILLE. Come, come, you're taking us for fools. Come down here, daughter.

GEORGE DANDIN. I swear before heaven that I was in the house, and that . . .

MME DE SOTENVILLE. Be quiet: such preposterous behaviour is not to be borne.

GEORGE DANDIN. Let lightning strike me down on this very spot if . . .

M. DE SOTENVILLE. Stop racking your brains for things to say, and start thinking about apologizing to your wife.

GEORGE DANDIN. Me? Apologize?

M. DE SOTENVILLE. Yes, apologize, and at once!

GEORGE DANDIN. What, am I to . . .?

M. DE SOTENVILLE. By God, if you answer me back, I'll soon show you what it is to trifle with us!

GEORGE DANDIN. Oh, George Dandin, my old friend!

[ANGÉLIQUE and CLAUDINE appear on stage.]

M. DE SOTENVILLE. Come here, daughter, so that your husband can apologize to you.

ANGÉLIQUE. Me? Forgive him for all that he's said to me? No, father, I could never bring myself to forgive him; I ask you to give me a separation from a husband with whom I can no longer bear to live.

CLAUDINE. How can you say no?

M. DE SOTENVILLE. Such separation, daughter, cannot be obtained without a great deal of scandal. You must show yourself to be better than him, and be patient this time.

ANGÉLIQUE. How can I be patient after suffering such indignity? No, father, I just can't consent to it.

M. DE SOTENVILLE. You must, daughter, because I tell you to.

ANGÉLIQUE. Those words prevent me from saying any more; you have absolute power over my wishes.

CLAUDINE. What submissiveness!

ANGÉLIQUE. It's tiresome to have to forget such insults; but however difficult it is for me, I must obey you.

CLAUDINE. Poor lamb!

M. DE SOTENVILLE. Come here.

ANGÉLIQUE. What you are making me do will have no effect; it will have to be done again tomorrow, you'll see.

M. DE SOTENVILLE. We'll put matters straight. Now, kneel down.

GEORGE DANDIN. Kneel?

M. DE SOTENVILLE. Yes, kneel down, right away.

GEORGE DANDIN [kneeling]. God! What do I have to say?

M. DE SOTENVILLE. 'Madame, I ask you to forgive me'

GEORGE DANDIN. 'Madame, I ask you to forgive me'

M. DE SOTENVILLE. 'For my appalling misjudgement'

GEORGE DANDIN. 'For my appalling misjudgement' [aside] 'in marrying you.'

M. DE SOTENVILLE. 'And I solemnly promise to behave better in future.'

GEORGE DANDIN. 'And I solemnly promise to behave better in future.'

M. DE SOTENVILLE. Make sure you do so; take note that this is the last act of impertinence we will put up with.

MME DE SOTENVILLE. By heavens! if you fall back into such ways, we'll soon teach you the respect you owe to your wife and to those of her blood.

M. DE SOTENVILLE. Dawn is breaking. Go back indoors, and make sure that you behave yourself.

[to MME DE SOTENVILLE] My dear, let's go back to bed.

[*All go out except* GEORGE DANDIN VIII

GEORGE DANDIN. Ah! I give up, and can't see any cure for it; when you've married, as I have, a vixen of a wife, your best course is to take a flying jump into the lake.

THE MISER

[*L'Avare*]

L'Avare, *comedy in five acts, was first produced at the Théâtre du
Palais-Royal, Paris, on 9 September 1668, with Molière in the
part of Harpagon.*

CHARACTERS

HARPAGON, *father of Cléante and Élise, and in love with Mariane*

CLÉANTE, *son of Harpagon, and in love with Mariane*

ÉLISE, *daughter of Harpagon, and in love with Valère*

VALÈRE, *son of Anselme, and in love with Élise*

MARIANE, *in love with Cléante, and loved by Harpagon*

ANSELME, *father of Valère and Mariane*

FROSINE, *a go-between*

MASTER SIMON, *an agent*

MASTER JACQUES, *cook and coachman to Harpagon*

LA FLÈCHE [*Arrow*]. *Valet to Cléante*

DAME CLAUDE, *servant to Harpagon*

BRINDAVOINE [*Oat-stalk*]. *Lackey to Harpagon*

LA MERLUCHE [*Stockfish*]. *Lackey to Harpagon*

A COMMISSIONER OF POLICE

HIS CLERK

The scene is set in Paris

ACT ONE

I

[VALÈRE *and* ÉLISE *discovered.*

VALÈRE. Can you be sad, my dear Élise, after giving me such sweet proofs of your affection? I am so happy, and yet I hear you sigh. Surely you do not regret having at last consented to our engagement?

ÉLISE. No, Valère, I can regret nothing I have done for you. I feel drawn on by a sweet, irresistible force that leaves me not even the wish to struggle. But, to tell you the truth, the future frightens me. I fear I may love you too much.

VALÈRE. But, my sweet Élise, what can you have to fear in loving me?

ÉLISE. Alas, a hundred things; my father's anger, the reproaches of my family, the disapproval of my friends. But, above all else, Valère, your own inconstancy, the cruel indifference with which your sex too often repays the too ardent offer of an innocent heart.

VALÈRE. Oh, do not do me the wrong of judging me by other men. Believe me capable of anything, Élise, rather than of failing in my affection for you. I love you too much for that. My love will last as long as my life.

ÉLISE. Ah, Valère, all men say that. In their words men are all alike. It is only in their actions that their different natures can be seen.

VALÈRE. Then, since our actions alone can prove our hearts, judge of my heart by mine; and do not condemn me in advance by harbouring unjust fears and exercising undue caution. Do not torment me, I beg you, with baseless suspicions. Give me time, and I will convince you, by a thousand proofs, of the sincerity of my feelings.

ÉLISE. Alas, we are only too easily persuaded by those we love! Yes, Valère, I believe your heart is incapable of betraying me. I believe you love me truly, and will be faithful. I cannot doubt it. My only fear is for what the world will say.

VALÈRE. But what is there to fear in that?

ÉLISE. Nothing, if everyone could see you as I do. You yourself are my best excuse. Your worth and a natural feeling of gratitude exonerate my heart from all blame. I can never forget the moment of deadly peril which brought us first together, your magnificent courage in risking your own life to save mine, the tender care you showed towards me when you had dragged me from the water, nor the unceasing homage of your ardent affection, which, forgetting family and country, and undeterred by any difficulties, keeps you still in Paris to the ruin of your career. When I think too that to be near me you have forgone your rank, and have even become a steward in my father's house, indifference is impossible. But, though in my eyes this is more than enough to justify our engagement, perhaps others will not see it as I do.

VALÈRE. It is only for my love that I ask any return; and, as for your scruples, your father's behaviour alone would be enough to excuse you before the world. His extraordinary avarice and the stingy way he treats his children would justify even greater rashness. Forgive me, darling Élise, for speaking so before you, but you know that on this point it is impossible to speak well of him. Once I have found my parents, it will be easy enough to obtain his consent. I am expecting news of them every day, and, if I hear nothing soon, I shall go in search of them myself.

ÉLISE. Oh, Valère, don't go away. Try rather to get into my father's good graces.

VALÈRE. I have been doing my best already. You know how artfully I contrived to get a footing here, my pretence of sympathy and similarity of outlook, the part I play every day in order to win his good opinion; and I am getting on remarkably well. I find that the shortest road to a man's goodwill is to humour his prejudices, pretend to share his opinions, pander to his faults and praise everything he does. One need never be afraid of going too far or showing one's hand too clearly. Flattery makes fools of the wisest people. There is nothing too extravagant or ridiculous for them to swallow, if it is only well seasoned with praise. It is true that sincerity suffers somewhat in the process; but, if we need their assistance, we must give in to their foibles; and, as that is the only way to win them, the fault is not with those who flatter, but with those who make it necessary.

ÉLISE. But why do you not try to win over my brother to our side, in case the servant should betray us?

VALÈRE. To humour them both would be too difficult. Their natures are so opposite it would be impossible to gain the confidence of both. But *you* might sound out your brother. You are great friends, and it should not be too hard for you to win his sympathy. Here he comes. Take this opportunity of speaking with him, but do not confide in him more than is absolutely necessary.

ÉLISE. I doubt if I shall have the courage to speak of it at all.

[VALÈRE *goes out. Enter* CLÉANTE.   II

CLÉANTE. I am glad to find you alone, sister. I have been dying to see you to tell you a secret.

ÉLISE. I am all attention. What is it you want to tell me?

CLÉANTE. A thousand things, my dear sister, but they may all be expressed in four words. I am in love.

ÉLISE. In love?

CLÉANTE. Yes, I am in love. But, before we go further, let me say this. I know that I am dependent on my father, whose wishes I am bound to respect. I know that we ought not to engage ourselves without the consent of those to whom we owe our existence. I know that Heaven has appointed them the guardians of our hearts, and that we may not dispose of them without their advice. I know that, being unprejudiced by passion, they are less likely to be deceived, and can judge what is good for us better than ourselves. I know that their wisdom and experience are more to be trusted than the blindness of our passion, and that the impetuosity of youth often makes us commit the most disastrous errors. I tell you all this, my dear sister, only to save you the trouble of telling it to me; for, to cut all short, my love will brook no interference, and I beg you to spare me your remonstrances.

ÉLISE. Are you engaged then to the one you love?

CLÉANTE. No, but my mind is made up, and once more I beg you not to try to dissuade me.

ÉLISE. Am I then so unnatural a monster?

CLÉANTE. No, my dear Élise, but you are not in love. You know nothing of that sweet violence with which tender love assails our hearts. You are too modest to understand.

ÉLISE. Alas, brother, do not speak to me of modesty! There is no one whom it does not desert at some time in their life, and, if you knew the truth, perhaps you would think me even more imprudent than yourself.

CLÉANTE. Would to God that your heart, like mine. . . . !

ÉLISE. Well, let me hear your story first. Tell me who it is you love.

CLÉANTE. It is a young girl who has lived in this neighbourhood only a short while, and who seems born for no other purpose than to make men fall in love. Nature, my dear sister, never formed a sweeter creature, and when I first set eyes on her I was thrown into ecstasy. Her name is Mariane, and she lives under the care of her dear old mother, who is nearly always ill and whom this charming girl loves with an almost unbelievable affection. The tenderness with which she waits on her, cherishes her and comforts her is the most affecting sight in the world, and there is an infinite charm in everything she does. In her slightest movement there is a grace, a sweetness, a simplicity which is quite adorable. Oh, my dear sister, I wish you could have seen her.

ÉLISE. I can picture her already from your description; but for me it is enough that you love her.

CLÉANTE. I have found out that they are far from well off, and it is only with the greatest economy they can make ends meet. Oh, my dear Élise, imagine the joy of helping someone one loves, of discreetly contributing towards the modest necessities of a deserving family; and then imagine the misery of being prevented by a father's stinginess from enjoying this satisfaction, and from giving this fascinating creature any proof of my affection.

ÉLISE. I can imagine it well enough.

CLÉANTE. It is really past bearing. Could anything be more outrageous than the niggardly way he treats us, the absolute penury in which we have to live? What is the good of having money when we cannot use it until we are too old to enjoy it; when in the meantime I am compelled to borrow right and left for very subsistence, and when, were it not for money-lenders, we should even be without decent clothes to our backs? I have been meaning for some time to ask you to come with me to put the matter to our father; and, if it has no effect, I am determined to run away from home with this charming creature, and risk whatever future Fate may send us. I am already doing my best to borrow some money, and if you, my dear sister, are in the same condition, and our father will not hear reason, we will both leave him and no longer be the slaves of his unbearable avarice.

ÉLISE. Every day he gives us more reason to regret our mother's death, and. . . .

—

CLÉANTE. I hear his voice. Come, tell me about your trouble; then we will come back together and try to persuade him to be more generous.

III   [*They withdraw. Enter* HARPAGON *and* LA FLÈCHE.

HARPAGON. Be off! And don't answer back. Get out of the house immediately, you scoundrel, you arch-thief!

LA FLÈCHE [*aside*]. I have never known such a wicked old man. I think he's possessed of the devil.

HARPAGON. What are you mumbling there?

LA FLÈCHE. Why are you turning away?

HARPAGON. Why, you rascal? You dare ask why? Get out quick before I hit you.

LA FLÈCHE. What have I done?

HARPAGON. Enough to make me wish to see the back of you.

LA FLÈCHE. Your son, my master, said I was to wait for him here.

HARPAGON. Then go and wait for him outside; but you shall no longer take refuge in my house, watching all that goes on, and trying to turn it to your own advantage. I won't have a spy prying into all my affairs; a fellow whose damned eyes follow all my movements, make notes of all my belongings, and are always on the look-out for something to steal.

LA FLÈCHE. How the devil do you suppose anyone could rob you? How can you be robbed when you keep everything under lock and key and mount guard over it night and day?

HARPAGON. I shall lock up what I like and mount guard as much as I please. Such habits are as good as informers to watch what is going on. [*Aside*]. I'm terrified he may suspect something about that money. [*Aloud*]. You're the very sort of man to go and spread a report that I have money hidden here.

LA FLÈCHE. You have money hidden?

HARPAGON. No, you scoundrel, I never said so. [*Aside*]. Oh, the rogue! [*Aloud*]. I said that was the kind of rumour you would spread out of spite.

LA FLÈCHE. What does it matter to us whether you have it or not? It never comes our way.

HARPAGON. So you fancy an argument? I'll box your ears if you answer me back. [*He lifts his hand in a threatening gesture*]. Get out.

LA FLÈCHE. Very well. I'm going.

HARPAGON. Wait. Let me make sure you've stolen nothing.

LA FLÈCHE. What should I steal?

HARPAGON. Let me see. Show me your hands.

LA FLÈCHE [*holding out his hands*]. There you are.

HARPAGON. Now the others.

LA FLÈCHE. The others?

HARPAGON. Yes, the others.

LA FLÈCHE [*quickly putting his hands behind his back, then holding them out again*]. There! Are you satisfied now?

HARPAGON [*pointing to* LA FLÈCHE'S *breeches*]. Haven't you got something in there?

LA FLÈCHE. You can look if you like.

HARPAGON [*feeling down outside his breeches*]. These wide breeches are great receivers of stolen goods. People should be hanged for wearing them.

LA FLÈCHE [*aside*]. It would serve such a man right for his fears to come true. Oh, how I would love to rob him!

HARPAGON. Eh?

LE FLÈCHE. What?

HARPAGON. What was that you said about robbing?

LA FLÈCHE. I said you had better make a thorough search to see if I have robbed you.

HARPAGON. That's what I intend to do. [*He feels in* LA FLÈCHE'S *pockets*].

LA FLÈCHE [*aside*]. The devil take all skinflints and their stinginess!

HARPAGON. What? What's that you say?

LA FLÈCHE. What was I saying?

HARPAGON. Yes. What were you saying about skinflints and stinginess?

LA FLÈCHE. I was asking the devil to take them.

HARPAGON. To whom were you referring?

LA FLÈCHE. To skinflints.

HARPAGON. And who are these skinflints?

LA FLÈCHE. Close-fisted cheeseparers.

HARPAGON. But whom do you mean by that?

LA FLÈCHE. Why do you want to know?

HARPAGON. Because I do.

LA FLÈCHE. Do you think I meant you?

HARPAGON. Never mind what I think. You shall tell me whom you were speaking to when you said that.

LA FLÈCHE. I was speaking to . . . my hat.

HARPAGON. I'll cuff you over the head.

LA FLÈCHE. What, would you stop me cursing the old skinflints?

HARPAGON. No; but I'll stop your impertinent chatter. Hold your tongue.

LA FLÈCHE. I named no names.

HARPAGON. I'll give you a thrashing if you say anything more.

LA FLÈCHE. If the cap fits, wear it.

HARPAGON. Will you be silent?

LA FLÈCHE. Yes, under protest.

—

HARPAGON. Hm!

LA FLÈCHE [showing HARPAGON a pocket in his tunic]. See, there's another pocket here. You'd better have a look.

HARPAGON. Come on, man. Don't make me search you. Give it up.

LA FLÈCHE. Give up what?

HARPAGON. What you have stolen.

LA FLÈCHE. I haven't stolen anything.

HARPAGON. You haven't?

LA FLÈCHE. Certainly not.

HARPAGON. Then go to the devil.

LA FLÈCHE [aside]. A courteous way of giving notice, I must say.

HARPAGON. I charge it to your conscience though.

[LA FLÈCHE goes out

A very dangerous character. I hate the sight of the limping cur.* It's a terrible anxiety to have a large sum of money on the premises. It's much better to have it all well invested, and only keep just enough for current expenses. Even with the whole house at one's disposal it's not at all easy to find a safe hiding place. I won't trust a strong box. That only attracts thieves. It's the first thing they go for.

[ÉLISE and CLÉANTE return in conversation at the back. IV
HARPAGON does not see them.

But I think it was a bit too risky to bury those ten thousand ecus I received yesterday in the garden. Ten thousand ecus in gold on the premises is enough to tempt ... [aside, catching sight of his children]. Oh, Heavens! I got carried away, and my nervousness has betrayed me. I believe I have spoken my thoughts aloud. [To them]. What do you want?

CLÉANTE. Nothing, father.

HARPAGON. Have you been there long?

ÉLISE. We have only just come in.

HARPAGON. Did you hear . . . ?

CLÉANTE. What, father?

HARPAGON. You know.

ÉLISE. What, papa?

HARPAGON. What I said just now.

CLÉANTE. No.

HARPAGON. I believe you did.

ÉLISE. No, really.

HARPAGON. You must have caught some of it. I was just remarking on the difficulty of getting money nowadays. I was saying one would be very lucky if one had ten thousand ecus in the house.

CLÉANTE. We hesitated to come in for fear of disturbing you.

HARPAGON. I tell you that, so that you won't get it the wrong way round and think I said that I *have* ten thousand ecus.

CLÉANTE. It's nothing to do with us.

HARPAGON. Would to God I *had* ten thousand ecus!

CLÉANTE. I can't imagine. . . .

HARPAGON. It would be a red letter day for me, I can tell you.

ÉLISE. That is a thing that. . . .

HARPAGON. Nothing would be more welcome.

CLÉANTE. I think. . . .

HARPAGON. It would put my affairs on a very different footing.

ÉLISE. You are. . . .

HARPAGON. I shouldn't be complaining then that times are bad.

CLÉANTE. Surely, father, you have no reason to complain. Everyone knows you are well enough off.

HARPAGON. What? I am well enough off? Anyone who says so is a liar. Nothing is more false. They are lying rascals who spread such reports.

ÉLISE. Don't be so angry.

HARPAGON. It's a nice thing that my own children should turn against me.

CLÉANTE. Is it turning against you to say you are well off?

HARPAGON. Yes. If you talk like that, and continue your extravagance, they'll be breaking into my house one of these days and cutting my throat in the belief that I'm rolling in money.

CLÉANTE. In what way am I extravagant?

HARPAGON. In what way? Can anything be more scandalous than the expensive way you dress? I was scolding your sister only yesterday, but you are worse still. It's enough to bring down a judgement on you. What you put on your back would bring in a good income. I have told you over and over again, my son, I am very displeased at the way you behave. You give yourself airs far beyond your station, and to be able to afford clothes like that you must be robbing me.

CLÉANTE. How do I rob you?

HARPAGON. I don't know; but where else do you get the money to keep up such a style?

CLÉANTE. Why, at the gaming table; and, as I am generally fairly lucky, I spend all my winnings on clothes.

HARPAGON. Such conduct is most reprehensible. If you are lucky at the tables you should take advantage of it, and put out your winnings at a decent rate of interest against a rainy day. I should like to know the use of all these ribbons, for instance, which flutter about you from top to toe.

Wouldn't a few buttons do well enough to keep up your breeches? Why spend money on wigs when you can wear your own hair for nothing? I should say, at a guess, you spend twenty pistoles at least on wigs and ribbons; and twenty pistoles would bring in eighteen livres, six sous, eight deniers a year, investing it at no higher than at eight per cent.

CLÉANTE. Yes, I daresay it would.

HARPAGON. Well, let that pass for the present. There is something else I want to say. [*Aside, seeing them make signs to each other*]. Eh? I believe they are in league to steal my purse. [*Aloud*]. What do those signs mean?

ÉLISE. My brother and I were discussing which should speak first. We both have something to say to you.

HARPAGON. And I have something to say to you too.

CLÉANTE. It is about marriage, father, that we wish to speak to you.

HARPAGON. It is about marriage too that I wish to speak to you.

ÉLISE. Oh, papa!

HARPAGON. Why that cry, girl? Is it the word or the thing that frightens you?

CLÉANTE. That depends on your intentions. We are afraid that our feelings may not agree with your choice.

HARPAGON. Oh, that's all right. There's nothing to be alarmed about. I know the very thing for you both. You will neither of you have any cause for complaint in what I mean to do. [*To* CLÉANTE]. Have you ever seen a young lady called Mariane who lives near here?

CLÉANTE. Yes, father, I have.

HARPAGON [*to* ÉLISE]. And you?

ÉLISE. I have heard of her.

HARPAGON. What do you think of the girl, my son?

CLÉANTE. Very charming indeed.

HARPAGON. Her face?

CLÉANTE. Open and full of intelligence.

HARPAGON. Her appearance, her manners?

CLÉANTE. Quite adorable.

HARPAGON. Don't you think a girl like that is worthy of serious consideration?

CLÉANTE. Most certainly I do.

HARPAGON. Wouldn't she make a desirable wife?

CLÉANTE. Very desirable indeed.

HARPAGON. Don't you think she is the kind of girl who would run her house well?

CLÉANTE. Not a doubt of it.

HARPAGON. And would make a man happy?

CLÉANTE. I am quite sure of that.

HARPAGON. There is one little difficulty. Her dowry is not so large as one could wish.

CLÉANTE. My dear father, the dowry is of no consequence when one is marrying the right person.

HARPAGON. Forgive me, but I can't altogether agree with you. But still, if the dowry is rather small, one can try and make up for it in other ways.

CLÉANTE. Yes, yes, of course.

HARPAGON. Well, I am glad that you agree with me, for her modesty and sweetness have quite won my heart, and I have decided to marry her, so long as she does not come entirely empty handed.

CLÉANTE. What?

HARPAGON. What?

CLÉANTE. You say you have decided. . . .

HARPAGON. To marry Mariane.

CLÉANTE. Who? You, you?

HARPAGON. Yes, I, I, I. Surely that's plain enough.

CLÉANTE. I feel a little dizzy. I'll go and lie down.

HARPAGON. Yes, that's right. Go and drink a large glass of cold water in the kitchen.

[CLÉANTE *goes out*

These elegant young fops! They've no more stamina than a chicken. There, my daughter, that's what I have decided for myself. For your brother I have chosen a certain widow, on whose behalf they came to negotiate with me this morning; and I intend to give you to Seigneur Anselme.

ÉLISE. Seigneur Anselme?

HARPAGON. Yes; a man mature, wise and prudent, not much over fifty, and, as I understand, extremely well-to-do.

ÉLISE [*curtsying*]. If you please, papa, I would rather not marry.

HARPAGON [*imitating her*]. If you please, my sweet, my darling daughter, I would rather that you did marry.

ÉLISE [*curtsying*]. Father, I beg you will excuse me.

HARPAGON [*imitating her*]. Daughter, I beg you will excuse me.

ÉLISE. I am Seigneur Anselme's very humble servant; but [*curtsying*] if it's all the same to you, I will never marry him.

HARPAGON. I am your daughtership's very humble servant; but [*imitating her*] if it's all the same to you, you shall marry him this very evening.

ÉLISE. This very evening?

HARPAGON. This very evening.

ÉLISE [*curtsying*]. Father, I tell you I will not.

HARPAGON [*imitating her*]. Daughter, I tell you you shall.

ÉLISE. No.

HARPAGON. Yes.

ÉLISE. I say no.

HARPAGON. I say yes.

ÉLISE. You will never make me do it.

HARPAGON. I most certainly will make you do it.

ÉLISE. I will kill myself sooner than marry a husband like that.

HARPAGON. You will not kill yourself, and you will marry him. But, Heavens above, what impertinence! That's a nice way for a daughter to speak to her father!

ÉLISE. There's a nice husband for a father to give his daughter away to!

HARPAGON. There's not a word to be said against him. I am sure everyone would approve my choice.

ÉLISE. And I'm sure it would not be approved by a single reasonable person.

HARPAGON [*seeing* VALÈRE *in the distance*]. There's Valère. Will you agree to be guided by his opinion?

ÉLISE. Yes, I'll agree to that.

HARPAGON. You will be ruled by what he says?

ÉLISE. Yes, I will be ruled by what he says.

HARPAGON. Very good then.

    [*Enter* VALÈRE.   V

Come here a moment, Valère. We want you to decide which of us is right, my daughter or I.

VALÈRE. Oh, you, Sir, undoubtedly.

HARPAGON. Do you know the question at issue?

VALÈRE. No, but you are rightness itself. You couldn't be wrong.

HARPAGON. I wish to marry her this evening to a man as rich as he is good, and the hussy tells me to my face that she won't have him. What do you say to that?

VALÈRE. What do I say?

HARPAGON. Yes.

VALÈRE. Well. . . .

HARPAGON. Well?

VALÈRE. I say that, as regards first principles, you are right. You could hardly help being right. But she too is not altogether in the wrong, and. . . .

HARPAGON. What? Seigneur Anselme is the most brilliant match. He is a gentleman of good birth, good-tempered, serious, intelligent, well-to-do, and not a child alive of his first marriage. Could she find a better?

VALÈRE. Yes, all that is true enough. But she could say, on her side, that it is all rather sudden, and that she needs a little time to see if her feelings. . . .

HARPAGON. Yes, yes, but we must grasp this opportunity while we have the chance. There is an advantage in this that I could not find anywhere else. He has agreed to take her without a dowry.

VALÈRE. Without a dowry?

HARPAGON. Yes.

VALÈRE. Oh, then I have nothing more to say. That settles the question. There is no resisting an argument like that.

HARPAGON. It will be a considerable saving for me.

VALÈRE. Of course. That's obvious. Still, your daughter might protest that marriage is a very serious business, that her whole future happiness depends on it, and that one should not enter rashly into a commitment which ends only with death.

HARPAGON. But without a dowry!

VALÈRE. Yes, that is of course final. Still, some people would think that in such a matter a girl's own inclination deserves some consideration, and that the great difference in their age, character and outlook makes such a marriage very liable to disaster.

HARPAGON. But without a dowry!

VALÈRE. Yes, that is quite unanswerable. Who could see it in any other light? Still, there are fathers who would consider a daughter's happiness rather than the money they would have to pay; who would hesitate to sacrifice her to their own interests, but would rather seek that conformity of temperament without which marriage is devoid of honour, peace, contentment, or . . .

HARPAGON. But without a dowry!

VALÈRE. True. There is no answer to that. Without a dowry. Such an argument is quite irresistible.

HARPAGON [*aside, looking out into the garden*]. I thought I heard a dog bark. I believe there's someone after my money. [*To* VALÈRE]. Don't go. I will be back immediately.

[*He goes out into the garden*

ÉLISE. Are you mad, Valère, to agree with him like that?

VALÈRE. I did it so as not to provoke him. We shall gain our end the better. To oppose him outright would be fatal. There are some minds which can only be led, not driven; some temperaments so stubborn and irrational that they shy away from the straight road of reason, and the only way to manage them is to guide them subtly in the desired direction. Pretend to agree to all he wishes; you will find that the wisest way, and. . . .

ÉLISE. But what of this marriage, Valère?

VALÈRE. We will find some pretext to break it off.

ÉLISE. But how can we, if it is to take place to-night?

VALÈRE. You must say you are ill and persuade him to postpone it.

ÉLISE. But they will see through that at once if they send for a doctor.

VALÈRE. Nonsense! What do doctors know? You can have any ailment you like, they will always give you reasons enough to account for it.

[HARPAGON *returns.*

HARPAGON. It was nothing after all, thank God!

VALÈRE [*not seeing him*]. If all else fails we can take refuge in flight; and, if your love, my sweet Élise, is strong enough. . . . [*Seeing* HARPAGON]. It is a daughter's duty to obey her father. She should never stop to consider what a husband is like; and, once the magic phrase *without a dowry* has been spoken, all question of choice is at an end.

HARPAGON. Most excellently put!

VALÈRE. I beg your pardon, Sir, if I have been too officious; if I have taken a liberty in putting it to her so strongly.

HARPAGON. No, no, I am delighted. I give you absolute control over her. [*To* ÉLISE, *who is going out*]. It's no good running away. The authority which Heaven gave me I resign to him. You are to obey him in everything.

VALÈRE. [*To* ÉLISE]. Disobey me now if you dare!

[ÉLISE *goes out*

I'll go after her, Sir, and continue my instruction.

HARPAGON. Do so. You will oblige me infinitely.

VALÈRE. She needs driving with a tight rein.

HARPAGON. She does indeed. You must. . . .

VALÈRE. Don't worry. I'm sure I can bring her to reason.

HARPAGON. Good, good. I have a little errand to do in town, but I will be back immediately.

VALÈRE [*following* ÉLISE *and speaking to her as he goes*]. Yes, money is the most important thing in the world. You ought to thank God for giving you such a father. He understands life. When a man offers to take a girl without a dowry it is quite unnecessary to enquire further. Youth, looks, birth, honour, sense and integrity are all included in that single phrase.

HARPAGON. Good boy, good boy! He speaks like an oracle. Happy the man who has such a steward!

ACT TWO

[*Enter* CLÉANTE *and* LA FLÈCHE.   I

CLÉANTE. Where have you been hiding yourself, you rascal? Didn't I tell you . . . ?

LA FLÈCHE. Yes, Sir, and here I came to wait your orders patiently; but that most ill-tempered of men, your father, drove me away. He wouldn't hear a word and threatened me with a beating.

CLÉANTE. Well, how have our plans been going? Things are more desperate than ever now. Since I saw you last I have discovered that my father is my rival.

LA FLÈCHE. Your father is in love?

CLÉANTE. Yes. I was so flabbergasted, it was all I could do to prevent his noticing it.

LA FLÈCHE. Him to meddle with love? What the devil can he be thinking of? Surely he can't be serious. Was love meant for men of his figure?

CLÉANTE. This craze of his must be a punishment for my sins.

LA FLÈCHE. But why didn't you tell him you were in love with the girl yourself?

CLÉANTE. So as not to awake his jealousy, and make it easier for me to prevent his marriage. What answer did you get?

LA FLÈCHE. Heavens, Sir, borrowers are very unlucky people! A man has a rough road to travel when forced, like you, to deal with usurers.

CLÉANTE. It has fallen through then?

LA FLÈCHE. No, not at all. Master Simon, the agent they recommended to you, and who, by the way, is a most busy and enterprising man, says he has done wonders for you. Your face alone, he told me, gave him confidence.

CLÉANTE. Then I shall have the fifteen thousand francs I asked for?

LA FLÈCHE. Yes; but there are one or two small conditions you must agree to, if you wish the thing to go through.

CLÉANTE. Did he take you to see the fellow who is lending the money?

LA FLÈCHE. Oh, Lord, things aren't done like that! He's even more anxious to keep his name dark than you are. You'd never believe the mystery there is in these sort of things. His name must not be mentioned at all. But they want you to meet him to-day in a rented house, so that he can hear from your own lips the particulars of your means and family. I've no doubt your father's name alone will be sufficient to do the trick.

CLÉANTE. And, above all, the property left me by my mother, which can't be taken from me.

LA FLÈCHE. Here are a few articles he dictated to the go-between, to be shown to you before going further. [*Reads*]. 'If the lender be satisfied with his security, and the borrower be of full age, of a family with ample means, settled income, and free from debt, a bond must be signed for the exact sum in presence of a notary of unimpeachable honesty, who, with this view, shall be chosen by the lender himself, to whom it is especially important that the deed be properly drawn up.'

CLÉANTE. Well, there's no objection to that.

LA FLÈCHE [*reads*]. 'The lender, not to overburden his conscience, is willing to lend his money at only five and a half per cent.'

CLÉANTE. Five and a half per cent? God, that's reasonable enough! There's no cause for complaint so far.

LA FLÈCHE. No. [*Reads*]. 'But, since the said lender has not the necessary sum by him, and since, in order to accommodate the borrower, he is himself compelled to borrow it from another at twenty per cent, it is agreed that the said original borrower shall pay this interest too without prejudice to the former; seeing that it is solely to oblige him that the said lender contracts this loan.'

CLÉANTE. The devil! Here's a usurer with a vengeance! Why, it's more than twenty-five per cent.

LA FLÈCHE. That's right; just as I warned you. You'd better think it over.

CLÉANTE. What do you mean, think it over? I need the money and I shall have to agree to anything.

LA FLÈCHE. That's what I told him.

CLÉANTE. Is there anything more?

LA FLÈCHE. Only one little article. [*Reads*]. 'Of the fifteen thousand francs required the lender can find only twelve thousand livres in cash; and, for the remaining thousand ecus, the borrower must take the clothes, linen and jewellery set forth in the following memorandum, and which the said lender has honestly valued at the lowest possible estimate.'

CLÉANTE. What does all that mean?

LA FLÈCHE. Just listen to the memorandum. [*Reads*]. 'Item: A four-post bedstead, hung with olive-coloured curtains, elegantly edged with Hungarian lace, with six chairs and counterpane to match; all in excellent condition and lined with taffeta shot red and blue. Item: A handsome bed tent of plain rose-coloured serge, with fringe and tassels of silk.'

CLÉANTE. What does he expect me to do with that?

LA FLÈCHE. Listen. [*Reads*]. 'Item: A piece of tapestry representing the loves of Gombaud and Macée.* Item: A large walnut wood table with twelve turned legs, which draws out at both ends; and the six stools belonging to it.'

CLÉANTE. What on earth. . . . ?

LA FLÈCHE. One moment! [*Reads*]. 'Item: Three heavy muskets, inlaid with mother of pearl, with rests to them. Item: A brick furnace with two retorts and three receptacles, very useful to people interested in distilling.'

CLÉANTE. Damnation take the fellow!

LA FLÈCHE. Don't get heated, don't get heated. [*Reads*]. 'Item: A Bologna lute, complete with all its strings, or nearly all. Item: A bagatelle board, draught board, and the goose game, as played by the Greeks; all excellent for passing the time when one has nothing to do. Item: A lizard's skin three and a half feet long stuffed with hay, a curiosity suitable for hanging from the ceiling of a room. All the above-mentioned articles honestly worth more than four thousand five hundred livres, and reduced to the value of a thousand ecus at the discretion of the lender.

CLÉANTE. The devil take the wily old brute and his discretion! Did you ever hear of such usury? Isn't he content with his exorbitant interest, but he must make me take every old worthless piece of junk about the place for three thousand livres? I shouldn't get two hundred ecus for the lot. But the worst of it is, I shall have to accept. The scoundrel has got a dagger at my throat. He can make me agree to anything.

LA FLÈCHE. Begging your pardon, master, it looks to me as if you were starting on the broad road Panurge* trod to ruin; borrowing money, buying dear, selling cheap and counting chickens before they are hatched.

CLÉANTE. Well, what else can I do? These are the sort of scrapes young men get into through the damned stinginess of their fathers; and then people are surprised that we long for them to die.

LA FLÈCHE. True enough, your father's meanness would provoke the most easy going nature in the world. I never had much taste for serious crime, thank Heaven, and, whenever my friends get mixed up in anything of that kind, I back out as quickly as I can, and steer clear of any roguery which has the whiff of the gallows about it. But I must say I feel a strong itch to rob your father. I'd look on it as a good deed.

CLÉANTE. Give me the memorandum. I would like to read it through again.

[*They retire backstage. Enter* HARPAGON *and* MASTER SIMON.]   II

SIMON. The young man is badly in need of money, Sir. The business is extremely urgent. He will agree to everything you suggest.

HARPAGON. But are you sure there is no risk, Master Simon? Do you know the young fellow's name, means and family?

SIMON. Well, no. I am not in a position to give you full information. It was purely by chance I came in touch with him. But he will tell you all that himself; and his man told me that you will be perfectly satisfied when you see him. All I know is this: his family is very rich, his mother is already dead, and, if you insist, he will guarantee his father's death within the next eight months.

HARPAGON. Hm! That doesn't sound too bad. Common charity, Master Simon, obliges us to accommodate our neighbours if we can.

SIMON. Naturally, naturally.

LA FLÈCHE [*aside, to* CLÉANTE]. What does this mean? Our Master Simon in conversation with your father?

CLÉANTE. Can someone have told him who I am? Have you betrayed me?

SIMON [*catching sight of* LA FLÈCHE]. Hullo, my friend! You seem in a great hurry. Who told you he lived here? [*To*

HARPAGON]. I never told them, Sir, either your name or where you lived. Still there's no harm done. They are discreet people, and you can come to terms at once.

HARPAGON. What's that?

SIMON. That is the young man who wants to borrow the fifteen thousand livres.

HARPAGON [*to* CLÉANTE]. What? Aren't you ashamed, you scoundrel, to have recourse to such disgraceful measures?

CLÉANTE. Aren't you ashamed, father, to engage in such an ignoble trade?

[MASTER SIMON *takes to his heels, and* LA FLÈCHE *hides.*

HARPAGON. Aren't you afraid to ruin yourself by such an enormous loan?

CLÉANTE. Aren't you afraid to make money by such wicked usury?

HARPAGON. I wonder you dare to look me in the face after this.

CLÉANTE. I wonder you dare to look the world in the face after this.

HARPAGON. Aren't you ashamed of your debauchery and extravagance, of shamefully squandering the money your parents have accumulated with so much toil and sweat?

CLÉANTE. Aren't you ashamed to disgrace your position by the bargains you drive, to sacrifice decency and reputation to the insatiable greed to add ecu to ecu, and to outswindle the most celebrated usurers in infamous methods of extortion?

HARPAGON. Out of my sight, you good for nothing, out of my sight!

CLÉANTE. Which in your opinion is the more criminal, he who buys money when he is in want, or he who steals money he does not need?

HARPAGON. Be off, be off! I'll not tolerate such insults.

[CLÉANTE *goes out*

I am not altogether sorry this has happened. It's a warning to me to keep a sharper eye on him than ever.

[*Enter* FROSINE.   III

FROSINE. Sir. . . .

HARPAGON. One moment. I will be back immediately. [*Aside*]. I had better go and see if my money is safe.

[*He goes out.* LA FLÈCHE *emerges from hiding*

LA FLÈCHE [*not seeing* FROSINE]. What a ridiculous coinci-   IV dence! He must have a big storeroom full of lumber somewhere. We didn't recognize a thing in that memorandum.

FROSINE. My dear La Flèche, is it you? Who ever thought of meeting you here?

LA FLÈCHE. Frosine! What are you doing here?

FROSINE. Why, what I do everywhere; I execute little commissions, make myself generally useful, and get as much profit as I can out of the few talents I possess. In this world, you know, we have to live by our wits. The only income Fate has given a woman like me comes from delicate negotiations and discreet dealing.

LA FLÈCHE. Have you business then with the master of the house?

FROSINE. Yes, I'm negotiating a small affair for him, which I hope will put something in my pocket.

LA FLÈCHE. Something in your pocket? Heavens, you will be very clever if you get anything out of him. I warn you money is very dear in this house.

FROSINE. Ah, but some kinds of service work wonders.

LA FLÈCHE. I daresay; but you don't yet know Seigneur Harpagon. Of all human beings Seigneur Harpagon is the least human. Of all mortals he is the hardest and most miserly. No service is great enough to make him put his hand in his pocket. Flattery, politeness, pretty speeches, professions of friendship as much as you please; but not a hint of money. No man's favours could be more worthless. Why, he has such a horror of the word *give* that he won't even say: *I give you*, but: *I lend you good day*.

FROSINE. Oh, let me alone. I know how to get round people. I know how to worm my way into their good graces, flatter their little weaknesses and find their soft spots.

LA FLÈCHE. None of that's any good here. I defy you to move him. He is a very Turk where his money is concerned; in fact, infinitely worse than any Turk. If you were to die on the spot, it wouldn't make the smallest impression on him. He loves money more than reputation, honour or honesty. The sight of a cadger is enough to make him fall in a fit. It's a mortal wound, a dagger in his vitals, and if . . . But here he comes. I'll get out of the way.

V   [*He goes out.* HARPAGON *returns.*

HARPAGON [*aside*]. Everything is all right. [*Aloud*]. Now, what is it, Frosine? .

FROSINE. Lord, how well you're looking! The very picture of health!

HARPAGON. Who? I?

FROSINE. I've never seen you look so fresh and lively.

HARPAGON. Really.

FROSINE. Why, you have never in your life looked as young as you do now. I've seen men of twenty-five look older than you.

HARPAGON. For all that, I shan't see sixty again, Frosine.

FROSINE. Well, what's sixty years? A mere nothing. It's the very prime of life. You have all your best years in front of you.

—

HARPAGON. True, but I could do with twenty less, don't you think?

FROSINE. Nonsense. There's no need of that. With your constitution you'll live to be a hundred.

HARPAGON. You really think so?

FROSINE. Certainly I do. There's every appearance of it. Wait! Yes, you've got the sign of long life between your eyes.

HARPAGON. Eh? You're an expert in those sorts of things?

FROSINE. Yes. Let me see your hand. Heavens! What a line of life!

HARPAGON. Is there?

FROSINE [*tracing it with her finger*]. Don't you see how long that line is?

HARPAGON. What does it mean?

FROSINE. Heavens, I said a hundred years; but I shouldn't be surprised if you saw the hundred and twenties.

HARPAGON. Is it possible?

FROSINE. They'll have to knock you on the head. You will live to bury both your children and your children's children.

HARPAGON. So much the better. Well, how goes our little affair?

FROSINE. Need you ask? Did you ever know me undertake a thing and not bring it off? Besides, I have a special gift for match-making. The parties don't exist that I couldn't bring together. Why, I believe, if I put my mind to it, I could marry the Grand Turk with the Republic of Venice. After all, this little affair wasn't so very difficult. As I am an acquaintance of theirs I had a good opportunity of talking about you to them both, and I told the mother how you had fallen in love with Mariane through seeing her at the window and passing down the street.

HARPAGON. And what did she say?

FROSINE. She was delighted at the idea; and, when I told her that you would like Mariane to be present at the signing of your daughter's marriage contract this evening, she agreed at once and put her in my charge.

HARPAGON. The fact is, Frosine, I am obliged to entertain Seigneur Anselme to supper to-night, and I should be glad to have her of the party.

FROSINE. Naturally. She can visit your daughter after dinner; then go on to the fair, as she intends, and return here for supper.

HARPAGON. Very well. They shall have my carriage and go together.

FROSINE. That would be the very thing.

HARPAGON. But, Frosine, did you sound the mother out about the dowry? Did you tell her that she must make a great effort, that she must be prepared for a great sacrifice on an occasion like this? For, you know, a man does not marry a girl unless she brings something into the marriage.

FROSINE. What! Why, she'll bring you twelve thousand livres a year.

HARPAGON. Twelve thousand livres a year?

FROSINE. Yes. In the first place, she has been accustomed to a very simple diet, such as salad, milk, cheese and apples. She will not be for ever requiring rich dinners, delicious soups, barley water, or the thousand other little delicacies another girl would expect. That's a saving of three thousand francs a year at least. Then in her dress she affects a plain neatness; she doesn't care for smart clothes, costly jewellery or handsome furniture which so many girls run after. That's a saving of more than four thousand livres a year. Then again she looks on gambling with positive horror, not at all a common attitude among women of to-day.—I know one in the next street who has lost twenty thousand francs at the tables this very year. But put it at a quarter of that amount. Five thousand francs a year at cards and four thousand francs in clothes and jewellery, that makes nine thousand livres; with a thousand ecus, we'll say, for table delicacies, there! doesn't that make up your full twelve thousand francs a year?

HARPAGON. Hm, it's quite useful. But it's not real money.

FROSINE. Not real money? I don't agree. Great economy will reign in your house, your wife's hatred of gambling is as good as a capital sum, and her simple style of dressing is a legacy in itself.

HARPAGON. It's ridiculous to count up all the money she won't spend, and call that her dowry. I'll give no receipt for what I don't receive. I must have something tangible.

FROSINE. Well, so you shall, enough and to spare. They mentioned some property abroad too. That will be yours of course.

HARPAGON. Ah, that's worth looking into. But, Frosine, there's still one thing I'm not quite easy about. The girl is young; and, as a rule, youth turns to youth and is happiest in its company. I'm afraid a man of my age will not be to her taste, and that might produce disagreeable consequences.

FROSINE. How little you know her! She has one more peculiarity that I must tell you. She positively loathes young men. All her love is for those of mature years.

HARPAGON. Really?

FROSINE. Yes. I wish you could hear her on the subject. She can't bear the sight of a young man; but nothing, she says, gives her greater delight than to see a beautiful old man with a majestic beard. The older he is the better she likes him. Whatever you do, don't make yourself out younger than you are. Sixty is her absolute minimum. Why, only four months ago she broke off her engagement on the very wedding day because her lover let out he was only fifty-six, and was going to sign the marriage contract without spectacles.

HARPAGON. Only for that?

FROSINE. Yes. She said fifty-six wasn't old enough for her, and she preferred noses with spectacles on the end.

HARPAGON. That is very unusual.

FROSINE. She carries it to the most extraordinary lengths. She has in her room several paintings and engravings; but what do you think are the subjects? Adonis, Cephalus, Paris or Apollo? Not on your life. Beautiful portraits of Saturn, King Priam, old Nestor, and father Anchises on the shoulders of his son.

HARPAGON. Well, that is splendid. I'm delighted to find her of that way of thinking. I should never have thought it. But indeed, if I'd been a woman, I shouldn't have cared for young men.

FROSINE. I should think not indeed. What is there to love in such rubbish? Why should we dote on the smooth skins of such puppyish fops? Where's the attraction I should like to know?

HARPAGON. I don't see any. I can't understand why some women fall so madly in love with them.

FROSINE. Sheer insanity. Is it commonsense to find youth attractive? You can't call these young fops men. Who could take any interest in such animals?

HARPAGON. I've always said it. With their milksop voices, their three little wisps of beard stuck out like cats' whiskers, their stringy wigs, their baggy breeches and their cut-away doublets!

FROSINE. What are they compared with men of your stamp? There's a man! There's something worth looking at! That is the style of figure and dress to inspire true love!

HARPAGON. You don't think I'm so bad looking then, eh?

FROSINE. Not so bad looking? You're ravishing. Your face would tempt an artist. Turn round a moment. Magnificent! Let me see you walk. There you are! A well-knit figure, free, graceful and distinguished. Not a suspicion of infirmity anywhere.

HARPAGON. I am pretty healthy, thank God! Only a touch of bronchitis now and then.

FROSINE. That's nothing. Your bronchitis is most becoming. You cough with great distinction.

HARPAGON. Tell me. Hasn't Mariane seen me yet? Hasn't she noticed me passing the house?

FROSINE. No, but we're always talking about you. I have described you to her in detail, praised you to the skies, and pointed out all the advantages of having a man like you for her husband.

HARPAGON. You've done very well, Frosine, and I'm most grateful to you.

FROSINE. Sir, I have a small favour to ask you. I am about to lose a lawsuit through lack of money, [HARPAGON's *face grows hard*] and a little help from you would just tip the scales. You can't conceive how delighted she will be to see you. [*He is radiant again*]. She'll be enraptured. She will positively dote on your old-fashioned ruff, and particularly the buttons which fasten your doublet to your breeches. That will make her quite mad about you. She will be in the seventh Heaven at having a suitor with buttons on his breeches.

HARPAGON. It's very gratifying to hear you say that.

FROSINE. This lawsuit, Sir, is of the greatest importance to me. [*His face grows hard again*]. I shall be ruined if I lose it, and a little timely assistance would save me. I would you could have seen her excitement when I described you. [*He grows radiant again*]. Her eyes sparkled with joy as I told over your charms, and I left her in a very fever of impatience for the marriage to take place.

HARPAGON. You have done me a great service, Frosine. I couldn't be more obliged to you.

FROSINE. I beg you, Sir, to give me the small assistance I ask. [*His face grows hard again*]. It will set me on my feet again, and I will be grateful to you for ever.

HARPAGON. Well, good-bye now. I must go and finish my correspondence.

FROSINE. I assure you, Sir, I shall never need your help more urgently.

HARPAGON. I will order my carriage to be ready to take you to the fair.

FROSINE. I wouldn't trouble you if I were not absolutely forced by necessity.

HARPAGON. And I will see you get an early supper. We mustn't have you falling ill.

FROSINE. Don't refuse me this favour, Sir. You can't imagine. . . .

HARPAGON. There's someone calling me. I must go. I'll see you again later.

[*He goes out*

FROSINE. May the devil shrivel you up with fever, you miserly dog! The old skinflint is deaf to all my prayers. But, for all that, I mustn't abandon the negotiations. There is still the other side. They are sure to pay me well.

ACT THREE

[HARPAGON *is discovered addressing* CLÉANTE, ÉLISE,   I
VALÈRE, MASTER JACQUES, LA MERLUCHE, BRIN-
DAVOINE *and* DAME CLAUDE, *who has a broom in her
hand.*

HARPAGON. Come here, all of you, and I will give you your
orders for the evening, and assign each his special work.
Dame Claude, we will begin with you. Your work, for
which I see you are already armed, will be to see that every
room is well swept and dusted; but don't polish the
furniture too hard, or you may wear it away. Also, during
supper, you will be in charge of the wine; and, if a bottle
goes astray, or anything is broken, I shall hold you responsible and deduct it from your wages.

JACQUES [*aside*]. A prudent punishment!

HARPAGON [*to* DAME CLAUDE]. Off you go.

[DAME CLAUDE *goes out*

Brindavoine and La Merluche, your work will be to rinse
out the glasses and carry round the wine, but only when
the guests are really thirsty; not like some officious lackeys
who are for ever inciting the company to drink, when, left
to themselves, they would never have thought of it. Take
no notice unless you are asked more than once, and then
be sure you have a large jug of water at hand.

JACQUES [*aside*]. That's wise. Wine undiluted always goes to
the head.

LA MERLUCHE. Shall we take off our overalls, master?

HARPAGON. Yes, when you see the guests arriving; but take
care not to spoil your clothes.

BRINDAVOINE. You'll remember, master, there's a large
grease-spot on the front of my doublet, where I upset the
lamp-oil.

LA MERLUCHE. And my breeches, master, are all holes behind, and, saving your reverence, you may see. . . .

HARPAGON [*to* LA MERLUCHE]. Quiet! You must keep your back to the wall, and present only your front to the company. [*To* BRINDAVOINE, *showing him how to hold his hat in front of his doublet to hide the spot*]. And you, hold your hat thus, while you're serving.

[BRINDAVOINE *and* LA MERLUCHE *go out*

Now, daughter, I want you to keep an eye on the dishes when they are cleared away, and see there is no waste. Such carefulness becomes a young girl. And be sure that you are ready to welcome my future wife when she comes to visit you and take you to the fair. Do you understand?

ÉLISE. Yes, Papa.

[*She goes out*

HARPAGON. As for you, young fop, whose behaviour of this morning I have been kind enough to overlook, see that she has no black looks from you either.

CLÉANTE. From me, father? Black looks? Whatever for?

HARPAGON. Oh, I know how children feel when their father marries again. I know how they feel towards their step-mother. But, if you want me to overlook your latest escapade, I recommend you to receive this lady pleasantly, and give her a hearty welcome.

CLÉANTE. Frankly, father, I cannot pretend to be pleased that she is to be my step-mother. I should lie if I said I was. But I give you my word I will greet her politely.

HARPAGON. Well, take care you do.

CLÉANTE. You shall have no cause for complaint, I promise you.

HARPAGON. You will find that the wisest plan.

[CLÉANTE *goes out*

—

Now, Master Jacques, I have left you to the last. Valère, I shall need your advice in this.

JACQUES. Are you speaking to me as your coachman, Sir, or as your cook, for I have the honour to be both?

HARPAGON. To both of them.

JACQUES. But which first?

HARPAGON. My cook.

JACQUES. One moment then, if you please. [*He removes his coachman's great coat and appears dressed as a cook*].

HARPAGON. What nonsensical ceremony is that?

JACQUES. I am ready to receive your orders, Sir.

HARPAGON. I am obliged to give a supper this evening, Master Jacques.

JACQUES [*aside*]. Wonders will never cease.

HARPAGON. Can you give us a good one?

JACQUES. Yes, if you give me plenty of money.

HARPAGON. The devil! Always money! They never say anything else. Money, money, money! It's the only word they know. Money! Always talking of money! Money is their bed-fellow, I believe.

VALÈRE. That's the silliest answer I ever heard. You will provide a good supper if you are given plenty of money? What's wonderful in that? It's the easiest thing in the world. Any fool could do as much. A really clever man would say he could provide a good supper cheaply.

JACQUES. A good supper cheaply?

VALÈRE. That's what I said.

JACQUES. Faith then, Master Steward, I'll be glad if you'll tell me the secret. Perhaps you'd care to accept my post as cook, as you wish to be general factotum here.

HARPAGON. Now, now! What shall we need?

JACQUES. Ask your steward there. He will provide you with a good supper cheaply.

HARPAGON. Come, answer me.

JACQUES. How many will you be at table?

HARPAGON. Eight or ten. But we need only provide for eight. When there is enough for eight there is enough for ten.

VALÈRE. That's perfectly true.

JACQUES. Well, we shall want four soups, and five entrées. Soups . . . entrées. . . .

HARPAGON. The devil! Here's enough to entertain the whole town!

JACQUES. Roast. . . .

HARPAGON [*placing his hand over his mouth*]. You villain! Would you eat me out of house and home?

JACQUES. Side dishes. . . .

HARPAGON [*with same gesture*]. What? More?

VALÈRE [*to* JACQUES]. Do you want to cram them all to bursting? Do you think our master has invited his guests to have them die of a surfeit? Study the laws of health. Ask the doctors if there is anything more prejudicial than eating to excess?

HARPAGON. True, true.

VALÈRE. Remember, Master Jacques, you and your like, that a table groaning under a superabundance of food is nothing but a death trap. Frugality must be the word if a host is to be a true friend to his guests. As an ancient philosopher has put it: *Man must eat to live, not live to eat.*

HARPAGON. Well said, well said! Let me embrace you for those words. I never heard a finer maxim in my life. *A man must live to eat, not eat to li.* . . . No, no, that's not it. How did you say it went?

VALÈRE. *A man must eat to live, not live to eat.*

—

HARPAGON [*to* JACQUES]. Yes, do you hear? [*To* VALÈRE]. Who was the great man who said that?

VALÈRE. I can't think of his name at the moment.

HARPAGON. Well, remember to write it down. I'll have it engraved in letters of gold over my dining-room chimney piece.

VALÈRE. I won't forget. And, as for the supper, leave it to me. I will see that everything is done properly.

HARPAGON. Excellent.

JACQUES. Oh, very well. So much the better. There'll be less work for me.

HARPAGON [*to* VALÈRE]. What we want are those filling sort of dishes that no one can eat much of; haricot mutton, nice and greasy, and a pie with lots of chestnuts in it.

VALÈRE. I will see to it.

HARPAGON. Now, Master Jacques, I want you to clean my carriage.

JACQUES. One moment, please. This is the coachman's business. [*He resumes his greatcoat*]. You said. . . .

HARPAGON. My carriage must be cleaned, and my horses got ready to go to the fair.

JACQUES. Your horses, Sir? Faith, they are in no condition to go anywhere. I won't say they are in the straw, poor beasts, for I should be telling a lie; they haven't got any. But you make them observe such strict fast days that they are nothing but shadows, the mere ghosts of horses.

HARPAGON. How can they be ill? They never do anything.

JACQUES. And because they do nothing, Sir, is that a reason why they must eat nothing? It would be far better for them, poor animals, to work hard and get good meals. It cuts me to the heart to see them so thin. I love my horses; and when I see them suffer it is the same as if it was myself.

I've been going short lately, Sir, to feed them; for it's not in me not to take pity on my fellow creatures.

HARPAGON. It won't be very hard work to go as far as the fair.

JACQUES. No, Sir, I haven't the heart to drive them; and I couldn't possibly use the whip on them in the state they're in. How do you expect them to drag a carriage when they can hardly drag themselves along?

VALÈRE. Sir, I will get Picard to drive them. We shall want Master Jacques here to cook the supper.

JACQUES. Very well. I would rather they died by someone else's hand than mine.

VALÈRE. Master Jacques is never at a loss for an answer.

JACQUES. Master Steward is never at a loss for a suggestion.

HARPAGON. Now, now, no quarrelling.

JACQUES. Sir, I hate a toady; and I can see that everything he does, the mean way he doles out the bread, wine, firewood, salt and candles is only to humour you and sneak into your favour. It makes me sick. I'm distressed every day by hearing the things people say about you, for I'm fond of you in spite of everything; and after my horses I love you better than anything in the world.

HARPAGON. Would you mind telling me what they say about me, Master Jacques?

JACQUES. Not at all, Sir, if I were sure you wouldn't be offended by it.

HARPAGON. Not in the least, I promise you.

JACQUES. Saving your presence, I'm sure it would make you angry.

HARPAGON. No, no, it wouldn't. On the contrary, I should be pleased. I like to know what people say about me.

JACQUES. Very well then, master, since you will have it, I will tell you quite frankly that you are a general laughing stock.

—

There are a hundred jokes about you going the rounds, and the neighbours never tire of picking your character to pieces and telling stories of your stinginess. One says you have special almanacks printed with twice as many saints' and ember days, so as to profit by the fasts you make them keep at home. Another that you always arrange to quarrel with your servants at the New Year, or when they are leaving your service, so that you may have a good excuse for giving them nothing. One tells how you had a neighbour's cat summonsed for eating the remains of a leg of mutton; another how one night you were surprised in an attempt to steal your horses' oats, and that your coachman, my predecessor, gave you a fearful drubbing in the darkness, and you didn't dare to say anything about it. But there's no use going on. It's the same everywhere. You are the fable and jest of the whole city, and you're never mentioned without being called miser, stinge, skinflint or old Shylock.

HARPAGON [beating JACQUES]. You're a silly, rascally, impudent knave.

JACQUES. There! What did I say? Didn't I warn you you'd be offended if I told you the truth?

HARPAGON. That will teach you to govern your tongue.

[He goes out   II

VALÈRE [laughing]. Aha, Master Jacques, you were ill rewarded for your frankness!

JACQUES. You mind your own business, Mister High and Mighty, till you've been here a bit longer. Keep your sneers for your own drubbing when you get it, and don't laugh at mine.

VALÈRE. Oh, my dear Master Jacques, don't be cross with me, I beg you.

JACQUES [aside]. He begins to sing small. I'll play the bully; and, if he's fool enough to be afraid of me, I'll make him smart a bit. [*Aloud*]. Do you know, Master Mocker, that I'm not at all amused; and, if you annoy me, I'll give you something to laugh at?

[*He drives* VALÈRE *to the back of the stage, threatening him.*

VALÈRE. Now, now, don't be angry.

JACQUES. Don't be angry? But what if I am angry?

VALÈRE [*in mock fear*]. Mercy!

JACQUES. You're an impertinent rascal.

VALÈRE. My dear Master Jacques!

JACQUES. Don't *My dear Master Jacques* me. If once I take a stick I'll beat the stuffing out of you.

VALÈRE. What! Beat me? [*He drives him back in his turn*].

JACQUES. No, no, I didn't mean that.

VALÈRE. Do you know, you fatuous fool, that I have a good mind to beat *you*?

JACQUES. Yes, I can see you have.

VALÈRE. You are nothing but a paltry cook.

JACQUES. I know, I know.

VALÈRE. You have mistaken your man, my friend.

JACQUES. I'm very sorry.

VALÈRE. So you'll beat me, will you?

JACQUES. I only said it in jest.

VALÈRE. I don't like your jests. [*Beating him*]. Perhaps that will teach you to make better ones in future.

[*He goes out*

JACQUES. The devil take sincerity! It is a bad trade. From this moment I give it up, and will never tell the truth again. I say nothing about my master, he has some right to beat me; but, as for this Steward, it won't be long before I have my revenge.

[*Enter* MARIANE *and* FROSINE.   III

FROSINE. Do you know if your master is at home, Master Jacques?

JACQUES. Yes, indeed he is. I've only too good reason to know it.

FROSINE. Then please tell him we are here.

[MASTER JACQUES *goes out*   IV

MARIANE. Oh, Frosine, I feel so wretched. I positively dread this interview.

FROSINE. But why should you be so upset?

MARIANE. Need you ask? Surely it is natural for me to dread the sight of the rack on which I am to die.

FROSINE. I quite appreciate that, if you want an easy death, Seigneur Harpagon is not exactly the means you would choose; but I can see well enough that you're still thinking of that young fellow you told me of.

MARIANE. Yes, Frosine, I cannot help it. His respectful manner when he called at our house has, I admit, made a deep impression on my heart.

FROSINE. But have you no idea who he is?

MARIANE. No, I don't know who he is; but I know it would not be difficult to fall in love with him. If I could make my own choice, I would rather have him than any other; and it is chiefly on his account that I so dread the thought of this other husband they have chosen for me.

FROSINE. Heavens, all these young fellows are attractive, and they can talk like a book; but most of them are as poor as church mice. You'd do far better to take an old husband who will make you rich. It's true that from one point of view it won't be so satisfactory, and you will have to put up with much that is disagreeable, but it won't be for long. His death will soon set you free to take a more agreeable husband who will make up for everything.

MARIANE. Oh but, Frosine, it's dreadful to have to wait for someone to die before one can be happy. And besides, Death is not always so accommodating.

FROSINE. Nonsense! You only marry him on the condition that he takes immediate steps to leave you a widow. That ought to be one of the articles of the contract. It would be outrageous of him to live longer than three months. But here he is himself.

MARIANE. Oh, Frosine, what a face!

V   [*Enter* HARPAGON.

HARPAGON. Do not be offended, my dear, that I come to you with my glasses on. I know your charms are visible enough, and there is no need of glasses to see them with; but you know it is with glasses we observe the stars, and to me you are a star, of all stars the brightest star that exists in the world of stars. Frosine, she doesn't say a word or show any kind of pleasure at seeing me.

FROSINE. She has not yet recovered from her surprise. Besides, you know, young girls are always shy at first of showing their real feelings.

HARPAGON. Ah, yes, I'd forgotten that. [*To* MARIANE]. Here is my daughter, sweetheart, come to welcome you.

VI   [*Enter* ÉLISE.

MARIANE. I should have come to see you before, Madame. . . .

ÉLISE. It was my duty, Madame, to call on you.

HARPAGON. She is a big girl, you see. But weeds always grow fast.

MARIANE [*aside to* FROSINE]. Oh, what a horrid old man!

HARPAGON [*to* FROSINE]. What did she say?

FROSINE. She thinks you're charming.

HARPAGON. You are too kind, my sweet.

MARIANE [*aside*]. The brute!

HARPAGON. I am most grateful for your good opinion.

MARIANE [*aside*]. I shall scream in another minute.

[*Enter* CLÉANTE, VALÈRE *and* BRINDAVOINE.   VII

HARPAGON. Here comes my son too to pay his respects.

MARIANE [*aside to* FROSINE]. Oh, Frosine, how wonderful! It's the very young man I told you of.

FROSINE [*to* MARIANE]. What an extraordinary coincidence!

HARPAGON. I can see you are surprised that my children are so old, but I shall soon be rid of them both.

CLÉANTE [*to* MARIANE]. I was very far from expecting a meeting like this, Madam. My father surprised me considerably when he told me his intentions this morning.

MARIANE. It is the same with me. The strange coincidence of such a meeting is as much a surprise to me as it is to you.

CLÉANTE [*aloud*]. Madam, my father could not have made a fairer choice, and I am overjoyed at the honour of making your acquaintance; but, for all that, I cannot pretend to be pleased with an arrangement by which you are to become my stepmother. I find the honour of such a relationship a little difficult to accept. Some people might think this rude; but I feel sure you will take it in the way it is meant, that it is not a marriage in which I could be expected to take much pleasure. Knowing my position, you cannot fail to appreciate how it interferes with my interests; and I hope you will not be offended when I tell you, with my father's permission, that, if it rested with me, such a marriage should never take place.

HARPAGON. There's a boorish way of greeting her! That's a nice thing to say!

MARIANE. I can only reply that my feelings are the same. If it is distasteful to you to have me for a stepmother, it is no less so to me to have you for a stepson. Pray do not think it is I who wish to cause you this annoyance. I should be very sorry to make you unhappy; and, if I were able to help myself, I promise you I should never consent to a marriage which was disagreeable to you.

HARPAGON. Well answered! A clumsy compliment calls for a reply in kind. I beg you will forgive my son's ineptitude, sweetheart. He is a young fool who does not realize what he is saying.

MARIANE. I am not offended in the least. On the contrary, it pleases me to hear him speak his real thoughts so frankly. Such a declaration is most welcome to me. I should certainly have thought less of him if he had said anything else.

HARPAGON. You are very kind so to excuse his faults. When he is older he will have more sense, and will see things in a different light.

CLÉANTE. No, father, I shall never change. I beg Madam to believe me.

HARPAGON. What a fool it is! He is only making it worse.

CLÉANTE. Would you have me false to myself?

HARPAGON. What? Again? I advise you to change your tune.

CLÉANTE. Very well then, father, if you wish me to change my tune, allow me, Madam, to put myself in my father's place, and to tell you that never in all the world have I seen anyone so charming as you. I can imagine no greater pleasure than to find favour in your eyes; and, if I might have the inestimable happiness to be your husband, I would not change places with the greatest king on earth. Yes, Madam, no fortune in the world could compare with the joy of having such a wife. There could be no greater bliss. There is nothing I would not do to win so sweet a prize; and the most insuperable obstacles. . . .

HARPAGON. That will do, my son, that will do.

CLÉANTE. I was only paying Madam a compliment in your name.

HARPAGON. Heavens above, I'm quite capable of speaking for myself! I don't need you as a proxy. Bring up some chairs.

FROSINE. No, no. We had better go to the fair at once, so as to be back the sooner, and have the rest of the evening to talk things over.

HARPAGON [*to* BRINDAVOINE]. Then have the horses harnessed.

[BRINDAVOINE *goes out*

HARPAGON [*to* MARIANE]. I hope you will excuse me, my love, for not offering you some slight refreshment before you go.

CLÉANTE. I thought of that, father; and I ordered some China oranges, sweet lemons and candied fruits to be sent for in your name.

HARPAGON [*aside to* VALÈRE]. Valère!

VALÈRE [*to* HARPAGON]. He must have taken leave of his senses.

CLÉANTE. Do you think it is not enough, father? I am sure Madam will have the kindness to overlook it.

MARIANE. It was not necessary at all.

CLÉANTE. Did you ever see a finer diamond, Madam, than that in my father's ring?

MARIANE. It sparkles most beautifully.

CLÉANTE [*taking the ring from his father's finger and giving it to her*]. Please examine it more closely.

MARIANE. It really is very beautiful. It flashes like fire.

CLÉANTE [*placing himself in front of her as she is about to return the ring*]. No, no, Madam. It could not be in fairer hands. My father makes you a present of it.

HARPAGON. What? I do?

CLÉANTE. Am I not right, father, in saying you wish Madam to keep it for love of you?

HARPAGON [*aside to his son*]. What do you mean?

CLÉANTE [*to* MARIANE]. A very unnecessary question. Of course he begs you will accept it.

MARIANE. Oh, but I can't. . . .

CLÉANTE. But you must. He certainly won't take it back again.

HARPAGON [*aside*]. Confound the young fool!

MARIANE. It would be. . . .

CLÉANTE [*always preventing her from returning the ring*]. No, no, you will offend him.

MARIANE. Please. . . .

CLÉANTE. Certainly not.

HARPAGON [*aside*]. May the devil . . . !

CLÉANTE. There now, you have offended him by your refusal.

HARPAGON [*aside to* CLÉANTE]. Oh, you villain!

CLÉANTE. You see he is so hurt.

HARPAGON [*aside to* CLÉANTE *and threatening him*]. You infernal thief!

CLÉANTE. It's not my fault, father. I'm doing my best to make her keep it, but she's so determined.

HARPAGON [*as before*]. You'll end up on the gallows.

CLÉANTE. You see, Madam; now he is angry with me.

HARPAGON [*as before*]. Oh, you abominable wretch!

CLÉANTE. You'll make him ill. For pity's sake, Madam, make no more objections.

FROSINE. Lord, what a fuss! Keep the ring if the gentleman wishes it.

MARIANE [*to* HARPAGON]. Very well then. Rather than make you angry, I will keep it now; but I will give it you back another day.

[*Re-enter* BRINDAVOINE. VIII

BRINDAVOINE. Sir, a man has come asking to speak to you.

HARPAGON. Tell him I'm engaged. Let him come back later.

BRINDAVOINE. He brings you money, he says.

HARPAGON [*to* MARIANE]. Excuse me a moment. I will be back immediately.

[BRINDAVOINE *goes out, and* HARPAGON *is following* IX *when* LA MERLUCHE *rushes in and knocks him over.*

LA MERCLUCHE. Monsieur. . . .

HARPAGON. Oh, he's killed me.

CLÉANTE. What is it, father? Have you hurt yourself?

HARPAGON. My debtors have bribed the rascal to break my neck.

VALÈRE. You're not hurt, Sir?

LA MERLUCHE. I beg your pardon, master. I thought it was my duty to come quickly.

HARPAGON. What do you want, you fool?

LA MERLUCHE. To tell you that neither of your horses is shod.

HARPAGON. Then take them to the nearest smith at once.

CLÉANTE. And while they are being shod, father, I will do the honours of the house for you, and take Madam into the garden, where the refreshments will be served.

[*All go out except* HARPAGON *and* VALÈRE

HARPAGON. Keep an eye on them, Valère. Save as much as you can, and I'll send it back to the shop.

VALÈRE. I'll do my best, Sir.

[*He goes out*

HARPAGON. Is the boy mad? Does he want to ruin his father?

ACT FOUR

I   [*Enter* CLÉANTE, MARIANE, ÉLISE *and* FROSINE.

CLÉANTE [*as they enter*]. It will be much safer to come back here. No one can overhear us, and we can talk openly.

ÉLISE. Yes, Madam, my brother has told me of his love for you. Well I know the misery and unhappiness when one's tenderest feelings are opposed, and I can assure you that you have my most heartfelt sympathy.

MARIANE. It is no small encouragement, Madam, to know I have a friend like you. I beg you will never take from me your generous friendship, which makes my wretched fate so much easier to bear.

FROSINE. Heavens, it is most unfortunate that neither of you told me all this before. I would never have let things go so far, and so prevented all this anxiety.

CLÉANTE. It can't be helped. It's just my infernal ill-luck. But, sweet Mariane, what are you going to do?

MARIANE. Alas, I am not in a position to do anything. In my present wretched state of dependence, there's nothing I *can* do but hope.

CLÉANTE. What? Have you no comfort for me in your heart but merely hope? No pity to make you strong? No kindness to give you courage? No affection to rouse you to an effort?

MARIANE. What am I to say? Put yourself in my place and tell me what to do. Advise me. Command me. I will be ruled by you. But I know you love me too much to urge me beyond the bounds of honour and propriety.

CLÉANTE. You tie my hands completely when you bind me by the laws of strict honour and scrupulous propriety.

MARIANE. But what else is there for me to do? Even if *I* were prepared to break the rigid code of conduct expected from our sex, I must have some consideration for my mother. She has brought me up with such loving care that I have not the heart to grieve her. Go to her. Try your very best to persuade her. I give you leave to do and say anything you like; and, if the avowal of my feelings will be of any help, I will willingly confess my love for you.

CLÉANTE. Dear Frosine, won't you help us?

FROSINE. Heavens, need you ask? Nothing would please me better. You know how sympathetic I am by nature. I haven't a heart of stone; and, when I see two young people who love each other and intend to act honourably, I am only too glad to give a little assistance. But what can I do in this case?

CLÉANTE. Do try to think of something.

MARIANE. You have so much experience.

ÉLISE. You must find some way of undoing what you have done.

FROSINE. It won't be at all easy. [*To* MARIANE]. Your mother is not altogether unreasonable, and might perhaps be persuaded to give you to the son instead of to the father; [*To* CLÉANTE] but the worst of it is, your father is your father.

CLÉANTE. That's certain.

FROSINE. What I mean is that he will turn vindictive if he is refused; and, after that, be bitterly opposed to your marriage. The surest way would be to induce him to change his mind, and break off the match himself.

CLÉANTE. Yes, you're right. That would be the best.

FROSINE. Of course I'm right. That's what we must do, but the devil's own difficulty is how to do it. Wait a moment. If we could only get hold of some woman, a little on the wrong side of forty, who had my talents and could act well enough to impersonate a lady of rank, with a suite of attendants—we could easily get them together—and some uncouth-sounding title, a marquise or vicomtesse of Lower Brittany, I'd guarantee to make your father believe that this was a rich lady, with an income of a hundred thousand ecus besides her estates, who was so desperately in love with him that, in order to marry him, she was willing to make over all her possessions to him in the marriage contract. I am sure he would fall into the trap, for, though he is very fond of you, he is fonder still of money; and, once we have tricked him into calling it off, it won't matter how soon the scales fall from his eyes when he comes to investigate our marquise's fortune.

CLÉANTE. Yes, that's quite a good idea.

FROSINE. Let me alone to manage it. I have just remembered a friend of mine who will play the part to perfection.

CLÉANTE. I'll be grateful to you all my life, Frosine, if you carry it through. But, dear Mariane, let us first do our best to persuade your mother. It won't be at all easy to break off this match. Leave nothing undone on your side, I beg of you. Appeal to the tender love she has for you. There is a persuasive heaven-sent charm in your eyes and voice that no one could resist. Try everything you can think of, endearments, prayers, caresses. I am sure she will refuse you nothing.

MARIANE. I will do the very best I can to move her.

II   [*Enter* HARPAGON *unseen.*

HARPAGON [*aside*]. What's that? My son kissing the hand of his prospective stepmother, and his prospective stepmother not objecting! That looks a bit suspicious.

ÉLISE. Here is papa.

HARPAGON. The carriage is ready now. You can start when you like.

CLÉANTE. As you are not going, father, I will escort them.

HARPAGON. No, no, they can go very well by themselves; and I want to talk to you.

[MARIANE, ÉLISE *and* FROSINE *go out* III

Come now, forget that she is to be your stepmother, and tell me quite honestly what you think of this lady.

CLÉANTE. What I think of her?

HARPAGON. Yes; of her manner, figure, looks and intelligence.

CLÉANTE. Oh, so so.

HARPAGON. No, no, be more explicit.

CLÉANTE. Very well then, to tell you the truth, father, I'm disappointed in her. Her manner is that of a professed coquette; her figure is clumsy, her beauty very mediocre and her intelligence very ordinary indeed. Don't think I say this to dissuade you; for, as stepmothers go, I like her as well as another.

HARPAGON. But you told her just now. . . .

CLÉANTE. I paid her a few compliments in your name, but that was to please you.

HARPAGON. Then you feel no attraction towards her?

CLÉANTE. I? None in the least.

HARPAGON. Ah, I am sorry for that; for it spoils a little plan of mine. Since I saw her here I have been thinking of my age, and it has occurred to me that people might criticize me for marrying so young a girl. This consideration has made me change my mind; but, as I asked for her hand and am committed so to speak, I would have given her to you if you had not found her so unattractive.

CLÉANTE. To me?

HARPAGON. Yes.

CLÉANTE. In marriage?

HARPAGON. In marriage.

CLÉANTE. It's true she is not much to my taste; but to please you, father, I would be quite willing to marry her.

HARPAGON. No, no, I'm more reasonable than you think. I don't want to put any pressure on you.

CLÉANTE. But, for love of you, I will make an effort to overcome my repugnance.

HARPAGON. No, no. A marriage could never be happy without affection.

CLÉANTE. But, father, perhaps it may come. You know they say that love is often the consequence of marriage.

HARPAGON. No. It is never safe to risk that on the man's side. There might be unpleasant complications to which I do not care to be exposed. Had you had any inclination for her, well and good, you should have married her instead; but, as that is not so, I will go back to my first plan and marry her myself.

CLÉANTE. Very well then, father, if that's the way it is, I'll be quite frank with you and tell you our secret. The truth is that I have been in love with her ever since one day when I saw her in the street. I was on the point of asking your permission to make her my wife when you forestalled me by announcing your own intentions, and I was naturally afraid of making you angry.

HARPAGON. What? Have you ever visited her?

CLÉANTE. Oh, yes, father.

HARPAGON. Often?

CLÉANTE. Often enough, for the short time I've known her.

HARPAGON. Did they receive you well?

CLÉANTE. Very well, but without knowing who I was. That's why Mariane was so surprised just now.

HARPAGON. Have you spoken to her of your love and of your wish to marry her?

—

CLÉANTE. Oh, yes. I had even begun to open negotiations with her mother.

HARPAGON. Did she listen to your proposal on behalf of her daughter?

CLÉANTE. Most graciously.

HARPAGON. And the daughter? Does she return your love?

CLÉANTE. As far as I can tell, father, I think she has some affection for me.

HARPAGON. [aside]. I am delighted to have discovered their secret. It is just what I wanted to know. [Aloud]. Very well, my son, do you want my answer to that? You must make up your mind to fall out of love again as quick as you can, to cease running after a young lady I intend for myself, and to resign yourself to marry the wife I have chosen for you without further ado.

CLÉANTE. Ah, so you've tricked me, have you, father? Very well then. As that is the case, I swear to you that I will never give up my love for Mariane. I will stop at absolutely nothing to gain my ends; and, though you have her mother on your side, perhaps I shall find some other way to help my cause.

HARPAGON. What, you good for nothing, have you the impudence to poach on my preserves?

CLÉANTE. It is you who are poaching on mine. I was in love with her first.

HARPAGON. Am I not your father? Do you owe me no respect?

CLÉANTE. This is not a case where sons must obey their fathers. Love is no respecter of persons.

HARPAGON. I'll see if a thick stick will make you respect me.

CLÉANTE. Threats won't do any good.

HARPAGON. You will give up Mariane.

CLÉANTE. I shall do nothing of the kind.

HARPAGON. So. Where's my stick?

IV   [*Enter* MASTER JACQUES.

JACQUES. Hey, hey, hey! What's all this, Gentlemen? What are you thinking of?

CLÉANTE. All that's quite useless.

JACQUES [*to* CLÉANTE]. Ah, Sir, be patient.

HARPAGON. How dare you speak to me like that?

JACQUES [*to* HARPAGON]. Oh, Sir, be calm.

CLÉANTE. I'll not take back one word.

JACQUES [*to* CLÉANTE]. What? This to your father?

HARPAGON. Let me get at him.

JACQUES [*to* HARPAGON]. What? Beat your son? It didn't matter about me.

HARPAGON. Come, Master Jacques, you shall judge between us, to prove I am in the right.

JACQUES. With all my heart, Sir. [*To* CLÉANTE]. Go a little further off, if you please.

HARPAGON. I am in love with a young lady and wish to marry her, and this good-for-nothing has the impertinence to love her too, and to persist in it in spite of me.

JACQUES. He is in the wrong.

HARPAGON. Isn't it a shocking thing for a son to compete with his father? Shouldn't common decency prevent him from interfering in my love affairs?

JACQUES. You're absolutely right. Let me have a word with him. Don't move.

CLÉANTE [*to* JACQUES *who approaches him*]. Very well. As he has chosen you to judge between us, I won't make any objection. It is immaterial to me who it is. But first, Master Jacques, I should like you to hear my side of the story.

JACQUES. I shall be honoured, Sir.

—

CLÉANTE. I am in love with a young girl who returns my affection, and has accepted the offer of my heart most tenderly; and now my father comes along to upset our happiness by asking for her for himself.

JACQUES. He is in the wrong unquestionably.

CLÉANTE. Shouldn't he be ashamed to think now of marrying? Courting does not suit him at his age. He should leave that to the younger generation.

JACQUES. You're absolutely right. He is making a fool of himself. Let me talk to him. [*To* HARPAGON]. You know, your son is not so bad as you make him out. He is quite reasonable. He acknowledges the respect he owes you, but he says he was carried away by the heat of the moment. He will be quite ready to agree to what you want, provided that you treat him a little better in the future, and find him a congenial wife.

HARPAGON. Ah, Master Jacques, tell him that, in that case, he will find me the most indulgent of fathers; and that, except for Mariane, he is at liberty to choose any girl that takes his fancy.

JACQUES. Leave it to me. [*To* CLÉANTE]. You know, your father is not so unreasonable as you think. He tells me it was your standing up to him that so enraged him. It was only of your manner that he was complaining; and, if you will go to work quietly and pay the respect and submission due to him as your father, he is willing to let you have your own way.

CLÉANTE. Ah, Master Jacques, tell him that, if he will only give up Mariane, he will find me the most submissive of sons; and I will never do anything again without asking his permission.

JACQUES [*to* HARPAGON]. It's all settled. He agrees to everything.

HARPAGON. That's splendid then.

—

JACQUES [*to* CLÉANTE]. It's all settled. He is quite satisfied with your promises.

CLÉANTE. Thank God for that!

JACQUES. You see, Gentlemen, all disagreement is at an end. You are now in complete agreement. Yet you were on the point of quarrelling purely through a misunderstanding.

CLÉANTE. Dear Master Jacques, I shall be grateful to you all my life.

JACQUES. Pray don't mention it, Sir.

HARPAGON. You have done me a service, Master Jacques, and one that deserves a reward. [*He feels in his pocket.* JACQUES *holds out his hand, but* HARPAGON *only draws out his handkerchief*]. Go now. I won't forget it, I promise you.

JACQUES. Your obedient servant, Sir.

V   [MASTER JACQUES *goes out*

CLÉANTE. Forgive me for losing my temper, father.

HARPAGON. Say no more about it.

CLÉANTE. I am extremely sorry.

HARPAGON. And I am delighted to find you amenable to reason.

CLÉANTE. It is very good of you to forgive me so soon.

HARPAGON. Parents willingly forgive their children when they return to dutiful ways.

CLÉANTE. And you will really overlook my impertinence?

HARPAGON. Your dutiful submission leaves me no alternative.

CLÉANTE. Oh, father, I'll never forget your goodness as long as I live.

HARPAGON. And I, my son, will never again deny you anything.

CLÉANTE. Dear father, there is nothing more for me to ask. You give me everything when you give me Mariane.

—

HARPAGON. What's that?

CLÉANTE. I say, father, that I am more than grateful. Your goodness in giving up Mariane leaves me nothing further to wish for.

HARPAGON. Who spoke of giving up Mariane?

CLÉANTE. You, father.

HARPAGON. I?

CLÉANTE. Why, yes.

HARPAGON. What? It was you promised to give her up.

CLÉANTE. I give her up?

HARPAGON. Yes.

CLÉANTE. Never!

HARPAGON. You've not withdrawn then, after all?

CLÉANTE. On the contrary, I'm more determined than ever.

HARPAGON. Oh, you wretch! So we're starting all over again?

CLÉANTE. Nothing will ever change me.

HARPAGON. You villain! I'll do something. . . .

CLÉANTE. Do anything you like.

HARPAGON. I forbid you ever to see me again.

CLÉANTE. Delighted.

HARPAGON. I wash my hands of you.

CLÉANTE. Wash away.

HARPAGON. You're no longer my son.

CLÉANTE. Very well.

HARPAGON. I disinherit you.

CLÉANTE. You must do as you please.

HARPAGON. I give you my curse!

CLÉANTE. I won't take any gifts from you.

VI   [HARPAGON *goes out.* LA FLÈCHE *comes in from the garden, carrying a cash-box.*

LA FLÈCHE. Ah, Sir, I've found you just in the nick of time. Come with me quick.

CLÉANTE. What's the matter?

LA FLÈCHE. Come quick, I say; we're in the devil's own luck.

CLÉANTE. How?

LA FLÈCHE. Here's what will do your business.

CLÉANTE. What?

LA FLÈCHE. I've had designs on this all day.

CLÉANTE. What is it?

LA FLÈCHE. Your father's hoard. I've stolen it.

CLÉANTE. How on earth did you manage that?

LA FLÈCHE. I'll tell you everything. But quick, let's run. I hear him calling.

VII   [CLÉANTE *and* LA FLÈCHE *run out.* HARPAGON'S *voice can be heard crying 'Thief' from the garden. He rushes in.*

HARPAGON [*as he comes in*]. Stop thief! Stop thief! After the villain! After the murderer! Justice, just Heaven! I am lost. I am killed. My throat is cut. My money is stolen. Who can it be? Where has he taken it? Where is he? Where is he hiding? What can I do to find him? Where can I go? Where can I not go? Is that him? Or that? Who's this? Stop! [*Catching himself by the arm*]. Give me back my money, thief. . . . Ah, it is myself. My brain's in a whirl; and I don't know where I am, who I am or what I am doing. Oh, my beloved money, my beloved money, my kind friend, they have taken you from me, and with you is gone all my being, all my comfort, all my joy. My world is at an end. There is nothing left for me to do on earth. Without you it is impossible for me to go on living. Yes, I am finished. I am dying. I am dead. I am buried. Will no one give me back my life by giving me back my beloved money, or telling me who has taken it? Eh? What do you say? There's no one there. The rascal who has done this must have timed it to the very hour, and chosen the very moment I was talking to my traitor of a son. I'll go call the police, and have all my household put to the torture, maids, valets, son, daughter, even myself. [*Looking at the audience*]. What a lot of people there are all round me! I suspect them all. Each one of them has the look of a thief. Eh? What's that they are saying there? Something about the man who has robbed me? What noise is that up there? Is it the thief? [*Addressing the audience*]. For pity's sake, if any of you know anything about him, I beseech you to tell me. Is he not hidden there among you? Ah, they all stare at me and grin. You can see they are all part of the gang. Come quick, constables, guards, judges, racks, gallows, hangmen. I'll have every one in the world hanged for this; and, if I don't get back my money, I'll string myself up beside them.

ACT FIVE

[*Enter* HARPAGON, *a* COMMISSIONER OF POLICE *and his clerk.*

COMMISSIONER. Leave it to me. I know my work. This is not the first time, Sir, I have had to do with a burglary. I wish I had as many sacks full of francs as I have sent men to the gallows.

HARPAGON. There's not a magistrate on the bench that's not involved in this; for, if I don't get back my money, I will demand justice on the law itself.

COMMISSIONER. We will do everything we can. You say this cash-box contained . . . ?

HARPAGON. Ten thousand ecus all told.

COMMISSIONER. Ten thousand ecus?

HARPAGON. Ten thousand ecus.

COMMISSIONER. It's a big robbery.

HARPAGON. No punishment could be too heavy for such a dreadful crime. If it goes unpunished the most sacred things in life will be in danger.

COMMISSIONER. Was this sum in cash?

HARPAGON. Yes. In good louis d'or and pistoles of full weight.

COMMISSIONER. Whom do you suspect?

HARPAGON. Everybody. You must put the whole town and suburbs under arrest.

COMMISSIONER. We must be very careful not to give the alarm prematurely. We must go to work quietly until we have some clues. After that the utmost rigour of the law shall be put in force to recover your property.

II   [*Enter* MASTER JACQUES.

JACQUES [*turning and speaking in the direction from which he has just entered*]. I shall be back immediately. His throat must be cut at once, and his feet broiled. Then plunge him into boiling water and hang him from the ceiling.

HARPAGON [*to* JACQUES]. Who? The rascal who has robbed me?

JACQUES. I was speaking of a sucking pig your steward has just sent me. I am going to make it into a nice tasty dish.

HARPAGON. We are thinking about something else just now. This gentleman would like to have a few words with you.

COMMISSIONER [*to* JACQUES]. Don't be alarmed. I'm not going to do you any harm. Let's just have a little quiet talk.

JACQUES. Is this gentleman one of your guests?

COMMISSIONER. You must keep back nothing from your master, my friend.

JACQUES. Heavens, Sir, I'll display the greatest triumphs of my art. You shall have the very best supper I can give you.

HARPAGON. That is not the question now.

JACQUES. If the fare is not so good as I could wish, that is Master Steward's fault, who has clipped my wings with the scissors of his economizing.

HARPAGON. We're not thinking about supper now, you fool. I want you to tell me about the money that's been stolen from me.

JACQUES. Someone has stolen your money?

HARPAGON. Yes, you rascal; and, unless you give it up, I swear that you shall hang.

COMMISSIONER. Come, come, Sir, don't threaten him. I can see by his face that he is an honest fellow. I am sure he will tell us all we want to know without our sending him to prison. If you speak the truth, my friend, no harm shall come to you, and you will be suitably rewarded by your master. He has been robbed to-day of a considerable sum of money, and it's impossible that you don't know something about it.

JACQUES [aside]. Here's the very opportunity I've been looking for to be revenged on Master Steward. Ever since he came he has been the favourite. No one else has had a look in. That beating too rankles in my mind.

HARPAGON. What are you muttering about?

COMMISSIONER. Let him alone. He is collecting his thoughts. I told you he was an honest fellow.

JACQUES. Well, Sir, if you want my opinion, I believe your precious Master Steward has done it.

HARPAGON. Valère?

JACQUES. Yes.

HARPAGON. Valère, whom I thought so faithful?

JACQUES. The very same. It's he has robbed you, I feel sure.

HARPAGON. What makes you think so?

JACQUES. What makes me think so?

HARPAGON. Yes.

JACQUES. I think so . . . er . . . because I think so.

COMMISSIONER. But you must give us your reasons.

HARPAGON. Have you seen him prowling round the place where my money was kept?

JACQUES. Yes, indeed I have. Where *did* you keep your money?

HARPAGON. In the garden.

JACQUES. The very place. I've often seen him prowling about the garden. What did you keep it in?

HARPAGON. A cash-box.

JACQUES. That's it! I've seen him with a cash-box.

HARPAGON. What was the cash-box like? I shall know at once if it's mine.

JACQUES. What was it like?

HARPAGON. Yes.

JACQUES. It was like . . . er . . . well . . . it was like a cash-box.

COMMISSIONER. Yes, yes, of course. But describe it.

JACQUES. It was a large cash-box.

HARPAGON. The one that's been stolen was small.

JACQUES. Oh well, yes; it was small in that sense. I called it large because of what it contained.

COMMISSIONER. What colour was it?

JACQUES. What colour?

COMMISSIONER. Yes.

JACQUES. Its colour . . . well, it was a kind of . . . [*To* HARPAGON] you remember?

HARPAGON. Eh?

JACQUES. Red, wasn't it?

HARPAGON. No, grey.

JACQUES. Yes, that's it; a reddish grey. That's what I meant.

HARPAGON. It's the very one. I'll swear to it. Write his evidence down, officer. Heavens! Whom will I ever be able to trust again? No one can be sure of anything any more. After this I shall believe myself capable of robbing myself.

JACQUES [to HARPAGON]. Oh, Sir, here he is! Whatever you do, don't tell him it was I who gave him away.

[*Enter* VALÈRE.   III

HARPAGON. Come, confess the blackest deed, the most horrible wickedness which has ever been committed.

VALÈRE. What do you mean, Sir?

HARPAGON. What, you treacherous rascal! Don't you blush for your crime?

VALÈRE. What crime are you speaking of?

HARPAGON. What crime am I speaking of, scoundrel? As if you didn't know well enough. It's no use attempting to deny it. It is all out. They've told me everything. How could you take advantage of my good nature, and worm your way into my house only to betray me?

VALÈRE. If they have told you everything, Sir, then I won't attempt to deny it.

JACQUES [*aside*]. What! Have I hit on the truth by mistake?

VALÈRE. I was going to speak to you about it, and waited only for a favourable opportunity. But, as it has come out, I beg you not to be angry, but to hear what I have to say.

HARPAGON. And what can you have to say, you abominable thief?

VALÈRE. Oh, Sir, I don't deserve to be called that. I have done you wrong, I admit; but after all my fault is pardonable.

HARPAGON. Pardonable? A treacherous and deliberately planned robbery?

VALÈRE. Please, Sir, don't be so angry. When you have heard me out, you will see there is not so much harm done after all.

HARPAGON. Not so much harm? My blood, my very being?

VALÈRE. Your blood, Sir, has not fallen into bad hands. My position is such that there is no harm done on that score. Nothing has been done that cannot easily be put right.

HARPAGON. Faith, I believe you! You shall instantly give back what you have stolen.

VALÈRE. Your honour, Sir, will be fully satisfied.

HARPAGON. There's no honour in the matter. Tell me who incited you to this?

VALÈRE. Ah, Sir, do you need to ask?

HARPAGON. Most certainly I do.

VALÈRE. A God who is himself the excuse for all he makes us do; Love.

HARPAGON. Love?

VALÈRE. Yes, Love.

HARPAGON. A worthy love, a worthy love, I swear; the love of my louis d'or!

VALÈRE. No, Sir, it was not your wealth that tempted me. I was not dazzled by that. I swear I will never ask you for anything more, if you will only let me keep what I have.

HARPAGON. No. Devil take me if I will! I will not let you keep what you have. Did you ever hear such insolence? To expect to keep his stolen booty!

VALÈRE. Do you call it theft?

HARPAGON. Do I call it theft? A treasure like that!

VALÈRE. A treasure, true; probably the most precious you have. But my gain need not be your loss. I beg you on my knees to give me this treasure so full of charms. Indeed goodness itself should urge you to consent.

HARPAGON. I shall do nothing of the sort. What an idea!

VALÈRE. We have promised eternal constancy, and sworn never to forsake each other.

HARPAGON. A worthy oath! A goodly promise!

VALÈRE. Yes, we belong to each other for ever.

HARPAGON. I'll quickly find a way to part you.

VALÈRE. Nothing but death can do that.

HARPAGON. You must be very keen to get my money.

VALÈRE. I have already told you, Sir, I was moved by no such consideration. My motives were not what you think. A far nobler feeling inspired me.

HARPAGON. You will observe it is for Christian charity that he covets my gold! But I will set him straight. The law will give me my rights, you brazen-faced villain.

VALÈRE. As to that, you must do as you please. I am ready to suffer the worst punishment you can inflict; but I beg you to believe that, if there is any harm, I alone am responsible, and your daughter is in no way to blame.

HARPAGON. Indeed, I should hope so. It would be shocking indeed if my daughter were an accomplice. But I will have my treasure back. You shall tell me where you have put my treasure.

VALÈRE. What do you mean, Sir? Your treasure is still at home.

HARPAGON [aside]. Oh, my beloved cash-box! [Aloud]. Not gone from the house, you say?

VALÈRE. No, Sir.

HARPAGON. Ah, then you have not touched. . . . ?

VALÈRE. I? Touched? You do me wrong, Sir. The passion which consumes me is too pure, too respectful.

HARPAGON [aside]. Passion for my cash-box!

VALÈRE. I would rather die than have an unworthy thought. Your treasure is too good, too modest for that.

HARPAGON [*aside*]. My cash-box too modest!

VALÈRE. All I ask is but to gaze on such beauty. No baser thought has profaned the love with which those sweet eyes have inspired me.

HARPAGON [*aside*]. The sweet eyes of my cash-box? The fellow talks like a lover of his mistress.

VALÈRE. Dame Claude knows everything, Sir. She will tell you. . . .

HARPAGON. What? My servant was in the plot?

VALÈRE. Yes, Sir, she was a witness to our engagement, and joined me in persuading your daughter to accept my love; though not until she was convinced of the honesty of my intentions.

HARPAGON [*aside*]. Does the fear of death make him rave? [*To* VALÈRE]. What has my daughter got to do with it?

VALÈRE. It was only after the utmost persuasion, Sir, that her modesty consented to my amorous desires.

HARPAGON. Whose modesty?

VALÈRE. Your daughter's. It was not until yesterday that I could persuade her to sign a promise of marriage.

HARPAGON. My daughter has signed a promise of marriage?

VALÈRE. Yes, Sir, and I have done the same.

HARPAGON. Good God! Another calamity!

JACQUES [*to the* COMMISSIONER]. Write it all down, officer, write it all down.

HARPAGON. Crime upon crime, disaster on disaster! [*To the* COMMISSIONER]. Come, officer, do your duty. I bring an action against him as a thief and a seducer.

VALÈRE. I have not deserved these names, and when it is known who I really am. . . .

[*Enter* ÉLISE, MARIANE *and* FROSINE.   IV

HARPAGON. Oh, you wicked girl, you don't deserve to have a father like me. This is how you put into practice the advice I have given you! You fall in love with an infamous thief, and sign a promise of marriage without my consent! But I will be a match for you both. [*To* ÉLISE]. The four walls of a convent will answer for your conduct in future. [*To* VALÈRE]. And you shall pay for your villainy on the gallows.

VALÈRE. Your unreasoning passion will not be the judge. I shall at least be heard before I am condemned.

HARPAGON. I was wrong when I said the gallows. You shall be broken alive upon the wheel.

ÉLISE [*falling on her knees before* HARPAGON]. Oh, father, I implore you not to be so cruel. Do not insist on the severest penalties a father's power can inflict. Do not give way to your first feelings of anger, but allow yourself time to realize what you are doing. You have quite mistaken this young gentleman. He is not what he appears; and, when I tell you that, but for him, you would have lost me long ago, you will no longer be angry with me for giving my life into his keeping. It was he, father, who saved me from drowning. You owe to him your daughter's very existence, and. . . .

HARPAGON. I don't give a brass farthing for that. Better for me if he had let you drown than do what he has done.

ÉLISE. Oh, father, I beseech you, by your love for me. . . .

HARPAGON. No. I won't hear a word. The law shall take its course.

JACQUES [*aside*]. Now you're going to pay me for that beating.

FROSINE [*aside*]. What a dreadful situation! .

V   [*Enter* ANSELME.

ANSELME. What is the matter, Seigneur Harpagon? You seem to be very upset.

HARPAGON. Ah, Seigneur Anselme, I am the most unfortunate of men. This evening's ceremony is altogether disrupted. I am ruined in my goods and in my honour. This treacherous scoundrel has violated all the most sacred rights. He has wormed his way into my house in the guise of a steward to steal my money and seduce my daughter.

VALÈRE. Who is thinking of your money? You're always dragging that in.

HARPAGON. They have signed together a promise of marriage. It is an offence against you, Seigneur Anselme. You ought to bring an action against him at your own expense and pursue him with all the rigour of the law to punish his presumption.

ANSELME. I have no desire to get a wife by force, or lay claim to a heart that belongs to another; but I am ready to embrace your interests as my own.

HARPAGON. Here, Sir, is a worthy commissioner of police, who, so he tells me, knows his business thoroughly. [*To* COMMISSIONER]. Charge him in proper form, officer; and make the offence as serious as you can.

VALÈRE. I don't see what crime can be made out of the love I bear your daughter; and, as for the punishment you believe I have incurred by our engagement, I can assure you that when they know who I am. . . .

HARPAGON. Oh, yes, I daresay. The world to-day is full of these pretended noblemen; impostors who take advantage of their obscurity, and impudently lay claim to the first noble name that occurs to them.

VALÈRE. I have too much self respect to take any name which does not belong to me. All Naples can bear witness to my parentage.

ANSELME. Not so fast. Take care what you say, young man. You risk a little more here than you are aware of. I happen to know Naples intimately, and can easily test the truth of your story.

VALÈRE [*proudly putting on his hat*]. I am not afraid of any man. If you know Naples, no doubt you have heard of Don Thomas D'Alburcy.

ANSELME. Most certainly I have heard of him. Few people knew him better than I did.

HARPAGON. A fig for Don Thomas, and Don What's your name too!

[HARPAGON, *seeing two candles alight at the same time, blows one out.*]

ANSELME. No. Let him continue. I want to hear what he has to say.

VALÈRE. I say that he is my father.

ANSELME. Don Thomas?

VALÈRE. Yes.

ANSELME. Don't be absurd. Invent another story which may serve you better. Don't imagine you will save yourself by this imposture.

VALÈRE. You are ill informed. It is no imposture. I advance nothing that I cannot easily prove.

ANSELME. What! You dare call yourself the son of Don Thomas D'Alburcy?

VALÈRE. Yes, I do. And I am ready to uphold the truth of it against the world.

ANSELME. Your effrontery is astounding. Know then, to your confusion, that it is sixteen years at least since the man you mention, with his wife and all his family, was lost at sea in an attempt to escape from the cruel persecutions which took place during the Neapolitan troubles, and which drove many noble families into exile.

VALÈRE. Very well. Then know, to *your* confusion, that his seven-year-old son and a servant were saved from the wreck by a Spanish ship, and that I am that son. The captain of this ship, taking pity on my misfortune, befriended me and brought me up as his own child; and, ever since I was old enough, I have been a soldier. A short time ago I received news that my father was not dead as I had always believed; and, as I passed through this city on my search to find him, a lucky fate allowed me a sight of the lovely Élise, to whose charms I became a willing slave; and the violence of my passion and her father's intractability induced me to take a situation in his household, and to send someone else in search of my parents.

ANSELME. But what proof have we, other than your own statements, that this is not an invention grafted on to a true story?

VALÈRE. The Spanish captain, a ruby seal that belonged to my father, an agate bracelet that my mother had clasped round my arm, and old Pedro, the servant who was saved with me from the wreck.

MARIANE. Then I, at any rate, can bear witness you are not an impostor. All you have just said proves you to be my long lost brother.

VALÈRE. You are my sister?

MARIANE. Yes. My heart has been in a flutter from the moment you first opened your lips. How overjoyed my mother will be to see you! She has told me over and over again of our family misfortunes. It was not our fate to be lost in that unhappy shipwreck any more than yours, but our lives were saved only at the expense of our liberty. As we drifted about, clinging to a mass of wreckage, my mother and I were taken aboard by pirates; and it was not until after ten years of slavery that a lucky chance delivered us, and we returned to Naples. Unable to obtain any news of our father, and finding that all our property had been sold, we went on to Genoa, where my mother tried to recover the meagre remains of a dissipated inheritance. And, at last, driven from there by the unkindness and dishonesty of her relations, she settled here in Paris, where her life has been nothing but a lingering misery.

ANSELME. Oh, Heaven, great is thy power! To thee only can miracles be ascribed! Embrace me, my children, and let us all rejoice together.

VALÈRE. Are you our father?

MARIANE. Is it for you my mother has wept so often?

ANSELME. Yes, my dear children, I am Don Thomas D'Alburcy. As you see, I too escaped from the wreck, and was lucky enough to save my moneybags along with me. After more than sixteen years of loneliness, believing you to be lost, I decided, by an alliance with a good and sweet lady, to seek consolation in a new family. As my life was no longer in Naples, and a lucky opportunity arose of selling my property there, I gave up all thoughts of ever returning and settled here instead, where, under the name of Anselme, I have tried to forget the misfortunes of that other name which had caused me so much unhappiness.

HARPAGON [*to* ANSELME]. Is that your son?

ANSELME. It is.

HARPAGON. Then I hold you responsible for the ten thousand ecus he has stolen from me.

ANSELME. *He* has stolen from you?

HARPAGON. Yes.

VALÈRE. Who told you that?

HARPAGON. Master Jacques.

VALÈRE. Do you say so?

JACQUES. I'm not saying a word, as you can see.

HARPAGON. He did say so. The Commissioner there has taken down his evidence.

VALÈRE. Do you really believe me capable of doing such a blackguardly thing?

HARPAGON. Capable or not capable, I want my money back.

VI   [*Enter* CLÉANTE *and* LA FLÈCHE.

CLÉANTE. Calm down, father, and withdraw these accusations. I have found out where your money is; and I come to tell you that, if you will consent to my marriage with Mariane, it shall be given back to you immediately.

HARPAGON. Where is it then?

CLÉANTE. Never mind. I will answer for its safety. I am only waiting to hear which you will choose, to let me marry Mariane or to lose your cash-box.

HARPAGON. Nothing has been taken out?

CLÉANTE. Nothing at all. So make up your mind to agree to this marriage. Her mother allows her to choose between us.

MARIANE. Ah, but more than her consent is needed now. Heaven has not only given me back a brother [*indicating* VALÈRE] but a father too [*indicating* ANSELME] and you must have his consent as well.

ANSELME. Heaven, my children, did not give me back to you to cross your natural affections. Seigneur Harpagon, you will easily understand that a girl would rather marry the son than the father. So waste no breath in useless opposition, but give your consent with me to this double wedding.

HARPAGON. I can't make up my mind until I have seen my cash-box.

CLÉANTE. You shall see it quite safe, with its contents untouched.

HARPAGON. I can't afford to give my children any money on their marriage.

ANSELME. I have enough for them, so don't let that distress you.

HARPAGON. You agree to bear all the expenses of these two weddings?

ANSELME. Willingly. Are you satisfied now?

HARPAGON. Very well, but on condition that you have a new suit made for me to go to church in.

ANSELME. With all my heart. Come then, let us all rejoice in the happiness this joyful day has brought us.

COMMISSIONER. One moment, Gentlemen! Wait a minute, if you please. Who is to pay me for these documents?

HARPAGON. Your documents are no use to us.

COMMISSIONER. That may be, but I didn't draw them up for nothing.

HARPAGON. Here's payment for you then. [*Indicating* JACQUES]. You can have this knave to hang.

JACQUES. Alas, what am I to do? I am beaten for telling the truth, and now they want to hang me for lying.

ANSELME. Seigneur Harpagon, you must forgive him this perjury.

HARPAGON. Will you pay the Commissioner then?

ANSELME. Yes, I'll pay him. And now let's go and see your mother, and tell her this happy news.

HARPAGON. And I'll go and gaze on my beloved gold.

THE WOULD-BE GENTLEMAN

[*Le Bourgeois gentilhomme*]

Le Bourgeois gentilhomme, *comedy-ballet in five acts, was first performed on 14 October 1670 in a room, which may still be visited, in the castle of Chambord in Touraine; being repeated on 29 November following in Paris. In the original production Molière played the part of M. Jourdain and the part of the Muphti was played by Lulli, who composed the music.*

CHARACTERS

M. JOURDAIN

MADAME JOURDAIN, *his wife*

LUCILE, *his daughter*

CLÉONTE, *in love with Lucile*

DORIMÈNE, *a Marquise*

DORANTE, *a Comte, in love with Dorimène*

NICOLE, *servant to M. Jourdain*

COVIELLE, *valet to Cléonte*

A MUSIC MASTER

HIS PUPIL

A DANCING MASTER

A MASTER-AT-ARMS

A PHILOSOPHY MASTER

A MASTER TAILOR

HIS ASSISTANT

TWO LACKEYS

THE MUPHTI

SINGERS, DANCERS

The scene is set in M. Jourdain's house in Paris

ACT ONE

The overture is played by a large orchestra. In the centre of the stage the MUSIC MASTER'S PUPIL *is sitting at a table, composing an air which* MONSIEUR JOURDAIN *has requested for a serenade. Enter* MUSIC MASTER, DANCING MASTER, *Three Singers, Two Violins, Four Dancers.*

MUSIC MASTER [*ushering in the musicians*]. Wait please in this ante-room until he comes.

DANCING MASTER [*ushering in the dancers*]. Wait in here too, if you please.

[*The musicians and dancers go into the ante-room.*

MUSIC MASTER [*to his pupil*]. Have you finished it?

PUPIL. Yes, Sir.

MUSIC MASTER. Let's see. . . . Ah, excellent!

DANCING MASTER. Is it something new?

MUSIC MASTER. Yes. It is an air for a serenade that I have asked him to compose for when our employer is awake.

DANCING MASTER. May we hear it?

MUSIC MASTER. You shall hear the whole thing, words and music, as soon as he comes. He won't be long now.

DANCING MASTER. Our posts are certainly no sinecures these days.

MUSIC MASTER. You're right. But this is the very sort of man we both needed. He's a safe income for us, is Monsieur Jourdain, with this craze for gentility and refinement he has got into his head. His demand for music and dancing should make us wish that all the rest of the world were like him.

DANCING MASTER. Not altogether. I could wish, for his own sake, that he were more capable of appreciating the value of the work we do for him.

MUSIC MASTER. It's true he doesn't appreciate it, but he pays for it. And that's what our arts need at the moment more than anything else.

DANCING MASTER. Personally, I confess that I like a little public recognition. I am by no means indifferent to applause. There is nothing so insufferably boring in any fine art as to exert oneself for fools, and have to listen to the comments and criticisms of a blockhead. The great joy is to work for people who are capable of perceiving the subtleties, who open their hearts to the beauties of a work, and whose approval is a gratifying return for the toil of creation. The most welcome reward one can receive for one's work is to have it recognized and received with flattering applause. There is nothing, to my mind, that pays us better for our pains. The praise of the cultured is infinitely sweet.

MUSIC MASTER. Oh, I'm with you there. It's just as sweet to me. There is nothing so gratifying as such applause. But that kind of incense won't keep the wolf from the door. No man can gain security by praise alone. There must be something more substantial; and the best kind of praise is the monetary kind that is given with the hand. I allow that this is a man whose perception is slight, who talks indiscriminately about everything, and who likes all the wrong things. But his money outweighs his judgement. His purse is discerning. His praise has a gilt edge to it. And you must admit this man without class or culture is of far more use to us than the cultivated fine gentleman who got us the job.

DANCING MASTER. Yes, there's certainly some truth in what you say, but you take too mercenary a view. To have an eye to the main chance is so degrading that no self-respecting man should ever descend to it.

MUSIC MASTER. For all that, you're very glad to get your wages, I notice.

—

DANCING MASTER. Granted; but I don't make it my sole aim. And I wish that, along with his cash, he had a little good taste as well.

MUSIC MASTER. I wish so too. And we are both of us working as hard as we can to that end. But, at any rate, he is giving us the means of making our reputations, and he will pay for the others for what the others will appreciate for him.

DANCING MASTER. Here he comes!

[MONSIEUR JOURDAIN *enters in dressing-gown and* II *night cap. He is followed by two lackeys who wait by the door.*

M. JOURDAIN. Well, Gentlemen, how goes everything? Have you got your little piece of nonsense ready for me?

DANCING MASTER. What do you mean? What little piece of nonsense?

M. JOURDAIN. Oh, the—er—what do you call it? Your prologue or dialogue of song and dance.

DANCING MASTER. Oh, I see.

MUSIC MASTER. Yes, here we are, Sir, quite ready.

[*The* MUSIC MASTER *and* DANCING MASTER *beckon the singers, dancers, and violins out of the ante-room.*

M. JOURDAIN. I am afraid I have had to keep you waiting. But the fact is I am being dressed to-day as a gentleman of fashion, and my tailor has sent me some silk stockings that I thought I should never get on.

MUSIC MASTER. It is our duty to wait your convenience.

M. JOURDAIN. I beg you will neither of you leave before my new suit arrives. I would like you to see me in it.

DANCING MASTER. Certainly, if you wish it, Sir.

M. JOURDAIN. You will see me decked out from head to foot in the very height of fashion.

MUSIC MASTER. We can well believe it, Sir.

—

M. JOURDAIN. I have had this Indian silk dressing-gown made for me.

DANCING MASTER. It is very beautiful.

M. JOURDAIN. My tailor tells me that people of fashion always go around like this of a morning.

MUSIC MASTER. It's wonderfully becoming.

M. JOURDAIN. Lackey! Hey there! Both my lackeys!

1ST LACKEY. What's your will, Sir?

M. JOURDAIN. Oh, nothing. I only wanted to make sure that you could hear me. [*To the* MUSIC *and* DANCING MAS-TERS]. What do you think of my liveries?

DANCING MASTER. Quite magnificent.

M. JOURDAIN [*opening his gown and showing casual dress consisting of a green velvet waistcoat and narrow red velvet breeches*]. This is just a little casual dress for doing my morning exercises.

MUSIC MASTER. Most distinguished.

M. JOURDAIN. Lackey!

1ST LACKEY. Sir?

M. JOURDAIN. T'other lackey!

2ND LACKEY. Sir?

M. JOURDAIN [*taking off his dressing gown*]. Take my gown. [*To the* MUSIC *and* DANCING MASTERS]. Do I look all right like that?

DANCING MASTER. Perfectly all right, Sir.

M. JOURDAIN. Then let's get down to business.

MUSIC MASTER [*introducing his pupil*]. I would first like you to hear an air he has just composed for the serenade you ordered. He is one of my pupils who has an admirable gift for that kind of thing.

M. JOURDAIN. I dare say. But you shouldn't leave a thing like that to a pupil. You yourself would be barely good enough for a work of that importance.

MUSIC MASTER. When I say 'pupil', Sir, pray do not misunderstand me. Such pupils are as able as the greatest masters, and the tune could not easily be bettered. Just listen.

M. JOURDAIN [to his lackeys]. Give me my gown. I shall hear better like that. No, wait. I think I shall be better without it. No, give it me back. Yes, that's better.

THE LADY [sings].
I pine night and day, and my pain is past bearing
Since your cruel beauty has chained me as your slave.
If your lovers, Iris, so unhappily are faring,
Alas for your foes! What mercy shall they have?

M. JOURDAIN. It sounds a little depressing. It makes me nod off. Couldn't you liven it up a bit here and there?

MUSIC MASTER. The air has to suit the words, Sir.

M. JOURDAIN. I learnt a lovely little thing the other day. Wait—er—how does it go?

DANCING MASTER. I haven't the least idea.

M. JOURDAIN. There was something about mutton in it.

DANCING MASTER. Mutton?

M. JOURDAIN. Yes. Ah, now I've got it!
[sings] *I thought Jeanneton*
Fair and sweet to be;
I thought Jeanneton
Sweeter than sweet mutton.
    Alas! Alas!
A hundred thousand times more cruel she
Than the tigers of the pass.

Pretty, isn't it?

MUSIC MASTER. Very pretty, indeed.

—

DANCING MASTER. And you sing it well, too.

M. JOURDAIN. Yet I never learnt music.

MUSIC MASTER. You should learn, Sir, the same as you do dancing. The two arts are very closely allied.

DANCING MASTER. And open the eyes of the soul to beauty.

M. JOURDAIN. Do persons of quality learn music as well?

MUSIC MASTER. Most certainly, Sir.

M. JOURDAIN. Then I'll learn it. Though I don't know what time I shall have for it; for, besides the master-at-arms who is teaching me to fence, I've engaged a master of philosophy who is to begin his lessons this very morning.

MUSIC MASTER. Philosophy is well enough. But music, Sir, music. . . .

DANCING MASTER. Music and dancing. Music and dancing. That is all that is necessary.

MUSIC MASTER. There is nothing so useful to a State as music.

DANCING MASTER. There is nothing so indispensable to mankind as dancing.

MUSIC MASTER. Without music the State would cease to function.

DANCING MASTER. Man can do nothing at all without dancing.

MUSIC MASTER. All the revolutions, all the wars in the world come solely from not learning music.

DANCING MASTER. All the misfortunes of mankind, all the disasters of which history is full, the bungling of politicians and the mistakes of great generals, all come through not learning to dance.

M. JOURDAIN. How is that?

MUSIC MASTER. Is not war due to a lack of agreement among men?

—

M. JOURDAIN. Yes, that's true enough.

MUSIC MASTER. Well, then, if everybody learnt music, wouldn't it be the means of settling their differences and bringing about universal peace in the world?

M. JOURDAIN. So it would.

DANCING MASTER. When a man makes a blunder, either in his family affairs, or in the government of a country, or in the command of an army, don't we say 'Such a one has made a false move or step'?

M. JOURDAIN. Yes, we do.

DANCING MASTER. And what makes a man make a false step if it isn't not knowing how to dance?

M. JOURDAIN. True enough. You're both of you absolutely right.

DANCING MASTER. It was only to make you appreciate the value of dancing and music.

M. JOURDAIN. I fully appreciate it now.

MUSIC MASTER. Then will you please give us your attention?

M. JOURDAIN. Willingly.

MUSIC MASTER. As I have told you already, this is just a little exercise I have devised to show the various passions which can be expressed by music.

M. JOURDAIN. I understand.

MUSIC MASTER [*To the singers*]. Come forward, please. [*To* M. JOURDAIN]. You must imagine that they are dressed as shepherds.

M. JOURDAIN. Why always shepherds? One never sees anything else.

DANCING MASTER. Whenever you have characters speaking to music, for the sake of plausibility, they must smack of the sheepcote. From time immemorial minstrelsy has been the special attribute of shepherds. It would be most unnatural to have princes or tradesmen venting their passions in song.

M. JOURDAIN. Well, well. Let's hear it.

MUSICAL DIALOGUE

[A Lady and two Men Singers]

The Lady.
    A heart in Love's strong chains imprisoned
      Is racked with cares to a cruel degree.
    They say that such sighings with pleasure are seasoned;
        Oh, most falsely reasoned!
    There's nothing so sweet as the life of the free.

1st Man.
    There's nothing so sweet as lovers' soft yearnings,
      Those amorous burnings
      That two hearts unite.
    Man can only be happy in treading Love's measure.
      If you put out Love's light
      You destroy all life's pleasure.

2nd Man.
    How sweet to be subject to Love's tender law
    If in his courts one faithful heart we saw!
      But, alas, for ever ranging free,
      Faithful shepherdess where is she?
    Inconstant sex! Unfit to live you prove;
    Because of thee I'll live no more to love.

1st Man.   *Beloved Flame!*
The Lady.   *Love's blessing o'er you!*
2nd Man.   *Your sex I blame.*
1st Man.   *How I adore you!*
The Lady.   *My soul delights in your person.*
2nd Man.   *You fill me with aversion.*
1st Man.   *Forsake this hate for love, dear shepherd, do.*
The Lady.   *I can, oh, I can show you*
        A shepherdess that's true.

2nd Man.	*Alas! May I believe you?*
The Lady.	*All women are not faithless.*
	I offer you my heart.
2nd Man.	*But how can you persuade me*
	That your love will ne'er depart?
The Lady.	*Let us make a gentle wager*
	Which of us two shall love the best.
2nd Man.	*May Good Fortune never favour*
	Who fails to stand the test!
All.	*May Love's bright torch for ever*
	Our gentle flames renew!
	How sweet to be a lover
	When two fond hearts are true!

M. JOURDAIN. Is that all?

MUSIC MASTER. Yes, Monsieur.

M. JOURDAIN. Very well put together. Very pretty little sentiments indeed.

DANCING MASTER. Now here is a little exercise designed to show the most graceful and varied movements and attitudes that can be comprised in a dance.

M. JOURDAIN. Are they shepherds too?

DANCING MASTER. They're anything you like to imagine. [*To the Dancers*]. Come along now.

BALLET

Four dancers execute all the different movements and steps that the DANCING MASTER *directs.*

ACT TWO

I   *The action is continuous.* MONSIEUR JOURDAIN, *the*
MUSIC MASTER *and the* DANCING MASTER *are*
discovered.

M. JOURDAIN. Brilliant! Those fellows frisk about capitally.

MUSIC MASTER. When dancing and singing are combined it
is even more effective. You will see something really fine
in the little ballet we have got up for you.

M. JOURDAIN. That will be for later. The lady, in whose
honour I ordered it, will be dining with me here.

DANCING MASTER. Everything is quite ready.

MUSIC MASTER. But, Sir, this is not enough. A gentleman
like yourself, magnificent in your style of living and with a
taste for the refinements of life, should put on a musical
soirée every Wednesday or Thursday.

M. JOURDAIN. Do people of rank do so?

MUSIC MASTER. Always, Sir.

M. JOURDAIN. Then I will do so too. You will be able to get
it up really well?

MUSIC MASTER. Assuredly, Sir. You will need three singers,
tenor, counter-tenor and bass, with a bass-viol, a theorbo,
a clavecin and two violins for the accompaniments.

M. JOURDAIN. Do let's have a marine trumpet too. I love the
marine trumpet, and it's very harmonious.

MUSIC MASTER. You must leave all that to us.

M. JOURDAIN. Be sure you don't forget to send me some
minstrels to sing during dinner.

MUSIC MASTER. You shall have everything as it should be.

M. JOURDAIN. But above all let the ballet be good.

MUSIC MASTER. You'll be delighted, Sir, especially with the minuets.

M. JOURDAIN. Oh, the minuet is my own speciality. Watch me. I'll dance it for you now. Come along, Master.

DANCING MASTER. A hat, Sir, if you please.

[M. JOURDAIN *takes a hat from one of the lackeys, and puts it on over his night cap. The* DANCING MASTER *takes his hand and makes him dance a minuet, singing the tune the while.*

La, la, la, la, la, la; la, la, la, la, la, la, la; la, la, la, la, la, la; la, la, la, la, la, la, la; la, la, la, la, la. Keep time, please. La, la, la, la, la. Leg straight, la, la, la. Don't move your shoulders so much. La, la, la, la, la, la, la, la, la, la. You hold your arms as if they were broken. La, la, la, la, la. Head up. Turn your toes out. La, la, la. Hold yourself straight.

M. JOURDAIN. Whew! How's that?

MUSIC MASTER. Perfect!

M. JOURDAIN. Oh, there's another thing. I want you to teach me how to make a bow to a Marquise. I shall have need of that presently.

DANCING MASTER. How to bow to a Marquise?

M. JOURDAIN. Yes. A Marquise called Dorimène.

DANCING MASTER. Give me your hand.

M. JOURDAIN. No, no. You do it for me. I shall remember.

DANCING MASTER. If you want to salute her very respectfully you must first take a step backward and bow; then three steps towards her, bowing each time, the last as low as her knees.

M. JOURDAIN. Show me. [*After the* DANCING MASTER *has made three bows*]. Good! That's splendid.

[*Enter a lackey.*

A LACKEY. The Master-at-arms is here, Sir.

M. JOURDAIN. Tell him to come in and give me my lesson. [*To the* MUSIC *and* DANCING MASTERS]. I should like you to see me at it.

II   [*The* MASTER-AT-ARMS *enters, followed by the other lackey carrying two foils.*

MASTER-AT-ARMS [*after taking the two foils from the lackey and handing one to* M. JOURDAIN]. Now, Sir, the salute. Body erect. Weight slightly resting on the left foot. Legs not quite so far apart. Feet in a line. Wrist held on a level with the hip. The point of your foil on a level with your shoulder. Arm not quite so far extended. Left hand held level with the eye. Left shoulder more to the front. Head erect. A confident look. Advance. Keep your balance. Touch my foil in quarte, lunge, riposte and on guard. One, two. As you were. Again. Firmer on your feet, and more attack. Retire. When you lunge, Monsieur, let your foil move forward first, the body presenting the smallest possible target to the enemy. One, two. Now. Touch my foil in tierce, lunge, riposte and on guard. Advance. Keep your balance. Advance. Lunge from there. One, two. As you were. Again. Retire. On guard, Sir, on guard. [*The* MASTER-AT-ARMS *lunges at him two or three times, saying 'on guard'.*

M. JOURDAIN. Whew! How's that?

MUSIC MASTER. You're marvellous at it.

MASTER-AT-ARMS. I have already told you that the whole secret of swordplay consists in two things, giving and not receiving. As I pointed out to you the other day by ocular demonstration, you cannot receive if you deflect your adversary's sword from the line of your body, which is just a simple matter of the movement of your wrist either this way or that.

M. JOURDAIN. So then a man has no need of courage, but can be sure of killing his man and of not being killed himself?

—

MASTER-AT-ARMS. Undoubtedly. Didn't you see the demonstration?

M. JOURDAIN. Yes, yes, I did.

MASTER-AT-ARMS. So now you can understand what great honour should be paid to us fencing masters in the State; and how far more important is the science of arms than such useless sciences as dancing and music.

DANCING MASTER. Just one moment, Master Swordsman. Please speak of dancing with a little more respect.

MUSIC MASTER. Kindly moderate your language when you speak of music.

MASTER-AT-ARMS. You've got a nerve to dare compare your sciences with mine.

MUSIC MASTER. Listen to His High and Mightiness!

DANCING MASTER. A funny little animal in a breastplate!

MASTER-AT-ARMS. I'll make you dance in a minute, my little Dancing Master. And you, too, my little fiddle scraper, I'll make you sing to some purpose.

DANCING MASTER. Master Metal Basher, I'll teach you your trade.

M. JOURDAIN [to the DANCING MASTER]. Are you crazy? To quarrel with him, who understands quarte and tierce, and can kill a man by ocular demonstration!

DANCING MASTER. I wouldn't give a farthing for his ocular demonstration, and his tierce, and his quarte!

M. JOURDAIN [to the DANCING MASTER]. Keep calm, I beg of you.

MASTER-AT-ARMS [to the DANCING MASTER]. What's that, you little impudent rascal?

M. JOURDAIN. Now, now, Master-at-arms!

DANCING MASTER [to the MASTER-AT-ARMS]. You great cart horse!

M. JOURDAIN. Now, Now, Dancing Master!

MASTER-AT-ARMS. If once I let myself go . . .

M. JOURDAIN [*to the* MASTER-AT-ARMS]. Gently! Gently!

DANCING MASTER. If once I set about you . . .

M. JOURDAIN [*to the* DANCING MASTER]. There! There!

MASTER-AT-ARMS. I'll give you such a thrashing.

M. JOURDAIN [*to the* MASTER-AT-ARMS]. For pity's sake!

DANCING MASTER. I'll wallop you within an inch of your life.

M. JOURDAIN. I beg of you!

MUSIC MASTER. Pray allow us to teach him better manners.

M. JOURDAIN [*to the* MUSIC MASTER]. Good Heavens, no; stop, stop!

III   [*Enter a* PHILOSOPHY MASTER.

Ah, Master Philosopher, you've come just at the right moment with your philosophy. Do please make peace between these people.

PHILOSOPHY MASTER. What is the matter, my masters? What is the question in dispute?

M. JOURDAIN. They are quarrelling about the importance of their several professions. They've been calling each other names already, and are just coming to blows.

PHILOSOPHY MASTER. My dear Sirs, is there really any occasion for such a display of temper? Haven't you read Seneca's learned treatise on the subject of wrath? What can be more shameful and degrading than a passion which transforms a man into a wild beast? All our actions should be governed by reason.

DANCING MASTER. Is he to come here, Sir, and insult us both; to sneer at dancing which I profess, and at music which is his profession?

—

PHILOSOPHY MASTER. A sensible man is superior to such insults. The best reply to abuse is patience and restraint.

MASTER-AT-ARMS. They have the audacity to compare their professions with mine.

PHILOSOPHY MASTER. And why should that upset you? Pride and status are not subjects for dispute among rational beings. The only worthwhile distinction among men is based on wisdom and virtue.

DANCING MASTER. I maintain that dancing is a science to which too much respect cannot be paid.

MUSIC MASTER. And I that music is a science which all centuries have delighted to honour.

MASTER-AT-ARMS. And I maintain, in both their teeth, that the science of arms is the most perfect and the most necessary of all the sciences in the world.

PHILOSOPHY MASTER. And where then does philosophy come in? You're three impertinent scoundrels to take that tone before me, and give the name of science to what is unworthy even of the name of liberal art. Why, they are nothing but the miserable trades of gladiator, minstrel and mountebank.

MASTER-AT-ARMS. Away, dog of a philosopher!

MUSIC MASTER. Away, you beggarly pedant!

DANCING MASTER. Away, you wretched little schoolteacher!

PHILOSOPHY MASTER. What's that you say, you villains. . . .?

[*The* PHILOSOPHY MASTER *hurls himself on them and all three shower blows on him.*

M. JOURDAIN. Master Philosopher!

PHILOSOPHY MASTER. Wretches, rogues, impudent rascals!

M. JOURDAIN. Master Philosopher!

MASTER-AT-ARMS. Plague take the animal!

M. JOURDAIN. Gentlemen!

PHILOSOPHY MASTER. Insolent ruffians!

M. JOURDAIN. Master Philosopher!

DANCING MASTER. The devil take the interfering fool!

M. JOURDAIN. Gentlemen!

PHILOSOPHY MASTER. Scoundrels!

M. JOURDAIN. Master Philosopher!

MUSIC MASTER. To Hell with the impertinent dog!

M. JOURDAIN. Gentlemen!

PHILOSOPHY MASTER. Rascally, beggarly, treacherous frauds!

M. JOURDAIN. Master Philosopher! Gentlemen! Master Philosopher! Gentlemen! Master Philosopher!

[*They go off fighting*

M. JOURDAIN. Oh, very well then, fight your bellyful. It's none of my business. I'm not going to ruin my new gown trying to separate you. I should be a fine fool to go in among them, and get a blow for my pains that would do me a mischief.

IV   [*Re-enter the* PHILOSOPHY MASTER.

PHILOSOPHY MASTER [*rearranging his neckband*]. Let's begin our lesson.

M. JOURDAIN. My dear Sir, I'm so sorry they have given you such a drubbing.

PHILOSOPHY MASTER. It's not worth mentioning. A philosopher is schooled to take everything as it comes. I shall write a satire against them in the style of Juvenal which will flay them alive. But enough of that! What is it you want to learn?

M. JOURDAIN. Everything. I have a longing to be learned. I'm furious to think that my parents didn't have me taught every kind of knowledge when I was a boy.

PHILOSOPHY MASTER. Well, that's quite reasonable; *nam sine doctrina vita est quasi mortis imago.* You understand that? You know Latin, of course.

M. JOURDAIN. Oh, yes. But act as if I didn't. Tell me what it means.

PHILOSOPHY MASTER. It means that 'without knowledge, life is but an image of death'.

M. JOURDAIN. That Latin has hit the mark.

PHILOSOPHY MASTER. Don't you know any of the rudiments of any of the branches of knowledge?

M. JOURDAIN. Oh, yes. I know how to read and write.

PHILOSOPHY MASTER. Well, what would you like to begin with? Shall I teach you logic?

M. JOURDAIN. What's logic?

PHILOSOPHY MASTER. It's the science that treats of the three operations of the mind.

M. JOURDAIN. And what are they, these three operations of the mind?

PHILOSOPHY MASTER. The first, the second and the third. The first to conceive by means of premises; the second to reason by means of categories; and the third to draw conclusions by means of figures: Barbara, Celarent, Darii, Ferio, Baralipton,* etc.

M. JOURDAIN. What repulsive sounding words! I don't like that logic at all. Teach me something prettier.

PHILOSOPHY MASTER. How about moral philosophy?

M. JOURDAIN. Moral philosophy?

PHILOSOPHY MASTER. Yes.

M. JOURDAIN. What's that about, moral philosophy?

PHILOSOPHY MASTER. It treats of happiness, teaches men to control their passions, and. . . .

M. JOURDAIN. No, no. I'll none of that. I'm as crotchety as the devil. No moral philosophy would have the smallest effect on me. Besides, I want to be as angry as I like, whenever the fit takes me.

PHILOSOPHY MASTER. Is it physics then you'd like to learn?

M. JOURDAIN. What does physics burble on about?

PHILOSOPHY MASTER. Physics explains the principles of natural phenomena and the properties of bodies. It deals with the nature of the elements, of metals, minerals, precious stones, plants and animals, and teaches us the cause of meteors, rainbows, will-o'-the wisps, comets, lightning, thunder, thunderbolts, rain, snow, hail, winds and tornadoes.

M. JOURDAIN. No, I don't like that. It's all too much of a hurly-burly.

PHILOSOPHY MASTER. Then what *do* you want me to teach you?

M. JOURDAIN. Teach me orthography.

PHILOSOPHY MASTER. Most willingly, if you wish it.

M. JOURDAIN. After that you can teach me to read the almanack, so that I may know when there is a moon and when there isn't.

PHILOSOPHY MASTER. Very well. In order to follow out your intentions properly and treat the question philosophically, we must begin, in strict order, with an exact knowledge of the nature of the letters and their correct pronunciation. And, thereupon, I must tell you that the letters are divided into vowels, because they express the different vocal sounds, and consonants, so called because they are sounded with the vowels and thus emphasize the various articulations of the voice. There are five vowels or voices: A, E, I, O, U.*

M. JOURDAIN. Yes. I follow that.

PHILOSOPHY MASTER. The vowel A is formed by opening wide the mouth; A.

M. JOURDAIN. A, A. Yes.

PHILOSOPHY MASTER. The vowel E is formed by approaching the lower jaw towards the upper jaw: A, E.

M. JOURDAIN. A, E. A, E. By Jove! So it is! Isn't that fine?

PHILOSOPHY MASTER. And the vowel I, by bringing the jaws even closer together, and stretching the two corners of the mouth up towards the ears: A, E, I.

M. JOURDAIN. A, E, I, I, I, I. True enough. Long live knowledge!

PHILOSOPHY MASTER. The vowel O is formed by reopening the jaws, and bringing the two corners of the mouth together: O.

M. JOURDAIN. O, O. Nothing could be more exact; A, E, I, O, I, O. Splendid! I, O; I, O.

PHILOSOPHY MASTER. The opening of the mouth makes a perfect little circle, just like an O.

M. JOURDAIN. O, O, O. Right you are. O. Oh, how delightful it is to have a little knowledge!

PHILOSOPHY MASTER. The vowel U is formed by bringing the teeth closer together, but without letting them touch, and shooting out the lips which are also brought nearer together without being entirely shut: U.

M. JOURDAIN. U, U. Nothing could be truer: U.

PHILOSOPHY MASTER. The lips shoot out just as if you were making a pout. So that if you want to mock at anyone by pouting at them, you have only to say U.

M. JOURDAIN. U, U. So you do. Oh, why didn't I begin to learn sooner? Then I should have known all that.

PHILOSOPHY MASTER. To-morrow we will have a look at the other letters, which are called consonants.

M. JOURDAIN. Is there the same sort of curious information to be had about them too?

PHILOSOPHY MASTER. Certainly. The consonant D, for instance, is formed by placing the tip of the tongue just inside the upper teeth: DA.

M. JOURDAIN. DA, DA, Yes. Excellent! Excellent!

PHILOSOPHY MASTER. F, by closing the upper teeth on the lower lip: FA.

M. JOURDAIN. FA, FA. Why, its absolutely as you say. Oh, father and mother, what a grudge I bear you for this!

PHILOSOPHY MASTER. And R, by bringing the tip of the tongue to the top of the palate, so that, being gently set in motion by the forcible expulsion of the breath, it yields and returns again to the same place, making a sort of trembling: R, RA.

M. JOURDAIN. R, R, RA, R, R, R, R, R, RA. True, true! You are a clever man! What a lot of time I've lost! R, R, R, RA.

PHILOSOPHY MASTER. I will explain to you the most fundamental principles of all these interesting things.

M. JOURDAIN. I beg you will. But now I'm going to tell you something in confidence. I am very much in love with a great lady of rank, and I want you to help me to write a little note, which I shall drop casually at her feet.

PHILOSOPHY MASTER. Very good.

M. JOURDAIN. I want it done in the most gallant style.

PHILOSOPHY MASTER. I understand. Do you wish to write to her in verse?

M. JOURDAIN. Oh no. Not in verse.

PHILOSOPHY MASTER. You want just prose.

M. JOURDAIN. No. I don't want either verse or prose.

PHILOSOPHY MASTER. But it must be one or the other.

M. JOURDAIN. Why?

PHILOSOPHY MASTER. Because, Sir, there are only two ways of expressing oneself, in prose or verse.

M. JOURDAIN. There's nothing except prose or verse?

PHILOSOPHY MASTER. No, Sir. Whatever is not prose is verse, and whatever is not verse is prose.

M. JOURDAIN. What is ordinary speech then?

PHILOSOPHY MASTER. Prose.

M. JOURDAIN. What! When I say: 'Nicole, fetch me my slippers, and give me my nightcap', is that prose?

PHILOSOPHY MASTER. Yes, Sir.

M. JOURDAIN. Good Heavens! Then I have been speaking prose for more than forty years without knowing it. I couldn't be more grateful to you for teaching me that. Now what I want to put in the note is: 'Fair Marquise, your beauty makes me die of love.' But I want it said prettily, put in an elegant way.

PHILOSOPHY MASTER. You can say that the sparks from her eyes reduce your heart to ashes; that, because of her, you are suffering night and day the agonies of a. . . .

M. JOURDAIN. No, no, no. I don't want any of that. I want only what I have just said: 'Fair Marquise, your beauty makes me die of love.'

PHILOSOPHY MASTER. But you must embroider it a bit.

M. JOURDAIN. No, I tell you. I want nothing else in the note but just those words, but arranged in a smart and up-to-date way. Let me hear the various ways in which they can be put, so that I can choose which I like best.

PHILOSOPHY MASTER. Well, first of all you can put them as you have said: 'Fair Marquise, your beauty makes me die of love'; or you can say: 'Of love makes me die, fair Marquise, your beauty'; or: 'Your beauty of love makes

me, fair Marquise, die'; or: 'Die your beauty, fair Marquise, of love makes me'; or: 'Makes me your beauty die,
fair Marquise, of love'.

M. JOURDAIN. But which is the best of all those?

PHILOSOPHY MASTER. The one you said: 'Fair Marquise,
your beauty makes me die of love.'

M. JOURDAIN. Yet it was without studying. I did all that at
the first go off. I thank you from the bottom of my heart.
Please come again early to-morrow.

PHILOSOPHY MASTER. I won't fail.

[He goes out

M. JOURDAIN [*to the lackey*]. Hasn't my suit come yet?

LACKEY. No, Sir.

M. JOURDAIN. That wretched tailor *would* keep me waiting
on a day I have such a lot to do. I am furious. A plague on
that ruffian of a tailor! A thousand curses on the tailor!
The devil take the tailor! If I had him here now, that
odious treacherous dog of a tailor, I'd. . . .

V   [*A* MASTER TAILOR *enters, followed by an assistant
carrying the suit of* M. JOURDAIN.

Ah, so there you are! I was just getting into a rage with
you.

TAILOR. I couldn't come before, Sir. And I put twenty men
on the job.

M. JOURDAIN. The silk stockings you sent me were so
narrow I've had all the trouble in the world to get them on.
There are two ladders in them already.

TAILOR. They will stretch.

M. JOURDAIN. Yes, I dare say, if I go on laddering them.
And the shoes you have made for me hurt like the devil.

TAILOR. Oh no, they don't, Sir.

M. JOURDAIN. What do you mean, they don't?

TAILOR. They don't hurt you at all.

M. JOURDAIN. I tell you they do hurt me.

TAILOR. You imagine it.

M. JOURDAIN. I imagine it because I feel it. And a very good reason too!

TAILOR. Here, Sir, is the finest and most tasteful Court suit ever made. It is a real masterpiece to have created a sober suit that isn't black. I'll give six tries to the cleverest tailors in Paris and they won't equal it.

M. JOURDAIN. Hey! What's this? You've put the flowers on upside down.

TAILOR. You never said you wanted them right way up.

M. JOURDAIN. Ought I to have done so?

TAILOR. Why, of course. All persons of rank have them like that.

M. JOURDAIN. Persons of rank have the flowers upside down?

TAILOR. Yes, Sir.

M. JOURDAIN. Oh, then that's all right.

TAILOR. I will put them right way up if you like.

M. JOURDAIN. No, no.

TAILOR. You have only to say the word.

M. JOURDAIN. No, no, I say. You have done quite right. Do you think the suit becoming?

TAILOR. What a question, Sir! I defy a painter with his brush to make you anything more perfect. I have an assistant who is the greatest genius in the world at shaping a pair of breeches; and another, for assembling a doublet, is the hero of our time.

M. JOURDAIN. Are the wig and feathers the right thing?

TAILOR. Everything is perfect.

M. JOURDAIN [*examining the* MASTER TAILOR]. Hey! What's this, what's this, Master Tailor? You're wearing a suit of the very same stuff as you made my last. I recognize it perfectly.

TAILOR. It was such a beautiful material, Sir, that I couldn't resist making myself a suit of it too.

M. JOURDAIN. That's all very well, but you had no right to make it out of my material.

TAILOR. Will you try your suit on?

M. JOURDAIN. Yes. Give it me.

TAILOR. One moment, Sir, if you please. That's not the way we do things here. I've brought my people along to dress you in rhythm. A suit like this has to be put on with ceremony. Come in there.

[*Four Tailor's Assistants enter dancing.*

Put on this gentleman's suit in the same way as you do for persons of rank.

[*The four tailor's assistants dance up to* M. JOURDAIN. *Two remove the breeches in which he does his exercises; the other two remove his waistcoat. After which, still in rhythm, they dress him in the new suit.* M. JOURDAIN *struts about among them, so that they may see the dress from every angle.*]

1ST ASSISTANT. Honoured gentleman, pray give the assistants something to drink.

M. JOURDAIN. What's that you call me?

ASSISTANT. Honoured gentleman.

M. JOURDAIN. Honoured gentleman! That's what it is to be dressed like a person of rank. You'd never be called 'Honoured gentleman' if you always went dressed like a shopkeeper. [*He gives him money*]. There! That is for 'Honoured gentelman'.

ASSISTANT. We are very grateful, My Lord.

—

M. JOURDAIN. My Lord! Oh! Oh! My Lord! One moment, my friend. 'My Lord' deserves something. It's not an insignificant little word that. There! That's what My Lord gives you.

ASSISTANT. My Lord, we will all go and drink your Grace's health.

M. JOURDAIN. Your Grace! Oh! Oh! Oh! Wait! Don't go. Come here. Your Grace! [*Aside*]. By Jove! If he goes as far as Highness he shall have the whole purse. [*Aloud*]. There! That's for my Grace.

ASSISTANT. We thank you most humbly, My Lord, for your generosity.

M. JOURDAIN. Perhaps it's just as well. I was going to give him the lot.

[*The four tailor's assistants dance with delight at the generosity of* M. JOURDAIN.]

ACT THREE

[MONSIEUR JOURDAIN *enters, followed by his two lackeys.*   I

M. JOURDAIN. I am going for a little walk in the town to show off my fine clothes. Follow me, and remember, both of you, to walk close at my heels, so that everyone may see you belong to me.

1ST LACKEY. Very good, Sir.

M. JOURDAIN. Call Nicole. I have some orders to give her. But, stay, here she comes!

[*Enter* NICOLE.   II

Nicole!

NICOLE. What's your will?

M. JOURDAIN. Listen, I. . . .

NICOLE [*laughing*]. Ha ha ha ha ha!

M. JOURDAIN. What are you laughing at?

NICOLE. Ha ha ha ha ha ha!

M. JOURDAIN. What's the matter with the little fool?

NICOLE. Ha ha ha! Aren't you all dolled up! Ha ha ha!

M. JOURDAIN. What?

NICOLE. Oh! Oh! Lord save us! Ha ha ha ha ha!

M. JOURDAIN. Are you laughing at me, you minx?

NICOLE. No, no, Sir. I should be very sorry to do that. Ha ha ha ha ha ha!

M. JOURDAIN. I'll box your ears if you don't stop that cackling.

NICOLE. I can't help it, Sir. Ha ha ha ha ha ha!

M. JOURDAIN. You won't stop?

NICOLE. I beg your Honour's pardon, but you look so funny that I can't keep it in. Ha ha ha!

M. JOURDAIN. What insolence!

NICOLE. You're a real figure of fun, decked out like that. Ha ha!

M. JOURDAIN. I. . . .

NICOLE. Don't be angry, Sir. Ha ha ha ha!

M. JOURDAIN. Now listen. If I hear even one more little snigger, I swear I'll give you the biggest slap you've ever had in your life.

NICOLE. Very well, Sir, I've done. I won't laugh any more.

M. JOURDAIN. Take care you don't. I want you to sweep. . . .

NICOLE. Ha ha!

M. JOURDAIN. To sweep out. . . .

NICOLE. Ha ha!

M. JOURDAIN. I want you, I say, to sweep out the room, and. . . .

—

NICOLE. Ha ha!

M. JOURDAIN. What! Again?

NICOLE. Oh, Sir, I'd far rather you slapped me and let me laugh myself out. It'd be better for me in the end. Ha ha ha ha ha!

M. JOURDAIN. I shall lose my temper in a minute.

NICOLE. For pity's sake, Sir, let me laugh. Ha ha ha!

M. JOURDAIN. If once I. . . .

NICOLE. Oh, Sir, if I don't laugh I shall burst. Ha ha ha!

M. JOURDAIN. Was there ever such an insolent hussy, to laugh in my face instead of listening to my orders?

NICOLE. What do you want me to do, Sir?

M. JOURDAIN. I want you, you little wretch, to put my house in order for the company that is coming this evening.

NICOLE. Oh, if that's what it is, I don't want to laugh any more. The company you bring here always make such a mess that the very word is enough to put me in a bad humour.

M. JOURDAIN. Do you expect me to shut my door to everybody just to please you?

NICOLE. There are certain people you definitely ought to shut it to.

[*Enter* MADAME JOURDAIN.   III

MADAME JOURDAIN. Oho! So this is the newest craze, husband? What, in the name of wonder, is all that frippery for? Do you care no longer what people think of you, to go bedizening yourself like that? You'll make yourself a perfect laughing stock.

M. JOURDAIN. No one will laugh but fools.

MADAME JOURDAIN. Do you think so? Then let me tell you they haven't waited until now. Your absurdities have been causing people amusement for a long time past.

M. JOURDAIN. And who are these *people* may I ask?

MADAME JOURDAIN. Everyone who has a little more judgement and common sense than you have. I am positively shocked at the way you are going on. I no longer recognize our house. One would think it was carnival every day. From morning till night there's such a squeaking and squawking of violins and singing as disturbs the whole neighbourhood.

NICOLE. What Madame says is perfectly true. I can no longer keep the place clean with all this rabble of people you bring into it. I think their shoes pick up mud in every corner of the town just to bring it all in here. Poor Françoise is quite exhausted scrubbing the boards that your fine masters dirty every morning.

M. JOURDAIN. Oho, my dear servant Nicole! You've got a very good gift of the gab for a girl from the country.

MADAME JOURDAIN. Nicole is quite right. She has more sense than you have. What do you want with a dancing master at your age, I should like to know?

NICOLE. Or a great brute of a sword slasher, who makes the whole house shake with his stampings, and kicks up all the floor tiles?

M. JOURDAIN. Hold your tongues, both of you.

MADAME JOURDAIN. Do you want to learn dancing for when you no longer have any legs?

NICOLE. Do you want to go and kill somebody?

M. JOURDAIN. Hold your tongues, I say. You're completely ignorant, the pair of you. You don't understand the advantage of these things.

MADAME JOURDAIN. You'd far better be thinking how to marry off your daughter. She is quite old enough to be provided for.

M. JOURDAIN. I shall think of marrying off my daughter when a suitable party presents himself. In the meantime I shall devote myself to acquiring knowledge.

NICOLE. I've heard too, Madame, that to-day, on top of everything, he has engaged a master of philosophy.

M. JOURDAIN. Perfectly true. I have. I want to know how to reason, so that I can hold my own among educated people.

MADAME JOURDAIN. One of these day, I suppose you'll be going to college and getting yourself spanked.

M. JOURDAIN. And why not? I'd willingly be spanked this minute in front of everybody to know what they learn at college.

NICOLE. You'd have a much better turned leg after all that, of course.

M. JOURDAIN. I should.

MADAME JOURDAIN. It would be such a help in managing your affairs.

M. JOURDAIN. Yes, it would. You talk like brute beasts, both of you. I'm quite ashamed of your ignorance. [*To* MADAME JOURDAIN]. For instance, have you any idea what you are speaking at this moment?

MADAME JOURDAIN. Yes. I know I am speaking good sense and that it's time you changed your way of life.

M. JOURDAIN. I don't mean that. I am asking you what sort of words you are using.

MADAME JOURDAIN. Very sensible words, which is more than can be said for your behaviour.

M. JOURDAIN. That's not what I mean, I tell you. What I am asking you, is this. The way I speak to you, what I am saying at this moment, what's that?

MADAME JOURDAIN. Balderdash.

M. JOURDAIN. No, no, that's not it. What we are saying to each other, the language we are speaking here and now?

MADAME JOURDAIN. Well?

M. JOURDAIN. What is it called?

MADAME JOURDAIN. It's called . . . whatever you like to call it.

M. JOURDAIN. It's prose, you idiot.

MADAME JOURDAIN. Prose?

M. JOURDAIN. Yes, prose. Everything that is prose is not verse; and everything that isn't verse is prose. There! So now you see what it is to have studied. [*To* NICOLE]. Now, you. Do you know what you must do to say U?

NICOLE. What do you mean?

M. JOURDAIN. What do you do when you say U?

NICOLE. What?

M. JOURDAIN. Say U, now.

NICOLE. Very well then, U.

M. JOURDAIN. What are you doing?

NICOLE. I'm saying U.

M. JOURDAIN. Yes. But when you say U, what is it you do?

NICOLE. I'm doing what you tell me.

M. JOURDAIN. Oh, what a thing it is to have to do with fools! You shoot out your lips and bring the upper and lower jaws closer together. U. Do you see? I make a pout. U.

NICOLE. Oh, that's very fine.

MADAME JOURDAIN. Very remarkable indeed.

M. JOURDAIN. It's another thing altogether when you say O, and DA, DA, and FA, FA.

MADAME JOURDAIN. What is all this rubbish?

NICOLE. What is it good for?

M. JOURDAIN. It makes my blood boil to see such ignorant women.

MADAME JOURDAIN. For shame! You ought to send all that rabble packing with their gibberish.

NICOLE. Especially that great scarecrow of a fencing master, who fills the whole house with dust.

M. JOURDAIN. Oh, so the fencing master sticks in your gizzard, does he? I'll show you your folly at once. [*He signs to a lackey to bring the foils and hands one to* NICOLE]. Now then. Ocular demonstration. The line of the body. When you are attacked in quarte you have only to do this, and when you are attacked in tierce you have only to do that. That's the way never to be killed. Isn't it worth something always to be sure of the outcome when you have to fight? Here, attack me now. I'll show you.

NICOLE. Very well. There!

[NICOLE *lunges several times at* M. JOURDAIN.

M. JOURDAIN. Hey, Hey! Be careful, be careful. Devil take the hussy!

NICOLE. You told me to attack you.

M. JOURDAIN. Yes. But you attacked in tierce before you attacked in quarte. And you didn't wait for me to parry.

MADAME JOURDAIN. Oh, you're crazy, husband, with your notions. This has all come since you took to frequenting the aristocracy.

M. JOURDAIN. I show my good sense in frequenting the aristocracy. It's better than hobnobbing with shopkeepers.

MADAME JOURDAIN. Oh, yes, to be sure. It's done you a lot of good! You have made a fine hand of it with this precious Comte you are so infatuated with.

M. JOURDAIN. Wait now. Be careful what you say. You don't know who you are speaking of when you speak of him. He is a person of more importance than you imagine. He is held in the highest consideration at Court, and talks to the King as familiarly as I am speaking to you now. It's a great feather in my cap for the world to see a man of that eminence come to my house so often, call me his dear friend and treat me as if I were his equal. You can't imagine how considerate he is. Why, the warm way he embraces me before everybody almost makes me ashamed.

MADAME JOURDAIN. Yes. I grant he is very considerate and affectionate. But he borrows your money.

M. JOURDAIN. Well, what of it? It is a great honour for me to lend money to a man of his rank. I could hardly do less for a lord who calls me his dear friend.

MADAME JOURDAIN. And what has this great lord done for you?

M. JOURDAIN. Things that would astonish people, if they knew.

MADAME JOURDAIN. Well, what?

M. JOURDAIN. It's not easy to explain. Let it be enough that any money I have lent him he will repay; and without undue delay either.

MADAME JOURDAIN. Do you think so?

M. JOURDAIN. Certainly. He told me so himself.

MADAME JOURDAIN. Oh yes. He won't fail to fail.

M. JOURDAIN. He swore it on his honour as a gentleman.

MADAME JOURDAIN. Fiddlesticks!

M. JOURDAIN. Oh, you are an obstinate woman. I tell you I feel quite confident he will keep his word.

MADAME JOURDAIN. And I feel quite confident that he won't. All this pretended affection is only to make a fool of you.

M. JOURDAIN. Sh! Here he is now.

MADAME JOURDAIN. That's all that was needed. I expect he's coming to borrow more money from you. The very sight of him puts me off my food.

M. JOURDAIN. Be quiet, I tell you.

[*Enter* DORANTE.

DORANTE. Monsieur Jourdain, my dear friend, how are you to-day?

M. JOURDAIN. Very well indeed, Sir, and very much at your service.

DORANTE. And Madame Jourdain, how is she?

MADAME JOURDAIN. Madame Jordain is as well as can be expected.

DORANTE. Why, Monsieur Jourdain, you *are* looking fine.

M. JOURDAIN. You see.

DORANTE. You look superb in that suit you are wearing. None of our young dandies at Court could hold a candle to you.

M. JOURDAIN. Aha! aha!

MADAME JOURDAIN [*aside*]. He knows which part of his back to scratch.

DORANTE. Turn round. Well, it *is* smart.

MADAME JOURDAIN [*aside*]. Yes, as big a fool from behind as from the front.

DORANTE. By God, Monsieur Jourdain, I could hardly wait to see you. There's no one for whom I have a greater respect. I was speaking of you this morning at the King's levée.

M. JOURDAIN. I am greatly honoured, Sir. [*To* MADAME JOURDAIN]. At the King's levée!

DORANTE. Pray put on your hat, Sir.

M. JOURDAIN. Sir, I hope I know my duty better.

DORANTE. Heavens! No ceremony between us, I beg of you.

M. JOURDAIN. Sir. . . .

DORANTE. Cover yourself, I beseech you, Monsieur Jourdain; you are my friend.

M. JOURDAIN. I am your servant, Sir.

DORANTE. I won't put on my hat unless you do.

M. JOURDAIN [*putting on his hat*]. I would rather be unmannerly than troublesome.

DORANTE. I am your debtor, as you know.

MADAME JOURDAIN [*aside*]. Yes, we know it only too well.

DORANTE. You have been so obliging as to lend me money on several occasions, and no one can do it with a better grace.

M. JOURDAIN. You must be joking, Sir.

DORANTE. But I never fail to pay back what I owe, and return the favour I receive.

M. JOURDAIN. I know it well, Sir.

DORANTE. I am anxious to settle my account with you, and I have come to-day to know how things stand between us.

M. JOURDAIN [*aside, to* MADAME JOURDAIN]. There you are wife! Just see how wrong you were.

DORANTE. I like to pay my debts at the earliest possible moment.

M. JOURDAIN [*aside, to* MADAME JOURDAIN]. What did I tell you?

DORANTE. Let's see now. How much do I owe you?

M. JOURDAIN [*aside, to* MADAME JOURDAIN]. Aren't you ashamed now of your ridiculous suspicions?

DORANTE. Can you remember the full amount of what you've lent me?

M. JOURDAIN. Yes, I think so. I made a little memorandum. Yes, here it is. Lent at one time two hundred louis.

DORANTE. Yes. I remember that.

M. JOURDAIN. At another time one hundred and twenty.

DORANTE. Yes.

M. JOURDAIN. And at another time again, one hundred and forty.

DORANTE. Yes, that's right.

M. JOURDAIN. Making altogether four hundred and sixty louis, which is five thousand and sixty livres.

DORANTE. Five thousand and sixty livres. Quite correct.

M. JOURDAIN. Then there was one thousand, eight hundred and thirty-two livres to your feather merchant.

DORANTE. Yes.

M. JOURDAIN. Two thousand, seven hundred and eighty livres to your tailor.

DORANTE. Yes.

M. JOURDAIN. Four thousand, three hundred and seventy-nine livres, twelve sols, eight deniers to your haberdasher.

DORANTE. True, twelve sols, eight deniers. Quite correct.

M. JOURDAIN. And one thousand, seven hundred and forty-eight livres, seven sols, four deniers to your sadler.

DORANTE. Good! Now what does all that come to?

M. JOURDAIN. Sum total—Fifteen thousand, eight hundred livres.

DORANTE. Sum total, fifteen thousand, eight hundred livres. Perfectly right. Now add the two hundred pistoles you are going to give me now. And that makes eighteen thousand francs which I will pay you at the earliest opportunity.

MADAME JOURDAIN [aside, to M. JOURDAIN]. There now, what did I tell you?

M. JOURDAIN [aside, to MADAME JOURDAIN]. Be quiet.

DORANTE. It won't inconvenience you, I hope, to let me have that amount?

M. JOURDAIN. Oh, no, not at all.

MADAME JOURDAIN [aside, to M. JOURDAIN]. The man is just milking you for all he can get.

M. JOURDAIN [*aside, to* MADAME JOURDAIN]. Hold your tongue.

DORANTE. If it does I can easily go to someone else.

M. JOURDAIN. No, no, Sir.

MADAME JOURDAIN [*aside, to* M. JOURDAIN]. He'll never rest till he's ruined you.

M. JOURDAIN [*aside, to* MADAME JOURDAIN]. Will you be quiet?

DORANTE. If you find it an embarrassment, you have only to say so.

M. JOURDAIN. Not the least in the world, Sir.

MADAME JOURDAIN [*aside, to* M. JOURDAIN]. He's a regular wheedler.

M. JOURDAIN [*aside, to* MADAME JOURDAIN]. Be quiet, I tell you.

MADAME JOURDAIN [*aside, to* M. JOURDAIN]. He'll squeeze the very last sou out of you.

M. JOURDAIN [*aside, to* MADAME JOURDAIN]. Will you hold your tongue?

DORANTE. I know several people who would be only too delighted to lend it me. But, as you are my best friend, I felt I should not be treating you fairly if I asked anyone else.

M. JOURDAIN. You do me too much honour, Sir. I'll go and fetch it now.

MADAME JOURDAIN [*aside, to* M. JOURDAIN]. What! You're going to give it to him?

M. JOURDAIN [*aside, to* MADAME JOURDAIN]. What else can I do? Would you have me refuse a man of his rank, who talked of me this morning at the King's levée?

MADAME JOURDAIN [*aside, to* M. JOURDAIN]. Bah! You're a proper fool.

[M. JOURDAIN *goes out* V

DORANTE. You look quite depressed, Madame Jourdain. What's the matter?

MADAME JOURDAIN. My head is bigger than my fist, Monsieur, and it's not swollen.

DORANTE. And where is Mademoiselle your daughter who I see is not here?

MADAME JOURDAIN. Mademoiselle my daughter is very well where she is.

DORANTE. How is she getting along?

MADAME JOURDAIN. On her two legs.

DORANTE. Wouldn't you like to bring her to Court one day to see the comedy and ballet?

MADAME JOURDAIN. Yes, indeed. We have a great longing to laugh. A great longing to laugh we have.

DORANTE. I'm sure, Madame Jourdain, you must have had lots of admirers in your youth, handsome and good-humoured as you were.

MADAME JOURDAIN. Is Madame Jourdain decrepit then? Is her head shaking with the palsy already?

DORANTE. By God! Madame Jourdain, a thousand pardons. I was forgetting that you were young. I am very absent-minded. I beg you will forgive my impertinence.

[*Re-enter* M. JOURDAIN. VI

M. JOURDAIN. [*to* DORANTE]. Here are two hundred louis.

DORANTE. Monsieur Jourdain, I am your most obedient servant. I will do everything I can to advance your interests at Court.

M. JOURDAIN. I am more than grateful, Sir.

DORANTE. And if Madame would care to see the royal entertainment, I will arrange for her to have the best seats.

MADAME JOURDAIN. Madame Jourdain kisses your hand.

DORANTE [*aside, to* M. JOURDAIN]. As I told you in my note, our lovely Marquise will be here later to sup with you and see the ballet. I have at last managed to persuade her to accept this proof of your devotion.

M. JOURDAIN. Come a little this way, if you please. I don't want my wife to hear.

DORANTE. It is eight days since I've seen you, so I've had no opportunity of telling you about the diamond you begged me to offer her on your behalf. It wasn't at all easy to overcome her scruples, and she has only to-day consented to accept it.

M. JOURDAIN. What does she think of it?

DORANTE. Oh, quite exquisite. And I shall be very surprised if the beauty of the gem does not move her very strongly in your favour.

M. JOURDAIN. Pray Heaven it may!

MADAME JOURDAIN [*to* NICOLE]. Once he has got his claws in him he can't let him go.

DORANTE. I have done my best to make her appreciate the richness of the gift and the greatness of your love for her.

M. JOURDAIN. Oh, Sir, your goodness overwhelms me. I am all confusion to think that a gentleman of your rank should condescend to do for me what you have done.

DORANTE. Nonsense! One doesn't stick at a trifle like that to oblige a friend. Wouldn't you do the same for me if occasion offered?

M. JOURDAIN. Most certainly I would, Sir, with all my heart.

MADAME JOURDAIN [*to* NICOLE]. His presence here is like a great weight on my shoulders.

DORANTE. With me friendship comes before everything. As soon as I knew of your passion for this adorable Marquise, I came forward at once, as her friend, to offer my services.

M. JOURDAIN. You certainly did. Your kindness puts me in your debt for ever.

MADAME JOURDAIN [*to* NICOLE]. Will he never go?

NICOLE. They like each other's company, I suppose.

DORANTE. You have certainly gone the right way to make an impression on her heart. Women love men to be extravagant in their service; and your continual bouquets and serenades, the magnificent firework display you gave for her on the water, the diamond you have just presented and the entertainment you are now preparing will all speak far more eloquently in your favour than anything you could say.

M. JOURDAIN. There is no expense I would spare if I could only find the way to her heart. A woman of rank has charms for me that ravish my very soul. No price would be too high to pay for such an honour.

MADAME JOURDAIN [*to* NICOLE]. What can they be talking about for so long? Try if you can get near enough to hear something.

DORANTE. You will soon be able to feast your eyes on her to your heart's content.

M. JOURDAIN. So that I may be quite free, I have arranged for my wife to dine with her sister, and pass the afternoon with her.

DORANTE. That was wise of you. Your wife being here would have made things very difficult. I have given all the necessary orders to the cook, and have made all arrangements for the ballet. It is of my own invention, and, if the execution only comes up to the conception, I can promise you that you will see. . . .

M. JOURDAIN [*seeing that* NICOLE *is listening, and giving her a box on the ears*]. Take that, you insolent little minx! [*To* DORANTE]. Let us leave the room, if you please.

[M. JOURDAIN *and* DORANTE *go out* VII

NICOLE. Heavens, Madame, my curiosity has got me a fine reward! But it's a true saying that there's no smoke without fire. I'll wager they are discussing something in which you are to be counted out.

MADAME JOURDAIN. This is not the first time, Nicole, that I've had reason to suspect my husband. I'm much mistaken if there's not some love affair in the wind, and I've been doing my best to ferret it out. But enough of that for the present! I want to talk about my daughter Lucile. As you know, Cléonte is in love with her. He is a young man I have a regard for, and I would like, if I can, to help him to get her.

NICOLE. Oh, Madame, I couldn't be more delighted to hear you say that; for, if you like the master, I like the man-servant, and I wish our marriage might take place at the same time as theirs.

MADAME JOURDAIN. Well then off you go and find him now, and tell him to come here immediately so that we may tackle my husband on the subject together.

NICOLE. You couldn't send me on a more welcome errand, Madame.

[MADAME JOURDAIN *goes out*

NICOLE. I am going to be the bearer of good news.

VIII   [*Enter* CLÉONTE *and* COVIELLE.

[*to* CLÉONTE]. Ah, there you are, the very man I was looking for! I am an ambassadress of happiness. I am sent. . . .

CLÉONTE. Away, you little traitress! I will no longer be made a fool of by your double dealing.

NICOLE. Is that the way you greet. . . .?

CLÉONTE. Away, I say! And tell your fickle mistress that never again shall she deceive the all too trusting Cléonte.

NICOLE. Why, what's all this confusion? My dear Covielle, do tell me what it's all about.

COVIELLE. Your dear Covielle, you wicked hussy! Out of my sight, you little wretch, and leave me in peace!

NICOLE. What, you too?

COVIELLE. Out of my sight, I say, and never dare to speak to me again!

NICOLE [*aside*]. Good lord! What's bitten them now, I wonder! I'll go at once and tell my mistress.

[*She goes out*   IX

CLÉONTE. It really is too bad. Is that the way to treat a suitor, the most faithful and devoted suitor in the whole world?

COVIELLE. It's monstrous the way they have behaved to us.

CLÉONTE. I showed her all the love and tenderness imaginable. She was all the world to me. My very soul was hers. My plans, my wishes, my pleasures were all in her. I spoke only of her. I thought only of her. I dreamt only of her. For her I drew my breath. My heart beat only for her. And this is how she repays me! For two whole days I am without sight of her, days that for me are like intolerable centuries. I meet her by chance. My heart bounds at the sight of her. My face is radiant with joy. I run to her in my delight. And the faithless creature turns her head away, and passes me by as if she'd never seen me in her life before.

COVIELLE. You take the very words out of my mouth.

CLÉONTE. Oh. Covielle, was there ever fickleness like that of the ungrateful Lucile?

COVIELLE. Or, like that of the wicked minx Nicole, Sir?

CLÉONTE. After all the sighs and vows I have paid to her beauty!

COVIELLE. After all the little jobs and chores I have done for her in her kitchen!

CLÉONTE. The tears I have shed at her very feet!

COVIELLE. The buckets of water I have drawn for her from the well!

CLÉONTE. The way I have put her every interest above my own!

COVIELLE. The way I have sweated, turning the spit in her place!

CLÉONTE. She turns from me with contempt.

COVIELLE. She turns her back on me with scorn.

CLÉONTE. Such inconstancy deserves the severest punishment.

COVIELLE. Such treachery deserves a good hiding.

CLÉONTE. Never dare to be so bold as to speak to me in her favour.

COVIELLE. Me, Sir? Not likely.

CLÉONTE. Never attempt to excuse her perfidy.

COVIELLE. No fear.

CLÉONTE. Nothing you can say in her defence will have the smallest effect.

COVIELLE. Me excuse her? I wouldn't think of it.

CLÉONTE. I will never forgive her, and I will have nothing more to do with her.

COVIELLE. My own sentiments exactly.

CLÉONTE. This precious Comte who visits her has turned her head, I suppose, and she has let herself be dazzled by his rank. But, my own sense of self-esteem will not allow her to have it all her own way. The world shall see that I can change as well as she can. She shan't have all the honour of jilting me.

COVIELLE. Capital! I am with you in everything you say.

CLÉONTE. Do everything you can to keep my anger alive and to fortify my resolution against the few stray embers of love that still burn in me. Make me see all that is worst in her. Draw her portrait in such a way as to make her contemptible, and complete my disgust by enumerating every fault you can possibly find in her.

COVIELLE. Her, Sir? Why she's nothing but a pretty, dolled up, affected piece. A fine object for you to be breaking your heart over! I see nothing in her but what is very ordinary. You could find a hundred others more worthy of your attention. In the first place, she has very small eyes. . . .

CLÉONTE. Yes, that's true. Her eyes are small. But they are full of fire. Their brilliance pierces you to the soul, and their expression is the most touching I have ever seen.

COVIELLE. She has a large mouth.

CLÉONTE. Yes, but it has a grace one looks for in vain in other mouths. Her mouth is the fountain of desire, the most attractive and adorable of all the mouths in the world.

COVIELLE. Then her figure. She's not tall, is she?

CLÉONTE. No. But her movements are free and graceful.

COVIELLE. There is a listlessness in her speech and gestures.

CLÉONTE. True. But there is a charm too. Her manners have an engaging fascination which quite captivates the heart.

COVIELLE. Her intelligence. . . .

CLÉONTE. Is full of delicate perception.

COVIELLE. Her conversation. . . .

CLÉONTE. Her conversation is enchanting.

COVIELLE. She's always much too serious.

CLÉONTE. Why, would you wish her to have a blowsy good humour and be for ever showing her teeth? There's nothing so infuriating as women who are always grinning.

COVIELLE. Well, you must admit she's capricious beyond anything that was ever seen.

CLÉONTE. Yes, I grant she is capricious. But how well it becomes her! From a pretty woman even caprice is supportable.

COVIELLE. Oh, very well then, if that is the way of it, I see you intend to go on loving her.

CLÉONTE. Me love her? I'd rather die. I'll hate her as much as I loved her.

COVIELLE. How are you going to manage that if you find her so perfect?

CLÉONTE. In that very thing shall be seen the greatness of my revenge. To leave her in her beauty, her charm, her adorable seduction will show the full strength of hatred of which my heart is capable. Here she comes!

X   [*Enter* LUCILE *and* NICOLE.]

NICOLE [*to* LUCILE]. I was absolutely flabbergasted.

LUCILE. It must be for the reason I told you, Nicole. But there he is.

CLÉONTE [*to* COVIELLE]. I won't even speak to her.

COVIELLE. I'll do just the same as you.

LUCILE. Why, Cléonte, what's the matter?

NICOLE. What is it, Covielle?

LUCILE. Why are you so strange?

NICOLE. Why are you in such a bad temper?

LUCILE. Are you dumb, Cléonte?

NICOLE. Has your tongue come unstuck, Covielle?

CLÉONTE. Was there ever such fickleness!

COVIELLE. The wicked little Judas!

LUCILE. I suppose it was our passing you just now that has upset you.

CLÉONTE [*to* COVIELLE]. Aha! So she knows what it is she's done.

NICOLE. Our manner this morning has given you the hump.

COVIELLE [*to* CLÉONTE]. She's guessed it.

LUCILE. Isn't that it, Cléonte? Isn't that what has made you so angry?

—

CLÉONTE. Yes, you false traitress, it is; since you must know the truth. But don't think to triumph in your infidelity. I mean to be the first to break with you. You shan't have the credit of jilting me. I shall no doubt find it hard to conquer my love. It will make me unhappy, and I shall suffer for a time. But I'll do it, never fear; and, rather than have the weakness to return to you again, I will stick a dagger in my heart.

COVIELLE [to NICOLE]. And I say the same.

LUCILE. Here's a fine to do about nothing! Shall I tell you, Cléonte, why I pretended not to see you this morning?

CLÉONTE [walking away to avoid LUCILE]. No. I won't hear a word.

NICOLE [to COVIELLE]. Do you know why we went by you without stopping?

COVIELLE [also walking away to avoid NICOLE]. No. I won't listen.

LUCILE [following CLÉONTE]. You should know that this morning. . . .

CLÉONTE [continuing to walk, without looking at LUCILE]. No, I say.

NICOLE [following COVIELLE]. Let me tell you. . . .

COVIELLE [also continuing to walk, without looking at NICOLE]. No, false minx.

LUCILE. Will you hear me?

CLÉONTE. No, I will not.

NICOLE. Let me speak.

COVIELLE. I'm deaf.

LUCILE. Cléonte.

CLÉONTE. No.

NICOLE. Covielle.

COVIELLE. I say 'No'.

LUCILE. Stay!

—

CLÉONTE. Not I.

NICOLE. Listen.

COVIELLE. Fiddlesticks!

LUCILE. One moment.

CLÉONTE. No.

NICOLE. Only a minute.

COVIELLE [*pretending to sing*]. La di da di da . . .

LUCILE. Let me explain.

CLÉONTE. No. It's all over.

NICOLE. Only one word.

COVIELLE. It's finished.

LUCILE [*stopping*]. Very well then, if you won't hear me, you can think what you like and do just as you please.

NICOLE [*stopping*]. If you're going to behave like that, you can have it your own way.

CLÉONTE [*turning towards* LUCILE]. Let us hear then the reason of such a charming salutation.

LUCILE [*walking away in her turn to avoid* CLÉONTE]. I don't choose to tell you now.

COVIELLE [*turning towards* NICOLE]. Let's know the why and wherefore.

NICOLE [*also walking away to avoid* COVIELLE]. No. It's too late.

CLÉONTE [*following* LUCILE]. Tell me. . . .

LUCILE [*continuing to walk, without looking at* CLÉONTE]. No. I won't tell you anything.

COVIELLE [*following* NICOLE]. Let me know. . .

NICOLE [*also continuing to walk, without looking at* COVIELLE]. No, I'll say nothing.

CLÉONTE. Please!

LUCILE. No, I tell you.

COVIELLE. Have pity!

NICOLE. Never!

CLÉONTE. I beg you.

LUCILE. Leave me alone.

COVIELLE. I beseech you.

NICOLE. Go away!

CLÉONTE. Lucile!

LUCILE. No.

COVIELLE. Nicole!

NICOLE. Not a word.

CLÉONTE. For God's sake!

LUCILE. I won't.

COVIELLE. Speak to me.

NICOLE. Certainly not.

CLÉONTE. Do please explain.

LUCILE. No. I shall do nothing of the kind.

COVIELLE. Cure my wounded heart.

NICOLE. No. I don't want to.

CLÉONTE. Very well then, since the pain I suffer means so little to you, and you scorn to justify the unworthy return you have made for my devotion, you see me, ungrateful girl, for the last time. I shall go away to a far country and die of love and grief.

COVIELLE [to NICOLE]. And, wherever he goes, I shall bring up the rear.

LUCILE [to CLÉONTE, who is going]. Cléonte!

NICOLE [to COVIELLE, who is following his master]. Covielle!

CLÉONTE [stopping]. Well?

COVIELLE [stopping]. Did you speak?

LUCILE. Where are you going?

CLÉONTE. Where I told you.

COVIELLE. We are going to our death.

LUCILE. You are going to your death, Cléonte?

CLÉONTE. Yes, cruel girl, since that is your pleasure.

LUCILE. My pleasure? My pleasure for you to die?

CLÉONTE. Yes. So it seems.

LUCILE. Who told you that?

CLÉONTE [*approaching* LUCILE]. Do you not wish my death when you refuse to dispel my suspicions.

LUCILE. But whose fault is that? If you had only listened to my explanation, you would have heard that the incident you complain of was due to the presence of an aged aunt, who is completely convinced that the mere approach of a man is fatal to a girl's reputation, and who is for ever preaching that men are devils to be fled from on sight.

NICOLE [*to* COVIELLE]. That is the whole truth of the matter.

CLÉONTE. Is that really the truth, Lucile?

COVIELLE [*to* NICOLE]. You're not making a fool of me?

LUCILE [*to* CLÉONTE]. As true as I stand here.

NICOLE [*to* COVIELLE]. That's exactly how it was.

COVIELLE [*to* CLÉONTE]. Do we surrender?

CLÉONTE. Oh, Lucile, one word from you and all my doubts are gone. We are easily persuaded by those we love.

COVIELLE. Yes the cunning little devils know how to rub us up the right way.

XI   [*Enter* MADAME JOURDAIN.

MADAME JOURDAIN. Ah, I am delighted to see you Cléonte, and you come just at the right moment. My husband will be here directly. So take this opportunity to ask him for Lucile.

—

CLÉONTE. Ah, Madame, such advice is welcome to me and conforms to my dearest wish. I cannot imagine a more agreeable command or a more precious favour.

[*Enter* M. JOURDAIN.   XII

Sir, for a long time I have intended asking you a favour, which is so essential to my happiness that, without the intervention of any third party, I wished to make my request to you in person. To come to the point, Sir, I beg you to accord me the inestimable privilege of becoming your son-in-law.

M. JOURDAIN. Before I reply, Sir, pray tell me one thing. Are you a gentleman by birth?

CLÉONTE. Monsieur, that is a question which most people would make no bones about answering in the affirmative. The word is easily said. The rank is assumed without scruple, and custom seems to smile on the practice. But I, Monsieur, take a more conscientious view of the matter. To an honourable man all imposture is odious. I consider that to make a secret of one's social position, to dress oneself up in borrowed robes and to attempt to pass for what one is not is the height of baseness. My parents were undoubtedly respectable, I have six years of honourable service in the army and I have the means to maintain a reasonable position in society; but, with all that, I will not assume a name to which others, in my place, would no doubt think themselves entitled. To be honest, Monsieur, I must tell you frankly that I am not in your sense a gentleman.

M. JOURDAIN. Give me your hand, Sir. My daughter is not for you.

CLÉONTE. What?

M. JOURDAIN. You are not a gentleman. You shan't have my daughter.

MADAME JOURDAIN. What's all this rubbish about gentlemen? Are we ourselves of the blood of St. Louis?

M. JOURDAIN. Be quiet, wife. I knew you'd interfere.

MADAME JOURDAIN. Do we not both come of respectable tradespeople?

M. JOURDAIN. I was expecting you to say some nonsense like that.

MADAME JOURDAIN. Was not your father in trade the same as mine?

M. JOURDAIN. A plague on the woman! She's always sticking her oar in. If your father was a shopkeeper, so much the worse for him. But for mine, they are ignorant rascals that say so. On one thing I am absolutely determined. My son-in-law shall be a proper gentleman.

MADAME JOURDAIN. What your daughter needs is a husband of her own class. Far better have a decent man who is handsome and well off than a gentleman who is needy and a freak.

NICOLE. That's true. The squire's son in our village is the most stupid and awkward idiot I've ever seen in my life.

M. JOURDAIN [to NICOLE]. Hold your tongue, you impertinent girl; you're always chipping in. I have money enough for my daughter. What I want is rank. I wish her to be a marquise.

MADAME JOURDAIN. A Marquise?

M. JOURDAIN. Yes, a Marquise.

MADAME JOURDAIN. Heaven forbid!

M. JOURDAIN. I am absolutely determined on it.

MADAME JOURDAIN. And I am equally determined against it. Marriages above one's station always end badly. I don't want my son-in-law ever to reproach my daughter with her parentage, or her children be ashamed to call me granny. If ever she came to visit me in all her grandeur, and missed bowing to one of the neighbours, there would be a hundred foolish tongues clacking at once. 'How stuck up Madame la Marquise has become all of a sudden!' they'd say. 'She's nothing but the daughter of Monsieur Jourdain, and was only too happy to play games with us when she was a child. She hasn't always been so high and mighty. Both her grandfathers sold cloth from premises outside the gate of St Innocent and piled up large fortunes for their children, for which they are no doubt paying dearly now in the other world. Honest folk don't get as rich as that.' I want no gossip of that sort. I want a man who will be grateful to me for letting him have my daughter, and to whom I can say: 'Sit down there, son-in-law, come and have a meal with me to-day.'

M. JOURDAIN. You have a petty soul and are happy to live in mediocrity. Not another word! My daughter shall be a Marquise in spite of everybody; and, if you put me in a temper, I'll make her a Duchess.

[*He goes out*

MADAME JOURDAIN. Don't lose heart, Cléonte. [*To* LUCILE]. Come with me, child, and tell your father firmly that, if you can't have Cléonte, you won't marry at all.

[MADAME JOURDAIN, LUCILE *and* NICOLE *go out*   XIII

COVIELLE. A nice mess you've made of things with your fine sentiments!

CLÉONTE. What else could I do? I have a conscience about it, and, in spite of what's happened, I'd do the same again.

COVIELLE. But why did you want to take it so seriously with a man like that? Don't you see that he is mad? Couldn't you have brought yourself to play up to his delusions?

CLÉONTE. True, but I didn't know one had to display a coat of arms to become the son-in-law of Monsieur Jourdain.

COVIELLE [*laughing*]. Ha ha ha!

CLÉONTE. What are you laughing at?

COVIELLE. At an idea that's just come into my head for fooling our fine gentleman and getting you what you want.

CLÉONTE. What's that?

COVIELLE. It's a gorgeous idea.

CLÉONTE. What is it then?

COVIELLE. There was a masquerade the other day, which is the very thing for our purpose, if I can only work it into a little trick I want to play on the old fool. It's a bit far fetched, it's true, but there's not much risk with him. We needn't be too careful. He is the kind of man who would fall in with anything and believe any nonsense we choose to tell him. I've got the actors and the costumes all ready, if only you'll let me set about it.

CLÉONTE. But tell me. . . .

COVIELLE. I'll tell you the whole thing. But let's be off. Here he is, coming back.

XIV   [*They go out. Enter* M. JOURDAIN.

M. JOURDAIN. What the devil is all the fuss about? All they can reproach me with is my love for aristocratic company; and there's nothing I like better. Where else do you see such politeness and distinction? I'd give two fingers of my hand to have been born a Comte or a Marquis.

    [*The lackey goes out.*

LACKEY. Sir, Monsieur le Comte is here with a lady.

M. JOURDAIN. What! Good Heavens! I have some orders to give. Tell them I'll be with them immediately.

XV   [*He goes out. Enter* DORANTE *and* DORIMÈNE.

LACKEY. My master says he will be with you immediately.

DORANTE. Very good!

                          [*The lackey goes out*

DORIMÈNE. Truly, Dorante, I am embarking on strange courses to follow you into a house in which I know no-one.

DORANTE. Where then would you choose, Madame, for my love to pay its homage, since the fear of scandal bars your own door and mine?

DORIMÈNE. But every day draws me insensibly on to accept even greater proofs of your passion. Regardless of my remonstrances you wear down my resistance; and you have a sweet persuasiveness which leads me, in spite of myself, to agree to everything you wish. At first it was assiduous visits; then came declarations, serenades and entertainments, and now it is expensive presents. It is in vain I remonstrate. You pursue your own way, and, little by little, you triumph over my resolution. I no longer know what to say, and I fear in the end you will entice me into marriage, for which I have such a settled aversion.

DORANTE. By God, Madame, you should be in that state already. You are a widow and dependent on no one but yourself. I am my own master and love you more than my life. Why should you not this very day consent to make me happy?

DORIMÈNE. Heavens, Dorante, many qualities are needed on both sides if two people are to live happily together. The most sensible people in the world have often found it difficult to achieve a union which was satisfactory to both.

DORANTE. It is frivolous in you, Madame, to imagine so many difficulties. Your first unfortunate experience is no criterion for the future.

DORIMÈNE. Well, whatever you say, the large sums you spend on me disturb me for two reasons. First, because they engage me further than I wish, and secondly, if I may say it without offence, because I am sure they are larger than you can afford. And I do not wish that.

DORANTE. Pshaw, Madame, trifles merely! It is not by such things as that. . . .

DORIMÈNE. I know quite well what I am talking about. Why, the diamond you have forced me to accept is of a value. . . .

DORANTE. Oh, Madame, I beg you will not rate so highly what, in my devotion, I find but too unworthy of you. Allow me. . . . Here is the master of the house.

—

XVI   [*Enter* M. JOURDAIN.

M. JOURDAIN [*finding, after he has made two bows, that he is too near to* DORIMÈNE]. A little further back, if you please, Madame.

DORIMÈNE. I don't understand.

M. JOURDAIN. A step further back, if you please.

DORIMÈNE. Why so, my dear Sir?

M. JOURDAIN. To give me room for the third one.

DORANTE. Monsieur Jourdain, you see, is quite at home in polite society, Madame.

M. JOURDAIN. Madame, it is a great honour for me to see myself so fortunate as to be so happy as to have the pleasure that you have had the kindness to accord me the favour of doing me the honour of honouring me with the privilege of your presence; and if I had only the merit to merit a merit such as yours, and Heaven, envious of my good fortune, had accorded me the joy of seeing myself worthy . . . to . . . to . . .

DORANTE. Monsieur Jourdain, enough, I beg of you. Madame does not care for compliments. She knows you are a man of wit. [*Aside, to* DORIMÈNE]. He is a worthy tradesman, quite ridiculous, as you see, in all his behaviour.

DORIMÈNE [*aside, to* DORANTE]. That's very easily seen.

DORANTE. Madame, I present to you my best friend.

M. JOURDAIN. You do me too much honour.

DORANTE. A man of the world, I can assure you.

DORIMÈNE. He has my regard.

M. JOURDAIN. I have done nothing yet, Madame, to deserve so great a favour.

DORANTE [*aside, to* M. JOURDAIN]. Whatever you do, don't say anything about the diamond you gave her.

M. JOURDAIN [*aside, to* DORANTE]. But shouldn't I ask her how she likes it?

DORANTE [*aside, to* M. JOURDAIN]. What! Not on your life! It would be in the worst of taste. To do the correct thing, you should behave as if it wasn't you who gave her the present at all. [*Aloud*]. Monsieur Jourdain says he is delighted to welcome you to his house, Madame.

DORIMÈNE. I am much honoured.

M. JOURDAIN [*aside, to* DORANTE]. I am most grateful to you, Sir, for being my intermediary.

DORANTE [*aside, to* M. JOURDAIN]. I had infinite trouble to persuade her to come.

M. JOURDAIN [*aside, to* DORANTE]. I don't know how to thank you.

DORANTE. He says, Madame, that he thinks you the most beautiful person in the world.

DORIMÈNE. He is too kind.

M. JOURDAIN. Madame, the kindness is yours, and . . .

DORANTE. Well, what about dinner?

[*Enter a lackey.*

LACKEY [*to* M. JOURDAIN]. Everything is ready, Sir.

DORANTE. Then let us sit down at once. Call in the musicians.

[*Six cooks, who have prepared the feast, dance, making the third entr'acte. After which they carry in a table, covered with dishes.*]

ACT FOUR

I   *The action is continuous.* DORIMÈNE, M. JOURDAIN, DORANTE, *Three Musicians and a Lackey are discovered.*

DORIMÈNE. Oh, Dorante, what a sumptuous repast!

M. JOURDAIN. A mere nothing, Madame. I only wish it were more worthy to be set before you.

   [DORIMÈNE, M. JOURDAIN *and* DORANTE *sit down to table.*

DORANTE. Monsieur Jourdain is right, Madame, and I am infinitely obliged to him for doing the honours of his house so well. I agree that the repast is unworthy of you. As I ordered it myself, and I lack in these matters the specialized knowledge of some of our friends, you have not, I fear, a very knowledgeable spread; and you will find a certain lack of balance and some barbarous lapses in good taste. Had Damis taken the work in hand, all would have been according to rule. Elegance and erudition would have been apparent everywhere; and he would have hastened to describe in the most accurate and minute detail every dish he offered you, so that you could not fail to recognize his high capacity in the science of good eating. He would have told you of pastry, brown all over, with high battlements of golden crust melting tenderly in the mouth; of wine strong and smooth to the taste, yet powerful enough to escape the charge of insipidity; of a quarter of mutton, garnished with parsley; of a loin of veal, fattened in the water meadows, long, white, delicate and crumbling in the mouth like almond paste; of partridges seasoned with a most surprising flavour; and, for his masterpiece, of a rich pearly broth, accompanied by a plump young turkey, flanked by young pigeons, and crowned with white onions with a flavouring of endive. But, as for me, I confess my ignorance. And, as

Monsieur Jourdain has so excellently put it, I wish the repast were more worthy to be offered you.

DORIMÈNE. The only reply I can make to your compliments is to go on eating.

M. JOURDAIN. Oh, what beautiful hands!

DORIMÈNE. The hands are very ordinary, Monsieur Jourdain. It must be the diamond you mean. That is exceedingly beautiful.

M. JOURDAIN. The diamond, Madame? Heaven forbid I should mention it! I hope I have better taste. The diamond is very poor stuff indeed.

DORIMÈNE. Then you must be very hard to please.

M. JOURDAIN. You are kind enough to . . .

DORANTE [*after a sign to* M. JOURDAIN]. Come, some wine for Monsieur Jourdain and for these gentlemen, who will do us the honour to sing us a drinking song.

DORIMÈNE. Music is the perfect accompaniment to a good dinner. I am being most royally entertained.

M. JOURDAIN. Madame, it is not . . .

DORANTE. Monsieur Jourdain, let us give our attention to these gentlemen. I warrant they will be more worth the hearing.

1ST AND 2ND MUSICIANS [*together, each with a glass in his hand*].

Some wine, sweet Phyllis; let the jug go round;
A glass held by you has a charm like none other;
You and the wine give a zest to each other,
And for both in my heart a new fervour is found.
Betwixt us three let's swear no cause shall sever
The bonds that bind us ever.

As it moistens your lips a new charm it receives,
And your lips from its kiss have a sweetness past telling.
For each, from my heart, new desires are welling

And a draught of you both of my senses bereaves.
Betwixt us three let's swear no cause shall sever
The bonds that bind us ever.

2ND AND 3RD MUSICIANS [*together*].

    Drink, jolly companions, let's drink!
    The fleeting hour invites us;
    The juicy grape delights us,
    We've less time than we think.

    When o'er the dark river Man passes,
    Wine, women and pleasure have fled.
    So come let us fill up our glasses!
    No man can drink when he's dead.

    Let pedants debate, if they can,
    The purest delights of existence.
    We found it without their assistance;
    To drink is the purpose of Man.

    Nor fighting nor spending nor thinking
    Our sorrows will ever disguise.
    True pleasure is only in drinking;
    That's where real happiness lies.

ALL THREE [*together*].

  Drink on, my lads, drink on; let's drink while we are able;
  Drink till our senses reel, and we fall under the table.

DORIMÈNE. I never heard better singing. It was quite enchanting.

M. JOURDAIN. I see something here, Madame, which is even more enchanting.

DORIMÈNE. Oho! Monsieur Jourdain is more gallant than I knew.

DORANTE Why, Madame, for what did you take Monsieur Jourdain?

M. JOURDAIN. I would she would take me for something I could whisper.

DORIMÈNE. What, again?

DORANTE [to DORIMÈNE]. You do not know him, Madame.

M. JOURDAIN. She may know me whenever she has the mind.

DORIMÈNE. Oh, I give up.

DORANTE. He is never at a loss for a repartee. Do you not see, Madame, that Monsieur Jourdain eats everything you have touched.

DORIMÈNE. Monsieur Jourdain ravishes me quite.

M. JOURDAIN. If I could ravish your heart, I would be . . .

[Enter MADAME JOURDAIN.   II

MADAME JOURDAIN. Oho, here's a pretty gathering! It's easy to see that I was not expected. So, my dear husband, this is why you were so anxious to pack me off to dine with my sister. I have just seen a theatre downstairs, and here is a spread fit for a wedding. It's plain now where the money goes. You entertain ladies with music and plays while I am asked to take a walk.

DORANTE. My dear Madame Jourdain, whatever are you talking about? You are very wide of the mark if you think that your husband is at this expense and that he is entertaining Madame. Allow me to inform you that I am the host. All he has done is to lend me his house for the occasion. You should really be more careful in what you say.

M. JOURDAIN. Yes; do you hear, you interfering hussy? It is Monsieur le Comte who is giving this dinner to Madame, who is a person of rank. He has honoured me by making use of my house, and inviting me to sit with them.

MADAME JOURDAIN. You won't take me in like that. I know what I know.

DORANTE. I beg you will get yourself a better pair of spectacles, Madame Jourdain.

MADAME JOURDAIN. I don't want any spectacles, Monsieur le Comte. I can see clear enough without them. I am no fool and I have seen for a long time what is going on. It is shameful for a great gentleman like you to encourage my husband in his silliness. And you too, Madame. It is neither good nor honest in you, a great lady, to sow discord in a household and allow my husband to fall in love with you.

DORIMÈNE. I don't know what this means at all. You must be out of your senses, Dorante, to expose me to the insulting suspicions of this madwoman.

[She goes out

DORANTE [*running after her*]. Madame! Hey, Madame! Where are you going?

M. JOURDAIN. Madame ... Monsieur le Comte, pray make her my excuses and try to persuade her to return.

[DORANTE goes out

Now look what you've done, you wretched creature. You have insulted me before everyone, and driven persons of rank out of my house.

MADAME JOURDAIN. I don't give a fig for their rank!

M. JOURDAIN. I don't know what stops me from battering in your skull with the remains of the dinner you have spoiled.

[Lackeys remove the table.

MADAME JOURDAIN. I don't care a brass farthing. I stand up for my rights, and every wife in the world will be on my side.

[She goes out

M. JOURDAIN. Yes, you're well advised to get out of my sight. She couldn't have come at a worse time. I was just in the vein to say some really good things. I never felt so witty in my life before. But what's this?

[*Enter* COVIELLE *in disguise.*

COVIELLE. I don't know, Sir, if I have the happiness to be known to you.

M. JOURDAIN. No, Sir.

CONVILLE [*measuring with his hand a foot from the ground*]. I knew you when you were so high.

M. JOURDAIN. Me?

COVIELLE. Yes. You were the finest-looking little child in the whole world. All the women used to take you in their arms and kiss you.

M. JOURDAIN. Kiss me?

COVIELLE. Yes. I was a great friend of your late lamented father.

M. JOURDAIN. My late lamented father?

COVIELLE. Yes. Ah, he was a great gentleman he was!

M. JOURDAIN. What's that you say?

COVIELLE. I said he was a great gentleman.

M. JOURDAIN. My father?

COVIELLE. Yes.

M. JOURDAIN. Did you know him well?

COVIELLE. Very well indeed.

M. JOURDAIN. And you knew him for a gentleman?

COVIELLE. Most certainly.

M. JOURDAIN. Then I don't know what's come over everybody.

COVIELLE. What do you mean?

M. JOURDAIN. Why, some people are so stupid as to make out he was a shopkeeper.

COVIELLE. Him a shopkeeper? It's pure calumny. He never was. All he did was that, being very good-natured, and knowledgeable in all sorts of stuffs and materials, he used to go about everywhere choosing such goods, had them brought to his house, and distributed them to his friends for money.

M. JOURDAIN. I am overjoyed to make your acquaintance, Sir. You will be able to bear witness that my father was a gentleman.

COVIELLE. I will maintain it before the whole world.

M. JOURDAIN. You will oblige me infinitely. What business brings you here?

COVIELLE. Since I knew that great gentleman, your father, as I have just told you, I have travelled all round the world.

M. JOURDAIN. All round the world?

COVIELLE. Yes.

M. JOURDAIN. That's a good long way off, I'll be bound.

COVIELLE. You're right. It is. I returned from the last of my voyages only four days ago, and, because of the interest I take in everything which concerns you, I have hastened to bring you a wonderful piece of news.

M. JOURDAIN. And what may that be?

COVILLE. You know that the son of the Grand Turk is here?

M. JOURDAIN. I? No.

COVIELLE. You surprise me. Why, he has a most magnificent following. Everyone is flocking to see him. He has been received in this country as a very great personage indeed.

M. JOURDAIN. Well, well. To think of that!

COVIELLE. But what makes it of such importance to you is that he has fallen in love with your daughter.

M. JOURDAIN. The son of the Grand Turk?

COVIELLE. Yes. And he wishes to be your son-in-law.

M. JOURDAIN. My son-in-law? The son of the Grand Turk?

COVIELLE. The son of the Grand Turk your son-in-law. I went to call on him, and, as I understand his language, we soon got quite intimate, and, after a little general conversation, he said: 'Acciam croc soler onch alla moustaph gidelum amanahem varahini oussere carbulath', which means: 'Do you know a beautiful young lady, the daughter of Monsieur Jourdain, a gentleman of Paris?'

M. JOURDAIN. The son of the Grand Turk said that about me?

COVIELLE. Yes. And when I told him that I knew you very well and had seen your daughter, 'Ah!' he said, 'Marababa sahem' which means: 'Oh, how I love her!'

M. JOURDAIN. 'Marababa sahem' means: 'Oh, how I love her?'

COVIELLE. Yes.

M. JOURDAIN. Faith, I'm glad you told me. I should never have guessed by myself that 'Marababa sahem' meant: 'Oh, how I love her!' What a fine language Turkish is!

COVIELLE. There couldn't be a finer. Do you know what 'cacaracamouchen' means?

M. JOURDAIN. Cacaracamouchen? No.

COVIELLE. It means: 'My dear soul.'

M. JOURDAIN. 'Cacaracamouchen' means: 'My dear soul'?

COVIELLE. Yes.

M. JOURDAIN. How wonderful! 'Cacaracamouchen: My dear soul.' Did you ever? I'm quite astounded.

COVIELLE. Well then, to bring my mission to a proper conclusion, he is coming to ask you for your daughter in marriage; and, so that he may have a father-in-law who is worthy of him, he is going to create you a Mamamouchi, which is a title of great dignity in his country.

M. JOURDAIN. Mamamouchi?

COVIELLE. Yes, Mamamouchi; that is to say in our language, Paladin. Paladin is one of those old . . . er . . . well, Paladin.

There is no nobler title in the world. You will be equal to all the great ones of the earth.

M. JOURDAIN. The son of the Grand Turk does me much honour. I beg you will take me to him so that I may thank him.

COVIELLE. What! But he is coming here.

M. JOURDAIN. Coming here?

COVIELLE. Yes. And he is bringing with him everything necessary for the ceremony of your installation.

M. JOURDAIN. He is not losing any time.

COVIELLE. His love will brook no delay.

M. JOURDAIN. The only thing that worries me is that my daughter is a pig-headed little fool who is infatuated with a certain Cléonte; and she swears she won't marry anyone else.

COVIELLE. She'll change her mind quick enough when she sees the son of the Grand Turk. And there's another marvellous thing. The son of the Grand Turk resembles this Cléonte very closely. I have seen him too. He was pointed out to me. And the love she has for the one may easily pass to the other, and ... But I hear him coming. He's here.

IV   [*Enter* CLÉONTE, *dressed as a Turk, with three pages in attendance.*

CLÉONTE. Ambousahim oqui boraf, Jordina, Salamalequi.

COVIELLE [*to* M. JOURDAIN]. That means: 'Monsieur Jourdain, may your heart be all the year like a rose tree in flower!' It's one of the pretty sayings they have in that country.

M. JOURDAIN. I am His Turkish Highness's very humble servant.

COVIELLE. Carigar camboto oustin moraf.

CLÉONTE. Oustin yoc catamalequi basum base alla moran.

COVIELLE. He says: 'May Heaven give you the strength of lions and the subtlety of serpents!'

M. JOURDAIN. His Turkish Highness does me too much honour. I wish him every kind of prosperity.

COVIELLE. Ossa binamen sadoc baballi oracaf ouram.

CLÉONTE. Bel-men.

COVIELLE. He says you must go with him at once to get ready for the ceremony, so that he may the sooner see your daughter and conclude the marriage.

M. JOURDAIN. Did he say all that in two words?

COVIELLE. Yes. The Turkish language is like that. It says a lot in very few words. Go with him at once. Don't lose a moment.

[CLÉONTE *with his train and* M. JOURDAIN *go out* V

COVIELLE. Ha! Ha! Ha! Faith, I could split my sides with laughing. What a fool! If he'd learnt his part by heart, he couldn't have played it better. Ha! Ha!

[*Enter* DORANTE.

I beg you will help us, Sir, in a little game we are playing.

DORANTE. Ha! Ha! Covielle. I wouldn't have recognized you. You *have* got yourself up.

COVIELLE. Yes, haven't I? Ha! Ha!

DORANTE. What are you laughing at?

COVIELLE. Something, Sir, that well deserves it.

DORANTE. What is it then?

COVIELLE. If I gave you a hundred guesses, Sir, you'd never guess the trick we're playing on Monsieur Jourdain to get him to give his daughter to my master.

DORANTE. I can't guess the trick, but I guess that it won't fail of its purpose, since you have the matter in hand.

COVIELLE. I see, Monsieur, that you know your Covielle.

DORANTE. Tell me all about it.

COVIELLE. Be good enough to come this way to leave room
for what I see coming. You will be able to watch part of the
story while I tell you the rest.

[*They withdraw*

The Turkish ceremony to ennoble M. JOURDAIN *is set to music
and is danced as the fourth entr'acte.*

*The Muphti, four Dervishes, six dancing Turks and six Turkish
musicians together with other Musicians playing Turkish instruments perform the ceremony.*

*The Muphti invokes Mahomet with the twelve Turks and four
Dervishes: after which* M. JOURDAIN *is led up to him, dressed
in Turkish costume but without a turban or sabre.*

THE MUPHTI [*to* M. JOURDAIN].

> If you savvee,
> Answer, answer.
> You no savvee,
> Keep your mouth shut.
> I am Muphti.
> Who may you be?
> Non comprenny?
> Keep your mouth shut.

*The Muphti asks the Turks present in the same language what is
M.* JOURDAIN'S *religion, and they confirm that he is a Muslim.
The Muphti then invokes Mahomet in lingua franca,* singing
the following:*

THE MUPHTI To Mahomet, for Giourdina,

> I will pray both morn and e'en-a
> I will make a Paladina
> Of Giourdina, of Giourdina;
> Turban give, and sabre-ina,
> Galley too, and brigantina,
> For defence of Palestina.
> To Mahomet, for Giourdina,
> I will pray both morn and e'en-a.

—

THE MUPHTI [*asking the Turks whether* M. JOURDAIN *will remain true to the Muslim religion, and singing the following*]

THE MUPHTI [*to* TURKS]. Good Turk is this Giourdina?

TURKS. Ay! By Alla! Ay! By Alla!

THE MUPHTI [*singing and dancing*]. Ha la ba, ba la chou, ba la ba, ba la da.

TURKS. Ha la ba, ba la chou, ba la ba, ba la da.

The Muphti prepares to give M. JOURDAIN *his turban, and sings:*

THE MUPHTI [*to* M. JOURDAIN]. You're no ill-doer?

TURKS. No, no, no.

THE MUPHTI. Nor dire deceiver?

TURKS. No, no no.

THE MUPHTI. This turban then receive-a.

TURKS. You're no ill-doer?
No, no, no.
Nor dire deceiver?
No, no, no.
This turban then receive-a.

The Muphti and the Dervishes put on their ceremonial turbans: the Muphti is given the Koran, and he makes a further invocation to Mahomet together with all the Turks present; then he gives M. JOURDAIN *his sabre and sings:*

THE MUPHTI. Thou art noble, 'tis no fake.
This sabre take.

TURKS [*drawing their sabres, and pretending to strike* M. JOURDAIN *with them*]
Thou art noble, 'tis no fake.
This sabre take.

The Muphti tells the Turks to beat M. JOURDAIN *with sticks, which they do in time*

THE MUPHTI. Bastonnada
Harder! Harder!

TURKS. Harder! Harder!
Bastonnada.

The Muphti, having had M. JOURDAIN *beaten, then sings*:

THE MUPHTI. Feel no shame-a,
This is the last stroke of the game-a.

TURKS. Feel no shame-a,
This is the last stroke of the game-a.

The Muphti begins yet another invocation, and retires at the end of the ceremony in the company of all the Turks, who dance, sing and play Turkish instruments.

ACT FIVE

I MONSIEUR JOURDAIN *discovered in his Turkish costume. Enter* MADAME JOURDAIN.

MADAME JOURDAIN. Heaven have mercy upon us! What a sight! What in the name of wonder is all this? Are you wearing this for a bet, or has the Carnival begun? For pity's sake tell me who has decked you out like that.

M. JOURDAIN. Did you ever hear such impertinence! To speak like that to a Mamamouchi!

MADAME JOURDAIN. A what?

M. JOURDAIN. You will have to pay me more respect in future. I have just been made a Mamamouchi.

MADAME JOURDAIN. What do you mean with your Mamamouchi?

M. JOURDAIN. Mamamouchi, I tell you. I am a Mamamouchi.

MADAME JOURDAIN. Well, what kind of animal is that?

M. JOURDAIN. Mamamouchi? In our language we should say Paladin.

MADAME JOURDAIN. Baladin? Do you mean to begin ballet dancing at your age?

—

M. JOURDAIN. Oh, what an ignorant woman! I said Paladin. It is a grand title they've given me. I have just been installed with the correct ceremonial.

MADAME JOURDAIN. What ceremonial?

M. JOURDAIN. 'To Mahomet for Jordina.'

MADAME JOURDAIN. Eh?

M. JOURDAIN. Jordina means Jourdain.

MADAME JOURDAIN. Well?

M. JOURDAIN. 'I will make a Paladina of Jordina.'

MADAME JOURDAIN. What?

M. JOURDAIN. 'Turban give and brigantina.'

MADAME JOURDAIN. I can't understand a word.

M. JOURDAIN. 'For defence of Palestina.'

MADAME JOURDAIN. But what does it mean?

M. JOURDAIN. 'Harder! Harder! Bastonnada.'

MADAME JOURDAIN. What is all this gibberish?

M. JOURDAIN. 'Feel no shame-a. This is the last stroke of the game-a.'

MADAME JOURDAIN. What on earth are you talking about?

M. JOURDAIN [*singing and dancing*]. Hou la ba, ba la chou, ba la ba, ba la da. [*He falls down*].

MADAME JOURDAIN. Heaven save us! My husband's gone mad.

M. JOURDAIN [*getting up*]. Be silent, you insolent woman, and show some respect for Monsieur the Mamamouchi.

[*He goes out*

MADAME JOURDAIN. He is out of his mind. I'll after him and prevent him leaving the house. [*Seeing* DORIMÈNE *and* DORANTE *coming*]. Heavens alive, here's the rest of the bunch! Troubles are coming upon us in battalions.

[*She goes out*

II   [*Enter* DORANTE *and* DORIMÈNE.

DORANTE. I promise you, Madame, you will see the funniest
thing you ever saw in your life. I don't believe, if you
searched the whole world, you could find a man as
crackbrained as he is. And then, Madame, we must do
what we can to forward the suit of young Cléonte by
playing up to his little game. He is an excellent young man
who should have our support.

DORIMÈNE. I have a great regard for him. He certainly
deserves to be happy.

DORANTE. And then, apart from that, Madame, there is the
ballet, which it would be a great pity to miss. I must have
your opinion as to how far my idea has been successful.

DORIMÈNE. I have already seen the most magnificent
preparations for it. But frankly, Dorante, I can no longer
permit this sort of thing. I am determined to put an end to
your extravagance, and by the means best calculated to
bring it about. I shall marry you at once. That method is
quite infallible. All such expenses come to an end with
marriage.

DORANTE. Oh, Madame, have you really come to so delicious
a resolve?

DORIMÈNE. It is for no reason in the world but to prevent
you ruining yourself. I can see that, without it, you will
soon not have a sou left.

DORANTE. I am infinitely touched, Madame, by your delicate
consideration for my financial state. Both it and my heart
are entirely at your service. You may do as you will with
either of them.

DORIMÈNE. I shall not fail, with both. But here is our man.
What a marvellous sight!

III   [*Enter* M. JOURDAIN.

DORANTE. Sir, we have come to congratulate you on your
new dignity, and to rejoice with you at your daughter's
marriage with the son of the Grand Turk.

M. JOURDAIN [*bowing in the Turkish manner*]. Sir, may you have the strength of serpents and the subtlety of lions!

DORIMÈNE. I am glad to be one of the first, Sir, to offer you my felicitations on your new high position.

M. JOURDAIN. Madame, I pray that your rose tree may flower all the year round. I am most grateful for the interest and honour that has been paid me, and I am delighted to see you here again that I may offer you my humblest apologies for the folly of my wife.

DORIMÈNE. I beg you will not mention it, Sir. Such feelings in her are only natural. Your love must be precious to her, and it is not to be wondered at that the possession of a man such as yourself should give her an occasional alarm.

M. JOURDAIN. You have the whole possession of my heart, Madame.

DORANTE. You see, Madame, that Monsieur Jourdain is not one of those people who are dazzled by good fortune. Even in his greatness he still remembers his friends.

DORIMÈNE. It is the true sign of a noble soul.

DORANTE. But where is His Turkish Highness? As your friends we would like to pay him our respects.

M. JOURDAIN. Here he comes now. I have sent to fetch my daughter that I may give him her hand.

[*Enter* CLÉONTE *in his Turkish dress.*   IV

DORANTE [*to* CLÉONTE]. Sir, we have come to make our bow to your Highness as the friends of your father-in-law. We are, most respectfully, your very humble servants.

M. JOURDAIN. Where is the interpreter to tell him who you are and what you say? He'll do your business for you. He speaks Turkish like a native. Where the devil has he got to? [*To* CLÉONTE]. Strouf, strif, strof, straf. Monsieur is a grande segnore, grande segnore, and Madame a granda dama, granda dama. [*Seeing that he is not understood*]. Ah!

[*To* CLÉONTE]. Monsieur he French Mamamouchi, and Madame French Mamamouchess. I'm sure I cannot make it clearer. Ah, good here's the interpreter!

[*Enter* COVIELLE *still in disguise.*

Where ever have you been? We couldn't say a word without you. [*Indicating* CLÉONTE]. Tell him that Monsieur and Madame are persons of the very highest quality who are come to greet him as my friends, and assure him of their goodwill. [*To* DORANTE *and* DORIMÈNE]. Just listen how he'll jabber away.

COVIELLE. Alabala crociam acci boram alabamen.

CLÉONTE. Catalequi tubal ourin soter amalouchan.

M. JOURDAIN [*to* DORIMÈNE *and* DORANTE]. You see?

COVIELLE. He says: 'May the rain of prosperity water the garden of your family for ever!'

M. JOURDAIN. Didn't I tell you he could speak Turkish?

DORIMÈNE. Wonderful!

V   [*Enter* LUCILE.

M. JOURDAIN. Come here, my daughter, and give your hand to Monsieur, who does you the honour to ask for you in marriage.

LUCILE. Heavens, father, what have you got on? Are you dressed for a comedy?

M. JOURDAIN. No. It is no comedy, but a very serious matter; and one which will bring you much honour. [*Indicating* CLÉONTE]. There stands your husband.

LUCILE. My husband?

M. JOURDAIN. Yes, your husband. Put your hand in his, and give thanks to Heaven for your good fortune.

LUCILE. I do not wish to marry.

M. JOURDAIN. But I do wish it, and I am your father.

LUCILE. I won't.

—

M. JOURDAIN. Now let's have no nonsense. Come, your hand.

LUCILE. No, father. I have told you already that no power on earth shall make me take any husband but Cléonte. I am ready to suffer anything rather than . . . [*Suddenly recognizing* CLÉONTE]. You are my father. You have a right to my obedience. Dispose of me as you will.

M. JOURDAIN. That's better. I am delighted to see you return to your duty so promptly. It is very gratifying to have such an obedient child.

[*Enter* MADAME JOURDAIN.   VI

MADAME JOURDAIN. What's this I hear? They tell me you are going to give your daughter to a fellow in fancy dress.

M. JOURDAIN. Hold your tongue, you silly creature. Will you never learn sense? You're always interfering with your foolish prejudices.

MADAME JOURDAIN. It's you who will never learn sense. You go from one act of madness to another. What are you up to here with all this rabble?

M. JOURDAIN. I am going to marry our daughter to the son of the Grand Turk.

MADAME JOURDAIN. The son of the Grand Turk?

M. JOURDAIN [*indicating* COVIELLE]. Yes. Pay him your respects at once through the interpreter there.

MADAME JOURDAIN. I don't need any interpreter. I'll tell him straight out that he shan't have my daughter.

M. JOURDAIN. Will you be quiet, woman!

DORANTE. Why, Madame Jourdain, will you set your face against such an honour as that? Will you refuse His Turkish Highness for a son-in-law?

MADAME JOURDAIN. Kindly mind your own business, Monsieur le Comte.

DORIMÈNE. Such a great compliment is not to be lightly rejected.

—

MADAME JOURDAIN. I'll thank you too, Madame, not to interfere in what doesn't concern you.

DORANTE. Our friendship makes us anxious for your welfare.

MADAME JOURDAIN. I shall get along very well without your friendship.

DORANTE. Your daughter has consented to obey her father.

MADAME JOURDAIN. My daughter consents to marry a Turk?

DORANTE. Most certainly.

MADAME JOURDAIN. She is able to forget Cléonte?

DORANTE. What will one *not* do to be a great lady?

MADAME JOURDAIN. If she could do such a thing I'd strangle her with my own hands.

M. JOURDAIN. Here's a lot of cackle! I say the marriage shall go forward.

MADAME JOURDAIN. And I say it shall not.

M. JOURDAIN. Babble! Babble! Babble!

LUCILE. Mother!

MADAME JOURDAIN. Go to, you're a hussy.

M. JOURDAIN [*to* MADAME JOURDAIN]. What! You call her names for obeying me!

MADAME JOURDAIN. Yes. She's as much mine as yours.

COVIELLE [*to* MADAME JOURDAIN]. Madame!

MADAME JOURDAIN. What do you want?

COVIELLE. One word only.

MADAME JOURDAIN. It will have no effect on me.

COVIELLE [*to* M. JOURDAIN]. Sir, if I may speak one word to her in private, I promise to make her agree to what you want.

MADAME JOURDAIN. I'll never agree.

COVIELLE. Only hear me.

MADAME JOURDAIN. No.

M. JOURDAIN [*to* MADAME JOURDAIN]. Will you listen to what he has to say?

MADAME JOURDAIN. No, I won't. I don't want to listen to what he has to say.

M. JOURDAIN. He will tell you . . .

MADAME JOURDAIN. I don't want him to tell me anything.

M. JOURDAIN. Was there ever such female obstinacy! What harm can it do you to listen to him?

COVIELLE. Only listen. Afterwards you can do what ever you like.

MADAME JOURDAIN. Oh, very well then. What is it?

COVIELLE [*aside, to* MADAME JOURDAIN]. We've been making signs to you for ever so long. Don't you see that we're only playing up to your husband's foibles, and making a fool of him? It's Cléonte himself who is the son of the Grand Turk.

MADAME JOURDAIN. Ha! Ha!

COVIELLE. And it is I, Covielle, who am the interpreter.

MADAME JOURDAIN. Oh, if that's how it is, I give in at once.

COVIELLE. Don't seem to notice anything.

MADAME JOURDAIN [*aloud*].Very well then, I agree. I consent to the marriage.

M. JOURDAIN. Good! Then everyone has come to their senses. [*To* MADAME JOURDAIN]. You wouldn't listen to him. I knew he would explain to you who the son of the Grand Turk was.

MADAME JOURDAIN. He has explained most admirably. I am more than satisfied. Let us send for the notary.

DORANTE. Well said! And so that you may feel quite at your ease, Madame Jourdain, and put away the jealousy you have conceived of your husband, Madame la Marquise and I will make use of the same notary to be married ourselves.

MADAME JOURDAIN. I consent to that too.

M. JOURDAIN [*aside, to* DORANTE]. Just to put her off the scent, eh?

DORANTE [*aside, to* M. JOURDAIN]. Yes, that's it. We must do something to keep her quiet.

M. JOURDAIN [*aside*]. Good! Good! [*Aloud*]. Let the notary be sent for.

DORANTE. And, until he comes, and while he is drawing up the contracts, let's see the ballet, and give this entertainment to His Turkish Highness.

M. JOURDAIN. An excellent idea! Come, let's take our places.

MADAME JOURDAIN. But what about Nicole?

M. JOURDAIN. I give her to the interpreter. And my wife—to anyone who will take her off my hands.

COVIELLE. Monsieur, I thank you with all my heart. [*Aside*]. If anyone is madder than this, I'll spread his fame as far as the antipodes.

The comedy finishes with the Ballet des Nations, *written in collaboration with Lulli and performed subsequently by the latter in 1672 as a prologue to his first opera* Les Fêtes de l'Amour et de Bacchus. *It is a mild satire directed against non-Parisians—Gascons, Swiss, Spaniards and Italians—and has no thematic links with the play.*

SCAPIN THE SCHEMER

[*Les Fourberies de Scapin*]

Les Fourberies de Scapin, *comedy in three acts, was first produced at the Théâtre du Palais-Royal, Paris, with Molière in the part of Scapin, on 24 May 1671.*

CHARACTERS

ARGANTE, *father of Octave and Zerbinette*

GÉRONTE, *father of Léandre and Hyacinthe*

OCTAVE, *son of Argante, in love with Hyacinthe*

LÉANDRE, *son of Géronte, in love with Zerbinette*

ZERBINETTE, *believed to be a gipsy, later recognized to be the daughter of Argante; and lover of Léandre*

HYACINTHE, *daughter of Géronte, in love with Octave*

SCAPIN, *a trickster, valet to Léandre*

SYLVESTRE, *valet to Octave*

NÉRINE, *Hyacinthe's nurse*

CARLE, *a trickster*

TWO PORTERS

The scene is set in Naples

ACT ONE

[*Enter* OCTAVE *and* SYLVESTRE.

OCTAVE. Could there be worse news for a suitor? My case is desperate indeed. You say, Sylvestre, you have just heard at the harbour that my father is coming home?

SYLVESTRE. Yes, Sir.

OCTAVE. He is expected to arrive this morning?

SYLVESTRE. This very morning.

OCTAVE. And he comes for the purpose of finding me a wife?

SYLVESTRE. Yes, Sir.

OCTAVE. A daughter of Seigneur Géronte?

SYLVESTRE. A daughter of Seigneur Géronte.

OCTAVE. That the girl has been sent for from Taranto?

SYLVESTRE. Yes.

OCTAVE. And you heard all this news from my uncle?

SYLVESTRE. From your uncle.

OCTAVE. Who had it from my father in a letter?

SYLVESTRE. In a letter.

OCTAVE. And my uncle knows all about our affairs?

SYLVESTRE. All about our affairs.

OCTAVE. Oh, for Heaven's sake, tell me everything straight out. Don't make me drag it out of you one word at a time.

SYLVESTRE. What more is there to say? You've described the situation quite correctly. You haven't forgotten a thing.

OCTAVE. Well, give me some advice then. Tell me what I am to do, in the difficult position in which I find myself.

SYLVESTRE. Upon my word, I'm as much at a loss as you are. I have as much need of advice myself.

OCTAVE. His coming home now has completely ruined me.

SYLVESTRE. Me too.

OCTAVE. When my father hears what I have done, I shall have a regular storm of reproaches showering about my ears.

SYLVESTRE. Reproaches break no bones. I would to God I could get off so cheaply! But it looks as if I should have to pay a bit dearer for your foolery. I think I see a gathering storm of blows ready to burst on my shoulders.

OCTAVE. How the hell am I to get out of this mess?

SYLVESTRE. You should have thought of that before you got into it.

OCTAVE. Oh, you make me sick with your ill-timed moralizing.

SYLVESTRE. You make me far sicker with your mad goings on.

OCTAVE. But what now? What am I to do? Where is there a way out?

II   [Enter SCAPIN.

SCAPIN. What is it, Seigneur Octave? What's the matter? What's all the fuss about? You seem in trouble.

OCTAVE. Oh, my dear Scapin, I am undone, ruined; I am the most unfortunate of men.

SCAPIN. How's that?

OCTAVE. Haven't you heard then?

SCAPIN. No. Not a word.

OCTAVE. My father is coming home with Seigneur Géronte, to find me a wife.

SCAPIN. Well, what is there so terrible in that?

OCTAVE. Alas, you little know why I am so upset!

SCAPIN. No, but I shall when you've told me; and I am an excellent comforter, always ready to sympathize with young gentlemen's troubles.

OCTAVE. Oh, Scapin, if you can only find some way of getting me out of this fix, I'll be beholden to you for more than my life.

SCAPIN. Well, to tell you the truth, there is very little I find impossible when I really set about it. There is no doubt that the gods have given me a genius for all those subtle schemes and inventive intrigues, which go by the name of trickery; and I can say without boasting that you would have to look far to find anyone quicker than myself at discovering expedients and devices, or who had gained a greater reputation in this noble art. But Lord! talent isn't rated at its true value nowadays, and, since a little mishap I had, I have given up such practices.

OCTAVE. Why, what was that, Scapin?

SCAPIN. A little affair which got me into trouble with the law.

OCTAVE. The law?

SCAPIN. Yes: we had a slight difference of opinion.

SYLVESTRE. You and the law?

SCAPIN. Yes. They treated me very badly; and I was so disgusted at the ingratitude of today's world that I decided to give it all up. But come, tell me about yourself.

OCTAVE. You remember, Scapin, how two months ago, my father and Seigneur Géronte went on a voyage together, to look after some business in which they both had an interest?

SCAPIN. Yes, I remember that.

OCTAVE. Léandre and I were left at home. I was to be looked after by Sylvestre here, and Léandre by you.

SCAPIN. Yes. And I have discharged my trust well.

OCTAVE. Shortly after, Léandre saw a young gipsy girl and fell in love with her.

SCAPIN. Yes. I know that too.

OCTAVE. As we were great friends, he soon took me into his confidence, and brought me to see the girl, whom I found to be pretty certainly, but not the pearl of beauty he wished me to find her. All day long he would talk of nothing but her, exaggerate her beauty and grace, praise her intelligence, and go into raptures over the charm of her conversation, which he would repeat, for my benefit, to the last syllable, and expect me to agree that it was perfection. Sometimes he would even quarrel with me for not being more impressed by what he told me, and reproach me for my indifference to the joys of love.

SCAPIN. I confess I don't yet see the drift of all this.

OCTAVE. One day, as we were on our way to see the good folk who were the young girl's guardians, we heard a sound of wailing and sobbing from a little house in a side street; we enquired what was happening, and a woman told us there were some strangers living there in such a pitiable condition that only hearts of stone could be unmoved by it.

SCAPIN. What on earth is all this rigmarole leading to?

OCTAVE. Being curious, I persuaded Léandre to come with me and see. We went into a room, where we saw an old woman lying at the point of death, a sobbing maid, and a young girl in a flood of tears, the most touchingly beautiful creature I have ever seen.

SCAPIN. Aha! Aha!

OCTAVE. Any other girl would have looked a perfect fright in such a state, for she had nothing on but a wretched little bodice and petticoat, made of common fustian, and a small yellow cap perched on the top of her head which allowed her hair to fall down over her shoulders in wild confusion.

But, in spite of this, her whole person seemed to me to be the perfection of attractiveness and grace.

SCAPIN. Aha! Now I see what we are getting at.

OCTAVE. If you had seen her, Scapin, in that state, you would have thought her adorable.

SCAPIN. I've no doubt at all of that; for, even though I didn't see her, I can well believe she was enchanting.

OCTAVE. Her tears were not that unpleasant kind which disfigure the face. She had a touching grace in her very weeping, and her grief was the most beautiful thing in the world.

SCAPIN. I'm sure it was.

OCTAVE. There wasn't a dry eye among us as she threw herself lovingly on the body of the dying woman and called her 'dearest mother'. No one could have been untouched by so sweet a nature.

SCAPIN. It certainly must have been very affecting. And so this same sweet nature made you fall in love with her.

OCTAVE. Oh, Scapin, a savage would have loved her.

SCAPIN. Of course. How could he help himself?

OCTAVE. I tried with a few words to comfort this sweet afflicted heart, and then we came away. I asked Léandre what he thought of her, and he answered coldly that he found her 'pretty enough'. Pretty enough indeed! His insensitivity annoyed me; but I was by no means anxious for him to see the effect her beauty had made on me.

SYLVESTRE. If you don't cut this short, we shall be here till to-morrow. Allow me to finish it in two words. His heart was on fire from that moment, and he couldn't live without going to console this bereaved person whom he found so attractive. The servant, now become the guardian by the mother's death, refuses to allow his frequent visits, and my master sinks into the depths of despair. He urges, begs, implores. All to no avail. She tells him that the girl, though utterly destitute and without protection, is of good family, and that, unless he intends to marry her, his advances cannot be considered. Opposition, of course, only makes the flame burn fiercer. He turns it over in his mind, weighs the pros and cons, makes up his mind at last, and there he is, a husband of three day's standing.

SCAPIN. I see.

SYLVESTRE. Now, add to this his father's sudden return, who was not expected for at least two months; the discovery that his uncle knows about his marriage; and the other match they want to make between my master and a daughter of Géronte by a second wife he is supposed to have married at Taranto.

OCTAVE. And add to that again the poverty in which the dear child is living, and my utter inability to find any means of supporting her.

SCAPIN. Is that all? Why, you are raising Cain over a mere bagatelle. There's nothing here to be so alarmed about. You should be ashamed to be stumped by such a trifle. What the devil? Do you mean to tell me that at your age your wits aren't equal to finding some ingenious little ruse to pull your chestnuts out of the fire? The devil take you, fool that you are! I wish I had had the opportunity in the old days to trick my elders and betters. I would have handled them both with the greatest of ease. Why, I was not that high [*measuring with his hand*] when I was already famous for tricks of that kind.

SYLVESTRE. I've not been blessed with your talents. I haven't your genuis for getting into trouble with the police.

OCTAVE. Here comes my darling Hyacinthe.

III   [*Enter* HYACINTHE.

HYACINTHE. Oh, Octave, is it true what Sylvestre has told Nérine, that your father is coming home and means to marry you to another?

OCTAVE. Yes, my sweet Hyacinthe, and I am appalled at the news. But what's this? You're crying? Why those tears? Surely you cannot doubt I will be faithful. Don't you know how much I love you?

HYACINTHE. Yes, Octave, I'm sure you love me now, but .... I am not sure that you will love me always.

OCTAVE. What? Could I love you at one moment, and not love you all my life?

HYACINTHE. I have been told, Octave, that our love lasts longer than yours, and that men's passions cool as easily as they are set on fire.

OCTAVE. Oh, my dear Hyacinthe, then my heart is not like other men's. I swear to you that I shall love you till my dying day.

HYACINTHE. I am willing to believe you mean what you say, and I don't doubt you are sincere. But I fear an influence which may outweigh in your heart all the tender feelings you have for me. You are dependent on a father who intends to marry you to another woman, and, if that were to happen, I should die.

OCTAVE. No father in the world, my darling Hyacinthe, can make me unfaithful to you; and, if necessary, I would be ready to fly the country this very day, rather than part from you. I have not seen the lady they have chosen for me, but I have already taken a violent dislike to her; and, without being cruel, I could wish that the sea might keep us apart for ever. Dry your eyes then, I beg you, my sweet Hyacinthe. It breaks my heart to see you cry.

HYACINTHE. Very well then, I will try to dry my tears, and wait patiently for whatever Fate sends us.

OCTAVE. Fate will be kind to us.

HYACINTHE. It cannot be against me, if you are true.

OCTAVE. I will be true, I promise you.

—

HYACINTHE. Then I shall be happy.

SCAPIN [*aside*]. A sensible girl, and not bad looking either.

OCTAVE [*indicating* SCAPIN]. Here is a man, who, if he only would agree to, could be of the greatest use to us.

SCAPIN. I have forsworn the world. But, if you both begged me very hard, perhaps. . . .

OCTAVE. If begging is all that's needed, I beg you with all my heart to find us a way out of this predicament.

SCAPIN [*to* HYACINTHE]. And have you nothing to say to me?

HYACINTHE. I beg you, by all you hold dearest in the world, to help us.

SCAPIN. I suppose I must give in, and take pity on you. Very well. I'll help you.

OCTAVE. I swear . . . .

SCAPIN. Shhh! [*To* HYACINTHE]. Go in now, and don't worry.

[HYACINTHE *goes out*

[*To* OCTAVE]. And you, brace yourself to face up your father.

OCTAVE. The very thought of it makes me tremble. I have a constitutional shyness I can't overcome.

SCAPIN. You must stand firm at the first shock, or he will take advantage of your weakness to treat you like a child. Come now. Try to look a little more confident. Be firm. Get answers ready for everything he can say.

OCTAVE. I'll do my best.

SCAPIN. Let's have a run through now, to get your hand in. I'll rehearse you in your part and see if you do it well. Come on. An air of determination. Head up. Eyes full of self-confidence.

OCTAVE. Like that?

SCAPIN. A little more still.

—

OCTAVE. So?

SCAPIN. That's better, Imagine now that I am your father, who has just arrived, and answer me boldly as you would him. 'What, you good-for-nothing, you rogue, you wretch, unworthy son of such a father, do you dare appear before me after your fine behaviour, after the cowardly trick you have played me in my absence? Is this the result of all my care, you knave; is this the fruit of my pains; the respect that you owe me, the respect that you pay me?'—Come on now—'You have the impertinence, you cheat, to plight your faith without your father's consent, to contract a clandestine marriage! Answer me, you scoundrel, answer me. Let's hear some of your fine excuses'—What the devil! You stand there tongue-tied.

OCTAVE. It's ... I can hardly believe it's not my father speaking.

SCAPIN. Well, that's the very reason you mustn't behave like a baby.

OCTAVE. I'll get a firmer hold on myself. I'll speak out like a man.

SCAPIN. Promise now.

OCTAVE. Yes, I promise.

SYLVESTRE. Here's your father coming now.

OCTAVE. Oh God! I'm undone.

[*He runs away*

SCAPIN. Hi, Octave! Wait, Octave! There now! He's run away. What a poor creature! We'll have to face the old man ourselves.

SYLVESTRE. What am I to say to him?

SCAPIN. Let me do the talking, and follow my lead.

[SYLVESTRE *retires backstage*

[*Enter* ARGANTE.   IV

ARGANTE [*who does not see them*]. Did anyone ever hear of such behaviour?

SCAPIN [*to* SYLVESTRE]. He has heard the whole thing already; and it's so much on his mind that he talks about it aloud to himself when he's alone.

ARGANTE. What appalling temerity!

SCAPIN [*to* SYLVESTRE]. Let's play the eavesdropper for a bit.

ARGANTE. I should very much like to know what excuses they will make for this fine marriage.

SCAPIN [*aside*]. We've got that all cut and dried.

ARGANTE. Will they try to deny it, I wonder?

SCAPIN [*aside*]. No, we never thought of it.

ARGANTE. Or attempt to justify it?

SCAPIN [*aside*]. We might have a shot at that.

ARGANTE. Will they try to fob me off with a cock-and-bull story?

SCAPIN [*aside*]. Perhaps.

ARGANTE. Nothing they say will have any effect.

SCAPIN. We'll see.

ARGANTE. They will never succeed in bringing me round.

SCAPIN. Don't be too sure.

ARGANTE. I'll soon clap up my good-for-nothing son in a safe place.

SCAPIN. We'll take precautions against that.

ARGANTE. And I'll thrash that rogue Sylvestre within an inch of his life.

SYLVESTRE. Yes, I should have been surprised if he had left me out of it.

ARGANTE [*suddenly seeing* SYLVESTRE]. Ah, there you are, my trusty tutor! A fine guardian you have been!

SCAPIN. I am delighted to see you home, Sir.

ARGANTE. Good day, Scapin. [*To* SYLVESTRE]. Well you've chosen a fine way to carry out my orders. My son has been behaving in a most exemplary manner while I have been away.

SCAPIN. You are looking the very picture of health.

ARGANTE. Well enough, well enough. [*To* SYLVESTRE]. Are you dumb, you rascal, are you dumb?

SCAPIN. Have you had a successful voyage?

ARGANTE. Yes, yes, very successful. Now let me tell this chap off in peace.

SCAPIN. Tell him off?

ARGANTE. Yes, tell him off.

SCAPIN. Whom then, Sir?

ARGANTE. That villain there.

SCAPIN. What on earth for?

ARGANTE. What! You haven't heard what's happened while I've been away?

SCAPIN. I did hear of some slight imprudence.

ARGANTE. Some slight imprudence? A thing of that importance?

SCAPIN. Yes, you have some cause for complaint.

ARGANTE. It is a piece of gross effrontery.

SCAPIN. True, true.

ARGANTE. To marry without his father's consent?

SCAPIN. Yes. I can see your point of view. But, if I were you, I shouldn't make a fuss about it.

ARGANTE. I don't share your opinion, I shall make a very great fuss about it. What! Haven't I every right in the world to be angry?

SCAPIN. Oh, as to that, I was very angry myself when I first heard about it. I took your side and even went to the length of telling the boy off. Ask *him* how I took him to task for his lack of consideration for a father whose very footsteps he ought to worship. You could hardly have put it more strongly yourself. But in the end I calmed down. Really there's not so much harm done after all.

ARGANTE. What's that you say? Not so much harm in going off and marrying a girl from goodness knows where on the spur of the moment?

SCAPIN. Well, it was his Fate, I suppose.

ARGANTE. Oh, of course there couldn't be a better excuse than that. A man has only to commit all the crimes imaginable, cheat, rob and murder, and then put everything down to Fate.

SCAPIN. You take me too literally. All I mean is that he found himself inexorably caught up by events.

ARGANTE. Why did he let himself be caught up?

SCAPIN. Can you expect him to be as prudent as you are? Young gentlemen will be young gentlemen. It's simply lack of experience that makes them make mistakes. Take our Léandre, for instance. He is going to do something even worse than your son in spite of everything I can do to stop him. Did you never sow wild oats when you were young, just like every one else? I think I've heard you were once a great lady's man yourself, and sowed a few wild oats with the best of them, and never began an affair without seeing it through to the end.

ARGANTE. That may be. But it never went further than a little flirtation. I never did what this young rogue has done.

SCAPIN. What would you have him do? He sees a young girl who is not indifferent to him—for in that he takes after you, you know; he is a great favourite with the ladies—he finds her attractive, visits her, flirts, sighs, falls passionately in love. She encourages him. He gets deeper and deeper in. Then all of a sudden in rush her relations, and, sword in hand, force him to marry her.

SYLVESTRE [aside]. Oh, the cunning rascal!

SCAPIN. Would you rather he had been killed? Surely it's better for him to be married than dead.

ARGANTE. No one told me it happened like that.

SCAPIN [*indicating* SYLVESTRE]. Ask him. He'll tell you the same.

ARGANTE [*to* SYLVESTRE]. He was compelled to marry her then?

SYLVESTRE. Yes, Sir.

SCAPIN. Would I tell you a lie?

ARGANTE. Then he must go at once and lay a complaint before a magistrate.

SCAPIN. That's the very thing he refuses to do.

ARGANTE. It would make it easier for me to get the marriage annulled.

SCAPIN. Get the marriage annulled?

ARGANTE. Of course.

SCAPIN. You'll never do that.

ARGANTE. Not do it?

SCAPIN. No.

ARGANTE. What! Shall I not have a father's rights, and justice for the violence done to my son?

SCAPIN. He'll never agree to it.

ARGANTE. Not agree?

SCAPIN. Never.

ARGANTE. My son?

SCAPIN. Your son. Would you have him own himself a coward, and that he was forced to do this thing? He'll take good care not to do that. Why, it would be a slur on his reputation, and make him unworthy to have you for his father.

ARGANTE. Rubbish!

SCAPIN. It's absolutely essential, for his honour and for yours, that the world should think he married her willingly.

ARGANTE. And I think it essential, both for my honour and his, that he should say the opposite.

SCAPIN. He certainly never will.

ARGANTE. I'll make him.

SCAPIN. He won't do it, I tell you.

ARGANTE. He shall do it, or I'll disinherit him.

SCAPIN. You mean that?

ARGANTE. I mean it.

SCAPIN. Very well.

ARGANTE. How is it very well?

SCAPIN. You won't disinherit him at all.

ARGANTE. I shan't disinherit him?

SCAPIN. No.

ARGANTE. No?

SCAPIN. No.

ARGANTE. Well! Here's a nice thing! I shall not disinherit my son?

SCAPIN. No, I tell you.

ARGANTE. Who will stop me?

SCAPIN. Yourself.

ARGANTE. Myself?

SCAPIN. Yes. You wouldn't have the heart.

ARGANTE. Oh, haven't I?

SCAPIN. You're joking.

ARGANTE. No, I'm not.

SCAPIN. A father's love will plead for him.

ARGANTE. It will do nothing of the sort.

SCAPIN. Yes, it will.

ARGANTE. I tell you it will not.

SCAPIN. Nonsense!

ARGANTE. It's no use saying 'Nonsense'.

SCAPIN. Oh, I know you. You're a tolerant man at bottom.

ARGANTE. I am not tolerant at all. I can be very hard when I like. Enough of this argument! It's making me lose my temper. [*To* SYLVESTRE]. Off with you, you scoundrel, and fetch my rogue of a son, while I look for Géronte, to tell him of my disgrace.

SCAPIN. If I can be of any service to you, Sir, you have only to let me know.

ARGANTE. I'm much obliged to you. [*Aside*]. Oh, why is he an only child? If only I had the daughter that Heaven took from me, I would make her my heir.

[*He goes out* V

SYLVESTRE. You're a great man, Scapin. It's all going splendidly. The only thing is, we are hard pressed for money. We must live. And there's a pack of creditors yapping after us as well.

SCAPIN. Leave it to me. I've thought it all out. All I want now is a man we can trust, to act out a certain part. Here, wait a minute! Pull your hat down over your eyes, like a villain, balance on one foot, put your hand on your hip, put a wild glare in your eye, and walk like a ham actor playing a king. That's right! Now come along with me. I'll show you how to make your face up and disguise your voice.

SYLVESTRE. For God's sake, don't get me into trouble with the law.

SCAPIN. Don't you worry. We'll share the risk together like brothers. It shall need more than a few years in the galleys to deter stout-hearted fellows like us.

ACT TWO

I   [*Enter* ARGANTE *and* GÉRONTE.

GÉRONTE. Yes, with this wind they should be here today. A sailor from Taranto told me that, when he left, my man was just about to set sail. But my daughter's arrival will find things very badly out of line with what we had intended. What you have just told me about your son has upset the whole plan.

ARGANTE. Don't let that disturb you. I'll soon get over that difficulty. I'm off to see about it now.

GÉRONTE. If you want my opinion, Seigneur Argante, we cannot be too careful about the way we bring up our children.

ARGANTE. No doubt. But what are you getting at?

GÉRONTE. Because, when a young man does wrong, it is very often the fault of the upbringing imposed on him by his father.

ARGANTE. It may be so sometimes. But what do you mean by that?

GÉRONTE. What do I mean?

ARGANTE. Yes.

GÉRONTE. Why, that if, like a good father, you had brought your son up properly, he would not have played this trick on you.

ARGANTE. Oh, thank you very much. You have brought up yours much better, I suppose.

GÉRONTE. Most certainly I have. I should be very angry indeed if he did anything like this.

ARGANTE. And what if this son that you have brought up so well had done something even worse than mine?

GÉRONTE. What's that?

ARGANTE. What then?

GÉRONTE. What do you mean by that?

ARGANTE. I mean, Seigneur Géronte, that you should not be so ready to criticize other people. It's a wise proverb that tells us that people in glass houses shouldn't throw stones.

GÉRONTE. This riddle is beyond me.

ARGANTE. It will soon be explained.

GÉRONTE. Have you heard something about my son?

ARGANTE. Suppose I had?

GÉRONTE. What is it then?

ARGANTE. Your man Scapin just mentioned it to me in passing. You can no doubt hear the details either from him or from someone else. I am going straight to consult a lawyer about the steps I ought to take in this affair. Good day to you.

[*He goes out*

GÉRONTE. What ever can it be? Something worse? I don't see what worse a son *can* do. To marry without the consent of one's father seems to me worse than anything one could imagine.

[*Enter* LÉANDRE.

Ah, there you are!

LÉANDRE [*running to embrace his father*]. Father! How glad I am to see you back!

GÉRONTE [*holding him off*]. Just a moment. There's a question I want to ask you.

LÉANDRE. Let me welcome you, and . . . .

GÉRONTE. Not so fast, I tell you.

LÉANDRE. What! You won't let me express how pleased I am to. . . .

GÉRONTE. No. There's a little mystery I want cleared up first.

LÉANDRE. What mystery?

GÉRONTE. Let me look at you.

LÉANDRE. What is it?

GÉRONTE. Look me right between the eyes.

LÉANDRE. Well?

GÉRONTE. Now tell me what has been going on?

LÉANDRE. Going on?

GÉRONTE. Yes. What have you been doing while I've been away?

LÉANDRE. What could I have done, father?

GÉRONTE. I am not saying what you could have done. I'm asking what you have done.

LÉANDRE. I? Nothing to give you any cause for complaint.

GÉRONTE. Nothing?

LÉANDRE. Nothing at all.

GÉRONTE. You are very sure of yourself.

LÉANDRE. Because I'm conscious of my own innocence.

GÉRONTE. Scapin, however, tells a different story.

LÉANDRE. Scapin?

GÉRONTE. Aha! That name makes you blush.

LÉANDRE. Scapin has told you something about me?

GÉRONTE. Well, I'm not going into it here and now. We'll settle it elsewhere. Go home now. I'll be back there straight away. If you disgrace me, you wastrel, I'll disown you for my son, and you can get used to the idea of never entering my presence again.

[*He goes out*

III   LÉANDRE. What monstrous treachery! A scoundrel who, of all men alive, should keep my secrets faithfully, is the very first to go and blab them to my father. But I swear to Heaven that I'll pay him back for it.

[*Enter* OCTAVE *and* SCAPIN.

OCTAVE. My dear Scapin, what a splendid fellow you are! I'm in your debt for ever. Fate is indeed my friend to send me such a resourceful ally.

LÉANDRE. Ah, so there you are, my treacherous friend. I'm delighted to see you.

SCAPIN. Your servant, Sir. You do me too much honour.

LÉANDRE [*drawing his sword*]. You make a joke of your villainy, do you? I'll teach you. . . .

SCAPIN [*falling to his knees*]. Sir!

OCTAVE [*coming between them*]. My dear Léandre!

LÉANDRE. Don't hold me back, Octave.

SCAPIN. Sir! Oh Sir!

OCTAVE. For Heaven's sake!

LÉANDRE. Hands off! Let me satisfy my thirst for revenge.

OCTAVE. Don't hurt him, Léandre, for my sake, I beg of you.

SCAPIN. What have I done to deserve this, Sir?

LÉANDRE. You know well enough, you sneak, you villain.

OCTAVE. Come, come now, Léandre.

LÉANDRE. No, Octave. He shall confess his treachery here and now. You didn't think I'd get to hear of it, you rogue; but I know the trick you have played on me; I've just been told about it, and, unless you admit it at once, I'll run you through on the spot.

SCAPIN. Oh, Sir, would you have the heart?

LÉANDRE. Speak then.

SCAPIN. I have done you some wrong, Sir?

LÉANDRE. Yes, rascal, and your conscience tells you only too well what it is.

SCAPIN. I swear to you I don't know what you mean.

LÉANDRE [*advancing on him*]. You don't know?

OCTAVE. Léandre!

SCAPIN Well, then, since you ask me, Sir, it was I and my friends who drank up the little cask of Spanish wine that was given you a few days ago. I made the hole, and poured water all round, so that you'd think the wine had run out.

LÉANDRE. Aha! So it was you drank my Spanish wine, and made me scold the maid so soundly, thinking she had done it?

SCAPIN. Yes, Sir. I beg you to overlook it.

LÉANDRE. I am delighted to hear it. But that is not the particular piece of knavery we are discussing at the moment.

SCAPIN. It's not that, Sir?

LÉANDRE. No. It is something much more important than that, and I intend you to tell me what it is.

SCAPIN. Sir, I can't think of anything else.

LÉANDRE [*threatening him*]. So you won't speak?

SCAPIN. Ah!

OCTAVE [*restraining him*]. Léandre.

SCAPIN. Well then, you remember three weeks ago, when you sent me out one evening to take a little watch to a young gipsy girl that you loved, and I came back with my face all bloody and my clothes covered with mud, and told you I'd fallen among thieves who had beaten me and stolen the watch? Well, I stole the watch, Sir.

LÉANDRE. You stole my watch?

SCAPIN. Yes, Sir, so that I should always be able to tell the time.

LÉANDRE. Oho, I am learning quite a lot of things today! What an honest valet I've got! But that's not what I mean either.

SCAPIN. It's not that?

LÉANDRE. No, scoundrel, it's something worse still.

SCAPIN [*aside*]. Hell!

LÉANDRE. Out with it now. I'm in a hurry.

SCAPIN. Sir, that is all.

LÉANDRE [*threatening him*]. That all?

OCTAVE. Now, now.

SCAPIN. Well then, Sir, you remember the bogeyman who gave you such a thrashing one night, six months ago, when you fell into a cellar in your flight and nearly broke your neck?

LÉANDRE. Well?

SCAPIN. I was the bogeyman, Sir.

LÉANDRE. You were the bogeyman, you treacherous villain?

SCAPIN. Yes, sir, but it was only to frighten you, and stop you sending us out every night, as you used to do.

LÉANDRE. I shall remember all this later on. But, come now, confess at once what you have told my father.

SCAPIN. Told your father?

LÉANDRE. Yes, you villain, told my father.

SCAPIN. But I have not even seen him since his return.

LÉANDRE. You haven't seen him?

SCAPIN. No, Sir.

LÉANDRE. You're lying.

SCAPIN. No, Sir, I'm not. Ask him yourself.

LÉANDRE. Why, it was he who told me.

SCAPIN. Begging your pardon then, he did not tell the truth.

    [*Enter* CARLE.   IV

CARLE. Sir, I bring you dreadful news.

LÉANDRE. What is it?

CARLE. The gipsies are carrying off your Zerbinette. She is crying her eyes out, and begged me to come and tell you that, unless you send them the money within two hours, you will lose her for ever.

LÉANDRE. Within two hours?

CARLE. Two hours.

[*He goes out*

LÉANDRE. Oh, my good Scapin, I beg you to help me.

SCAPIN [*rising and passing haughtily in front of* LÉANDRE]. 'Ah, my good Scapin!' I am 'my good Scapin' now that you need my help.

LÉANDRE. I'll forgive you everything, and worse still if you have done it.

SCAPIN. No. Don't forgive me anything. Run me through. I'd rather you took my life.

LÉANDRE. On the contrary, I beg you to save mine by ensuring my happiness.

SCAPIN. No, no. Better run me through.

LÉANDRE. I know your worth too well. I implore you to use your marvellous ingenuity, which I have never known to fail.

SCAPIN. No. Kill me, I tell you.

LÉANDRE. Forget all that, for mercy's sake, and set your wits to work.

OCTAVE. Scapin, you must do something for him.

SCAPIN. How can I, after the way he has treated me?

LÉANDRE. I beg you to forget my ill temper, and help me once more.

OCTAVE. For my sake too, Scapin.

SCAPIN. I feel too hurt.

OCTAVE. You must forget and forgive.

LÉANDRE. Have you the heart to desert me, Scapin, in this terrible crisis?

SCAPIN. Suddenly, for no reason at all, to turn on me like that!

LÉANDRE. I was wrong, I own it.

SCAPIN. To call me traitor, scoundrel, villain, knave!

LÉANDRE. I most deeply regret it.

SCAPIN. To threaten to run me through with your sword!

LÉANDRE. I humbly beg your pardon, Scapin. Don't desert me now, I beseech you. See, I beg you on my knees.

OCTAVE. You can't hold out after that, Scapin.

SCAPIN. Oh, very well then. Get up. And another time think before you speak.

LÉANDRE. You'll help me?

SCAPIN. I'll think about it.

LÉANDRE. But there's not a minute to be lost.

SCAPIN. Don't you worry. How much do you need?

LÉANDRE. Five hundred ecus.

SCAPIN. And you?

OCTAVE. Two hundred pistoles.

SCAPIN. I shall have to try to get the money from your fathers. [To OCTAVE]. As far as yours is concerned, I see the way already. [To LÉANDRE]. And there should be even less difficulty with yours, for, though he's as tight-fisted as the devil, you know how little sense he's got, thank God! and I can easily make him believe anything I please. Don't let that offend you. There's not the slightest suspicion of resemblance between you, and you know well enough that everyone thinks he only owns you for his son to avoid a scandal.

LÉANDRE. Come now, Scapin.

SCAPIN. Aha! That shocks you, does it? You can't mean it. But here comes Octave's father. We'll try him first, as he

is here. Away, both of you. [*To* OCTAVE]. And send
Sylvestre along, as soon as your can, to play his part.

> [OCTAVE *and* LÉANDRE *go out,* SCAPIN *retires back-stage. Then enter* ARGANTE.

V   Here he comes, and he's talking to himself.

ARGANTE [*thinking he is alone*]. How could he have so little
decency and consideration as to blunder into a marriage of
that kind? What idiots young men are!

SCAPIN. Your servant, Sir.

ARGANTE. Ah, good day, Scapin.

SCAPIN. I expect you are still thinking about this scrape of
your son's.

ARGANTE. Yes. I'm really furious about it.

SCAPIN. Life is a valley of troubles, Sir. It's best to be
prepared for everything. Many years ago I heard a maxim
of a sage of old, which I have never forgotten.

ARGANTE. What was that?

SCAPIN. That if the father of a family has been away from
home for ever so short a time, he should resign himself in
advance to every possible disaster on his return; his house
burnt down, his strong box stolen, his wife dead, his son a
cripple, his daughter seduced; and for any one of these
things that hasn't happened he should thank his good
fortune. In my homespun philosophy I have always followed this advice, and I never return home without being
prepared for a bad reception; reproaches, abuse, a kick up
the backside, or a sound thrashing, and I thank my lucky
stars for anything I escape.

ARGANTE. That's all very well, but this preposterous marriage, which ruins all our plans, is more than I can put up
with; and I have just been to see a lawyer about getting my
son out of it.

SCAPIN. Heavens, Sir, if you'll take my advice, you will try and settle the business in some other way. You know what lawsuits are in this country. You'll get yourself into the most awful tangle.

ARGANTE. Yes, I see that too. But what other way is there?

SCAPIN. I believe I've found one. I was so sorry for your disappointment that I have been racking my brains eversince to find some way out of the difficulty; for I can't bear to see a good father saddened by his children, and I've always had a special regard for you.

ARGANTE. That's exceedingly kind of you.

SCAPIN. I have got in touch with the girl's brother. He is one of these soldiers of fortune, who are all cut and thrust, talk of nothing but killing, and make no more bones about finishing a man off than drinking a glass of wine. I tackled him on the subject, showed him how the charge of rape would make it easy for the marriage to be annulled, pointed out your rights as a father, and how your money and influence would almost certainly tip the scales in your favour. In the end I worked on him to such an extent that he took note of the financial proposition I put to him, and he has agreed to the annulment of the marriage, if only you will pay him well.

ARGANTE. How much does he want?

SCAPIN. Oh, at first he was for asking something quite ridiculous.

ARGANTE. What?

SCAPIN. Oh, it's quite out of the question.

ARGANTE. Well, how much?

SCAPIN. He mentioned nothing less than five or six hundred pistoles.

ARGANTE. Five or six hundred bouts of fever, more like! Does he think I'm a fool?

SCAPIN. That's just what I told him. I refused such extravagant propositions out of hand, and gave him clearly to understand that you were not a simpleton to be done out of five or six hundred pistoles. At last, after a good deal of argument, we came down to this: 'The time has come', he said, 'for me to join the army. I have to get my equipment together, and my urgent need of money will make me agree to almost anything. I must have a horse, and it would be impossible to get one that was any good for less than sixty pistoles.'

ARGANTE. Well, I'm willing to give sixty pistoles.

SCAPIN. 'I must have harness, of course, and a pair of pistols. That will come to twenty pistoles more.'

ARGANTE. Twenty pistoles and sixty, that would be eighty.

SCAPIN. Exactly.

ARGANTE. It's a good deal. But very well then, I agree to that.

SCAPIN. 'I must also have a mount for my batman, which will come to another thirty.'

ARGANTE. Devil take the fellow! Let him walk! I'll give him nothing at all.

SCAPIN. Monsieur!

ARGANTE. No. He is an impudent scoundrel.

SCAPIN. Would you have his servant go on foot?

ARGANTE. He may go as he pleases, and his master too.

SCAPIN. Merciful heavens, Sir, don't throw everything over for such a trifle as that. Don't go to law, I beg of you. Give it all rather than get into the lawyers' clutches.

ARGANTE. Oh, very well then. I'll give the extra thirty.

SCAPIN. 'Then', he said, 'I shall need a mule to carry. . . .'

ARGANTE. The devil take him, and his mule too! This is really too much. I shall go to court.

SCAPIN. For pity's sake, Monsieur. . . .

ARGANTE. No. My mind is made up.

SCAPIN. Monsieur, only a tiny little mule.

ARGANTE. I won't even give him a donkey.

SCAPIN. Think. . . .

ARGANTE. No. I would rather go to court.

SCAPIN. Oh, don't say that, Monsieur! Don't embark on anything like that. Just think of all the dishonest practices of the law, the number of appeals and different legal processes, the tiresome procedure, the ravenous rabble, through whose clutches you must pass; sergeants-at-law, attorneys, advocates, registrars, deputies, assessors, judges and their clerks. Any one of these is capable, on the slightest provocation, of queering the best case in the world. A sergeant will serve you with trumped-up writs on which you will be condemned without your knowledge. Your attorney will be got at by the other side, and will sell the case for ready money. Your advocate, bribed as well, will be out of the way when the case comes on, or will raise questions to confuse the issue and lead nowhere. The registrar will register decisions against you by default. The assessor's clerk will make away with documents, or the assessor himself will write a false report. And when, by the skin of your teeth, you have come through all this, you will be flabbergasted to find that the judges have been canvassed against you, either by pious hypocrites or women they love. Oh, Monsieur, if you can, I beseech you to keep away from this Hell on earth. To go to law is to be damned while you are still alive, and the very thought of such a thing would be enough to send me off into voluntary exile as fast as my feet could carry me.

ARGANTE. How much did he say for the mule?

SCAPIN. Monsieur, for the mule, his own horse and that of his man, the harness, pistols, and to settle a small account he owes his landlady, two hundred pistoles in all.

ARGANTE. Two hundred pistoles?

SCAPIN. Yes.

ARGANTE [*angrily walking to and fro*]. No. We'll go to court.

SCAPIN. Think it over.

ARGANTE. I'll go to court.

SCAPIN. Don't plunge yourself into. . . .

ARGANTE. I intend to go to law, I tell you.

SCAPIN. But a lawsuit will cost you quite as much. There will be the writ, its registration, the power of attorney, the appearance, the consultations, the attorney's time, the discussions and pleadings of the advocates, engrossments of the huge piles of documents, the deputies' reports, the judges' fees, registrations, provisional judgements, warrants, verdicts, stamps, signatures, and copies by the clerks, without mentioning all the folk you'll have to bribe. Pay this man his money and there you are quit of the whole business.

ARGANTE. What! Two hundred pistoles?

SCAPIN. You'll be the winner by it. I have worked out, in my head, all the expenses of the law courts; and I find that by giving your man his two hundred pistoles you will be at least a hundred and fifty to the good, not to speak of all the worry and vexation you'll be spared. Then think of all the indiscreet revelations these smooth-tongued, rascally lawyers come out with in front of everybody. I'd rather pay three hundred pistoles than go to court.

ARGANTE. That's nonsense. I defy the lawyers to say anything against me.

SCAPIN. Well, please yourself. But, if I were you, I should steer clear of the law.

ARGANTE. I'll never pay two hundred pistoles.

SCAPIN. Why, here's the very man himself.

[SYLVESTRE *enters, dressed as a soldier of fortune.* VI
ARGANTE *retires backstage.*

SYLVESTRE. Scapin, what sort of a man is this Argante, Octave's father?

SCAPIN. Why do you ask, Sir?

SYLVESTRE. They tell me he is going to sue me, and have my sister's marriage dissolved by law.

SCAPIN. I don't know about that. But he won't pay two hundred pistoles. He says it's too much.

SYLVESTRE. Death, blood and wounds! If I meet him, I'll chop him up for dogmeat, though they break me on the wheel for it.

[ARGANTE *has crept up trembling, and tries to hide behind* SCAPIN.

SCAPIN. Octave's father, sir, is a man of spirit, and perhaps would not be so easily frightened.

SYLVESTRE. What? Blood and bones! If he stood there, I'd run him through the guts. [*seeing* ARGANTE]. Who is that?

SCAPIN. That's not him, Sir, that's not him.

SYLVESTRE. One of his friends perhaps.

SCAPIN. No, Sir; on the contrary, it is his bitterest enemy.

SYLVESTRE. His bitterest enemy?

SCAPIN. Yes.

SYLVESTRE. By Heaven! I'm delighted to hear it. [*To* ARGANTE]. You are an enemy of this rascal of an Argante, eh, Sir.

SCAPIN. I'll answer for that.

SYLVESTRE [*roughly shaking hands with* ARGANTE]. I'm proud to shake you by the hand, Sir. By my sword I swear, by every oath I know, before this day shall close I'll rid you of this cursed rogue, this scoundrel of an Argante! Rely on me.

—

SCAPIN. In this country, Monsieur, violence is not permitted.

SYLVESTRE. I don't care a fig! I have nothing to lose.

SCAPIN. You won't catch him alone. He has plenty of friends and servants to take his part.

SYLVESTRE. All the better, damn my soul! That's what I want. [*Drawing his sword*]. Death and Hell! If only I could meet him now with all his rabble round him! Let him appear now, hedged in with thirty guards, and let them all come on! What, knaves do you dare attack me? Come on, by God! Kill! Kill! [*Lunging on all sides as if he were fighting with several men at once*]. No quarter! Steady! Lunge! Sure foot. Steady eye. Ah, knaves! Ah, scum! That tickled you. I'll give you your fill. Bear up, you dogs, bear up! Come, lunge! Again! Here! There! What, you fall back? Stand your ground, damn you, stand your ground!

SCAPIN. Hey, hey, Sir, we're not of their party!

SYLVESTRE. I'll teach you to dare play tricks with me.

[*He goes out*

SCAPIN. There you are, you see! All those people killed for the sake of two hundred pistoles! I wish you luck, that's all.

ARGANTE [*trembling*]. Scapin.

SCAPIN. Eh?

ARGANTE. I'll pay him the two hundred pistoles.

SCAPIN. I'm glad to hear it, for your own sake.

ARGANTE. Let's go after him. I have them on me.

SCAPIN. You have only to give them to me. It would be a slur on your honour for you to appear in it now, after you have pretended to be someone else. And besides if you make yourself known, I'm afraid he may take it into his head to ask for more.

ARGANTE. Still, I should like to see the money given.

SCAPIN. Why? Don't you trust me?

ARGANTE. Yes, yes, but . . .

SCAPIN. Come now, Sir, either I am a rogue or I am an honest man. I must be one of the two. Why should I wish to deceive you? What interest can I have in the affair but to serve you and my master, with whom you hope to be allied? But, if you are not going to trust me, I'll wash my hands of the whole business, and you can find someone else to manage your affairs.

ARGANTE [giving him the money]. Oh, very well then, here it is.

SCAPIN. No, Sir. Better not trust me with your money. I would rather you found someone else.

ARGANTE. Come, take it.

SCAPIN. No. Don't trust me. How do you know I shan't steal it?

ARGANTE. Take it, I say. Don't keep me arguing any longer. But be sure you get a receipt from him.

SCAPIN. You can leave all that to me. I'm not a fool.

ARGANTE. I'll wait for you then at home.

SCAPIN. I'll follow you there.

[ARGANTE *goes out*

That's one. Now I've only to find the other. And, by the Lord, here he comes! It looks as if Fate were driving them into my hands, one after the other.

[*Enter* GÉRONTE.   VII

SCAPIN [*pretending not to see him*]. Oh, Heavens! What a terrible misfortune! Oh, unhappy father! Poor Géronte! What will he do?

GÉRONTE [*aside*]. What's that he's saying about me, with that gloomy face?

SCAPIN. Will no one tell me where to find Seigneur Géronte?

GÉRONTE. Why, what is it, Scapin?

SCAPIN [*running across the stage, pretending not to see or hear* GÉRONTE]. Oh, where can I find him, to tell him of this calamity?

GÉRONTE [*running after him*]. What is it, man, what is it?

SCAPIN. I can't find him anywhere. I've been all round the town.

GÉRONTE. Here I am, man, here I am.

SCAPIN. He must have gone into hiding. He's certainly not to be found.

GÉRONTE [*stopping him*]. Hey, steady! Are you so blind that you can't see me?

SCAPIN. Ah, Sir, I couldn't find you anywhere.

GÉRONTE. Why, I've been standing in front of you for the last hour. What ever is the matter?

SCAPIN. Sir. . . .

GÉRONTE. What?

SCAPIN. Sir, your son. . . .

GÉRONTE. Well? My son. . . .?

SCAPIN. Has met with the most terrible accident.

GÉRONTE. What?

SCAPIN. An hour or two ago I found him looking very downcast at something you had said to him, I don't know what, something in which you had mixed me up to my discredit by the way; and, in order to raise his spirits, I suggested a stroll by the harbour. There, amongst other things, we caught sight of a Turkish galley, very sumptuously fitted up. A good-looking young Turk invited us on board and held out his hand to help us up the gangway. We went below, where he hospitably offered us refreshment, setting before us the most delicious fruit, and some of the best wine we had ever tasted.

GÉRONTE. Well, what is there so terrible in all this?

SCAPIN. Ah, Sir, I'm coming to that now. While we were at table he gave orders for the galley to put to sea, and when we were some way out, he dropped me overboard into a skiff and sent me to tell you that unless you immediately send him five hundred ecus by me he will carry your son as a slave to Algiers.

GÉRONTE. The devil! Five hundred ecus?

SCAPIN. Yes, Sir. And what is worse still, he gives me only two hours to get it in.

GÉRONTE. Oh, villainous Turk! What monstrous robbery!

SCAPIN. Loving him as you do, you must do what you can to rescue him from slavery. There's not a moment to be lost.

GÉRONTE. But what the devil was he doing in that galley?

SCAPIN. He never dreamed that such a thing would happen.

GÉRONTE. Quick, Scapin, go back to this Turk, and tell him I'll have the law on him.

SCAPIN. Law on the high seas? You must be joking.

GÉRONTE. Well, what the devil was he doing in that galley?

SCAPIN. Men are driven at times by an evil Fate.

GÉRONTE. Scapin, you must do what a faithful servant would do in this crisis, you must indeed.

SCAPIN. What, Sir?

GÉRONTE. You must go and tell this Turk to send me back my son, and that you will take his place until I can collect the money.

SCAPIN. What? Use your common sense, Sir. Do you suppose the Turk is such a fool as to accept a wretch like me in the place of your son?

GÉRONTE. What the devil was he doing in that galley?

SCAPIN. He never suspected this. Remember I have only two hours, Sir.

GÉRONTE. You say he demands. . . .

SCAPIN. Five hundred ecus.

GÉRONTE. Five hundred ecus! Has he no conscience at all?

SCAPIN. Yes. A Turk's conscience.

GÉRONTE. Does he know how much five hundred ecus are?

SCAPIN. Yes, Sir. One thousand five hundred livres.

GÉRONTE. Does the scoundrel think that one thousand five hundred livres can be picked up in the street?

SCAPIN. It's no use expecting these sort of people to hear reason.

GÉRONTE. But what the devil was he doing in that galley?

SCAPIN. True; but, one can't foresee everything! For mercy's sake, Sir, hurry up.

GÉRONTE. Oh, very well then. Here's the key of my cupboard. [Giving him a key].

SCAPIN. That's better.

GÉRONTE. Open it.

SCAPIN. Yes.

GÉRONTE. You will find a big key in the left hand corner. It's the key of the attic.

SCAPIN. Yes, yes.

GÉRONTE. Take all the clothes that are in the big basket, and sell them to the rag and bone man to ransom my son.

SCAPIN [giving him back the key]. What, Monsieur, are you crazy? I should not get a hundred francs for the lot. And besides, you know how short a time he has given me.

GÉRONTE. But what the devil was he doing in that galley?

SCAPIN. Oh, not that question again! Give the galley a rest. Think how time is going, and the risk you run of losing your son. Oh, my poor master, perhaps I shall never see you again! Perhaps, even now, they are dragging you, a slave, to Algiers. But Heaven is my witness that I did my best; and, if you are not ransomed, your father's want of affection is alone to blame.

GÉRONTE. Wait here, Scapin. I will go and fetch the money.

SCAPIN. Be quick then, Sir, be quick. I tremble to hear the clock strike.

GÉRONTE. Four hundred ecus, you said?

SCAPIN. No. Five hundred ecus.

GÉRONTE. Five hundred ecus?

SCAPIN. Yes.

GÉRONTE. What the devil was he doing in that galley?

SCAPIN. Oh, do make haste.

GÉRONTE. Couldn't he have gone some other way for his stroll?

SCAPIN. Be quick. Be quick.

GÉRONTE. Oh, that cursed galley!

SCAPIN [aside]. He's got that galley on the brain.

GÉRONTE. Wait, Scapin. I had forgotten that I have just received that very sum in gold, but I didn't expect to be robbed of it so soon. [Taking his purse from his pocket and offering it to SCAPIN]. Here, take it, and go ransom my son.

SCAPIN [holding out his hand]. Give it to me quick then, Sir.

GÉRONTE [keeping his purse back]. But tell this Turk from me he is a scoundrel.

SCAPIN [as before]. Yes.

GÉRONTE [as before]. An infamous dog.

SCAPIN. Yes, yes.

GÉRONTE. A thief, an infidel.

SCAPIN. I'll tell him.

GÉRONTE. That he is wringing five hundred ecus out of me against all justice and equity.

SCAPIN. Yes.

—

GÉRONTE. That I am only lending him the money.

SCAPIN. Very well.

GÉRONTE. And that, if I ever catch him, I'll be revenged on him.

SCAPIN. Yes, yes.

GÉRONTE [*putting the purse back into his pocket and going away*]. Then off with you at once, and bring back my son.

SCAPIN [*running after him*]. Hey, Sir!

GÉRONTE. What is it?

SCAPIN. Where is the money?

GÉRONTE. Didn't I give it to you?

SCAPIN. No. You have just put it back into your pocket.

GÉRONTE [*giving the money*]. Ah, grief has made me distracted.

SCAPIN. That's clear enough.

GÉRONTE. What the devil was he doing in that galley? Oh, damned galley! Infamous Turk! The devil take him!

[*He goes out*

SCAPIN. It's clear that those five hundred ecus stick in his gullet. But I'm not quits with him even yet. He shall pay some other way for the lie he told about me to his son.

VIII   [*Enter* OCTAVE *and* LÉANDRE.

OCTAVE. Well, Scapin, has your trick been successful?

LÉANDRE. Have you been able to do anything for me?

SCAPIN [*to* OCTAVE]. Here are two hundred pistoles I've wheedled out of your father. [*He gives him the money*].

OCTAVE. Oh, wonderful!

SCAPIN [*to* LÉANDRE]. For you—I've been able to do nothing.

LÉANDRE [*turning to go*]. Then I'll go and hang myself. I have nothing left to live for if Zerbinette is taken from me.

SCAPIN. Hi, hi, not so fast! Lord, how hasty you are!

LÉANDRE [*coming back*]. What do you want with me?

SCAPIN. I have done your little commission after all.

LÉANDRE. You have? Oh, Scapin, you have restored me to life.

SCAPIN. But only on condition that you allow me to pay back your father for the trick he played me.

LÉANDRE. Yes, yes. Anything you like.

SCAPIN. You promise, before a witness?

LÉANDRE. Yes, yes, I promise.

SCAPIN [*giving him the money*]. There then! There are your five hundred ecus.

LÉANDRE. Let's go immediately and ransom my darling Zerbinette.

ACT THREE

[*Enter* ZERBINETTE, HYACINTHE, SCAPIN *and* SYLVESTRE.

SYLVESTRE. Your suitors are anxious for you to lodge together, and we are simply carrying out their orders.

HYACINTHE [*to* ZERBINETTE]. I have no fault to find with such an arrangement. I am delighted to welcome such a companion; and I should be only too happy if the friendship between the ones we love might be cemented by our own.

ZERBINETTE. I accept your offer with pleasure. I will never refuse a hand held out in friendship.

SCAPIN. And how about a hand held out in love?

ZERBINETTE. Love? Ah, that is another matter. There the risk is greater, and I feel more diffidence.

SCAPIN. Yes, my master is suffering through that same diffidence now. But surely what he has just done for you ought to give you courage to answer his passion kindly.

ZERBINETTE. I still do not altogether trust him. And what he has done is not enough to make me feel quite safe. I am naturally light-hearted and never stop laughing; but, for all that, I can be serious on some subjects, and your master is greatly mistaken if he thinks he has only to buy me from captivity to make me his. It will cost him other things than money; and, before I can return his love in the way he wishes, he must plight me his troth and submit to a certain necessary ceremony.

SCAPIN. Why, that's exactly what he wants. He proposes to you in all good faith and honour. I shouldn't have been party to the affair, if he had had any other idea.

ZERBINETTE. I'm ready to believe it, since you tell me so. But I doubt if his father will agree.

SCAPIN. Oh, we'll find some way of arranging it.

HYACINTHE [to ZERBINETTE]. The similarity of our positions should bind us still closer together, for we both have the same obstacles to fear, and are both subject to the same ill-fortune.

ZERBINETTE. You have this advantage at least that you know whose daughter you are, and can be sure that, once your family is known, all your difficulties will be smoothed away, and you will have no trouble in getting recognition for a marriage which has already taken place. But I can find no comfort in what I am; and my present situation will do little to reassure a father whose sole aim is money.

HYACINTHE. But you have one advantage too, that the man you love has not been tempted with another match.

ZERBINETTE. Inconstancy is not the worst one has to fear. A girl will always trust her own charms to hold on to the man who loves her. But, if his father is against the match, all the charm in the world will count for nothing.

HYACINTHE. Oh, why is true affection always crossed? How sweet it would be to love, if there were nothing to break the tender chains which bind two hearts together!

SCAPIN. There I disagree with you. In love, nothing can be worse than a dead calm. Undiluted happiness is apt to become tedious. Life must have its ups and downs, and obstacles only sharpen the appetite and increase the enjoyment.

ZERBINETTE. Oh, Scapin, do tell us about the clever trick you played on that old skinflint, to cheat him of his money. You know how dearly I love a story.

SCAPIN. Sylvestre can tell you as well as I. I'm looking forward to a little revenge of my own, and want to work it out.

SYLVESTRE. You are a light-hearted devil! Why are you always getting into these mischievous scrapes?

SCAPIN. I'm addicted to living dangerously.

SYLVESTRE. If you take my advice, you'll give it up.

SCAPIN. Perhaps. But I'm going to take my own advice.

SYLVESTRE. What the devil is the fun to be now?

SCAPIN. What the devil is it to do with you?

SYLVESTRE. Only that I see you running the risk of a good thrashing for no reason at all.

SCAPIN. Well, it's my back will suffer, not yours.

SYLVESTRE. Oh, I admit that your back is your own property, and you can do what you like with it.

SCAPIN. I never consider that sort of risk. I hate these faint hearts who are always thinking of the consequences and never risk anything.

ZERBINETTE. We shall need your help too.

SCAPIN. I won't fail you. I'll join you presently. But no man shall boast he made me give myself away and blurt out other people's secrets into the bargain.

[SYLVESTRE, HYACINTHE *and* ZERBINETTE *go into a* II *house. Then enter* GÉRONTE.

GÉRONTE. Ah, well met, Scapin. Have you settled that business of my son?

SCAPIN. Your son, Sir, is safe enough. It's you who are in danger now, very great danger; and I would give a lot to see you safe again in your own house.

GÉRONTE. Why, what do you mean?

SCAPIN. At this very moment they are looking for you everywhere to do you in.

GÉRONTE. Me?

SCAPIN. Yes.

GÉRONTE. Who are they?

SCAPIN. You remember the brother of the girl Octave married? He believes that your ambition to supplant his sister by a daughter of your own is the main reason for annulling the marriage; and he has openly declared his intention of being revenged on you, and taking your life to avenge his honour. All his friends, soldiers of fortune like himself, are looking for you everywhere, and enquiring your whereabouts from everyone they meet. I've several times heard members of his band asking the passers-by, and there are patrols on all the roads leading to your house, so that you won't be able to go home, or stir a step to right or left without falling into their hands.

GÉRONTE. Oh, my good Scapin, what am I to do?

SCAPIN. I don't know, Monsieur. It's a fearful position for you to be in. I tremble all over when I think of it, and. . . .Wait, what's that? [going to back, as if to see if anyone is coming].

GÉRONTE [trembling]. What is it?

SCAPIN [coming back]. No, it's nothing.

GÉRONTE. Can't you think of any way to save me?

SCAPIN. There is one way; but I should run a great risk of being killed myself.

GÉRONTE. Oh, Scapin, now is your opportunity to prove yourself a faithful servant. Don't fail me, I beg of you.

SCAPIN. I don't want to, I have a high regard for you, as you know. I shouldn't like to think I had left you in the lurch.

GÉRONTE. You shan't go unrewarded, I promise you. You shall have this suit I'm wearing, when I've worn it a little longer.

SCAPIN. Listen. This is the scheme I've thought of. You must get into this sack, and. . . .

GÉRONTE. Oh, what's that?

SCAPIN. No, no, no, there's no one there. Get in here, and take care not to move a muscle. I'll hoist you on my back like a sack of goods, and carry you right through your enemies up to your own door. Once inside, we can barricade the house and send for help against these villains.

GÉRONTE. Yes. That's a good idea.

SCAPIN. It's perfect. You'll see in a minute. [*Aside*]. Now you are going to pay me back for that lie.

GÉRONTE. What's that you say?

SCAPIN. I was saying your enemies will be nicely taken in. Get well down, and, for Heaven's sake, don't show yourself or move an inch, whatever happens.

GÉRONTE. No, no. I'll take good care not to. . . .

SCAPIN. Inside, quick! [GÉRONTE *gets into the sack*]. Here's one of those cut-throats looking for you now. [*Disguising his voice*]. 'Will no one tell me where to find this Géronte, that I may rid the world of him?' [*In his natural voice*]. Don't move! [*The words in inverted commas are said in a disguised voice, the rest in his natural voice*]. 'Damnation! I'll find him though he's hiding in the bowels of the earth.' Don't show yourself. 'Hi there, man with the sack!' Sir. 'I'll give you a louis if you'll tell me where this Géronte is.' Do you want Seigneur Géronte? 'Yes, by God, I do want him!' What for, Sir? 'What for?' Yes. 'Hell and damnation! I'm going to beat him to death.' Oh, Sir, you can't beat a gentleman like him. He's not the kind of man to be treated like that. 'What, that villain of a Géronte, that knave, that scoundrel?' Seigneur Géronte, Sir, is neither a villain, knave nor scoundrel, and you ought not to speak so, if you please. 'What, you dare to bandy words with me?' I defend the character of a man of honour, Sir, as is my duty. 'Are you a friend of this Géronte then?' Yes, Monsieur I am. 'Death and Hell! you are a friend of his, are you? [*He thrashes* GÉRONTE *in the sack*]. Take that for him, then.' Oooh! ooh! Sir! oh! oh! Sir, gently, gently. Oooh! 'Go, take him that from me. Good day to you, Sir.' Oh, devil take the brute! Ooh!

GÉRONTE [*putting out his head*]. Oh, Scapin, I can't stand any more of this.

SCAPIN. Oh, Sir, my shoulders are a mass of bruises.

GÉRONTE. What? It was my shoulders he was hitting.

SCAPIN. No, no, mine, Sir.

GÉRONTE. What are you talking about? I felt the blows and can feel them still.

SCAPIN. No, no. It was only the end of the stick that touched you.

GÉRONTE. Well, couldn't you stand further away from the sack, so as to spare me. . . .

SCAPIN [*pushing his head down again into the sack*]. Look out, here comes another! He looks like a foreigner, 'Ouf! here haf I all day been zeeking, and cannot vind zis Géronte devil.' Keep your head well down. 'Ha, you, mine vriend, if you please, do you know vhere is zis Géronte I seek?' No, Sir, I haven't the least idea. 'Is zat really zo? I not vant much wiz him. Just to give him a leetle present of a dozen stripes or zo on ze back, and three or vour leetle zord thrusts through ze belly.' I assure you, Sir, I don't know where he is. 'I zink I zee zomezing move in zat zack.' There's nothing there, Sir. 'There is somezing zere, I'm zertain.' No, no, Sir. 'I haf desire pass my zord through zat zack.' No, no, please. 'Show me zen, you, vat is inzide.' Certainly not, Sir. 'Zertainly not?' You have no right to ask to see what I'm carrying. 'But I wish to zee it.' You shan't see it. 'Ah, zere's knafery here!' It's nothing but some old clothes that belong to me. 'Show me, zen.' I won't. 'You von't?' No. 'I'll gif you zen zis stick across your zhoulders.' I laugh at threats, Sir. 'Ho! You zink zat funny, eh?' [*He thrashes* GÉRONTE *in the sack*]. Oh! ooh! oh! ooh! Sir! oh! oh! ooh! 'Zats for you, mine vriend, to teach you to be inzolent.' Oh! Perdition take all foreigners! Ooh!

GÉRONTE [*putting out his head*]. I'm black and blue all over.

SCAPIN. Oh, I'm half-dead!

GÉRONTE. Why the devil must they thrash me.

SCAPIN [*pushing his head down again into the sack*]. Look out! Here come half a dozen of them, all together. [*Speaking as for several people*]. 'Come along, we must find this Géronte. Look everywhere. Don't spare shoe leather. Comb the whole town. Break in anywhere. Ransack every corner. Which way shall we go? This way. No. Down here. To the left. To the right. No, no. Yes, yes.' Keep yourself out of sight. 'Ah, friends, here's his valet! Come, fellow, you must tell us where your master is.' Oh, Gentlemen, don't hurt me! 'Come on, tell us where he is. Out with it at once. Be quick! Speak, man, speak.' Oh, Gentlemen, gently! [GÉRONTE *quietly puts his head out of the sack and sees* SCAPIN'S *trick*].

SCAPIN [*continues, not seeing him*]. 'If you don't bring us to your master at once, we'll give you the biggest thrashing you've ever had in your life.' I would rather suffer anything than betray my master. 'We'll beat you then.' I don't care. 'You want to be beaten?' I won't betray my master. 'Ah, so you will have it then, will you? There—' Oh! [*As he is about to strike,* GÉRONTE *comes out of the sack and* SCAPIN *takes to his heels*].

GÉRONTE. You treacherous, rascally villain! He's half killed me, the blackguard!

III   [ZERBINETTE *runs laughing out of the house*

ZERBINETTE [*not seeing* GÉRONTE]. Ha ha! I must have a breath of fresh air.

GÉRONTE [*aside*]. You shall pay for it, I promise you.

ZERBINETTE [*as before*]. Ha, ha, ha, ha! I never heard such a funny story. What a silly dupe the old man is!

GÉRONTE. It's not funny at all. Stop laughing, do you hear.

ZERBINETTE. Why, whatever do you mean, Sir?

GÉRONTE. You have no right to laugh at me.

ZERBINETTE. Laugh at you?

GÉRONTE. Yes.

ZERBINETTE. Whoever dreamt of laughing at you?

GÉRONTE. How dare you come here and laugh in my face?

ZERBINETTE. It has nothing to do with you. I was laughing at a story I have just heard. I don't know if it's because I'm concerned in the affair, but I've never heard anything so good as this trick a son has just played on his father to do him out of money.

GÉRONTE. A trick played by a son on his father to do him out of money?

ZERBINETTE. Yes. I have a great mind to tell you the whole thing. I love telling funny stories.

GÉRONTE. I should like very much to hear it.

ZERBINETTE. Very well then. There can't be any harm in my telling you, for it won't be long before it all comes out. I was brought up among a band of those people called gipsies, who wander all over the country telling fortunes, and frequently doing all sorts of other things as well. When we arrived in this town a young man saw me and fell in love with me. He followed me everywhere; and, like all young men, imagined that he had only to say the word and I should be his immediately. I happened to have a little self-respect, however, and he soon found out his mistake. He applied to the people I was travelling with, and they agreed to part with me for a sum of money. But unfortunately, my suitor was in the condition of so many sons of good families, extremely hard up. He has a father who, though rich enough, is a regular old stinge, the most awful old skinflint—Wait a minute! I should remember his name. You'll probably know. Can you think of anyone in this town particularly noted for being tight with his money?

GÉRONTE. No.

ZERBINETTE. His name ends with ron . . . ronte. . .Or-ronte. No Gé . . . Géronte; yes, Géronte. That's it. That's his name. That's the old fogey I mean. Well, to return to what I was saying. Our people were going to leave the town to-day, and my suitor would have lost me through want of money, if he hadn't been helped by a servant of his, who cunningly wheedled it out of his father. I remember the servant's name perfectly well. He is called Scapin; a gem of a man, who deserves all the praise he gets.

GÉRONTE [aside]. Oh, the scoundrel! the villain!

ZERBINETTE. This was the way he tricked the old fool. Ha! Ha! I can't think of it without laughing. [Laughing, holding her sides]. He went to this tight-fisted old creature and told him that, while walking with his son by the harbour, they had been invited on board a galley by a young Turk; and that, while they were being entertained below, the galley had put to sea, and he had been sent ashore in a skiff to tell the old man that, unless he immediately sent five hundred ecus, his son would be carried off to Algiers. Now the old fogey was in the most awful quandary, what with his affection for his son and his affection for his money.

The five hundred ecus were so many daggers in his heart. He couldn't make up his mind to part with so much, and his misery made him suggest a hundred ridiculous ways of ransoming his son. First he was for sending the law after the Turk on the high seas. Then he begged the valet to offer himself in his son's place, until he could get the money together, though of course he never intended to pay it. Then, to make-up the five hundred ecus, he was for sacrificing four or five old suits, which all together were not worth thirty. The valet pointed out the silliness of each suggestion, and the whole time he kept on moaning, 'But what the devil was he doing in that galley? Oh, cursed galley! Treacherous Turk!' In the end, after every kind of evasion, and many groans and sighs—But you're not laughing. Don't you think it's funny?

GÉRONTE. I think the young man is an insolent dog, who shall be well punished by his father for the trick he has played him; the gipsy girl a silly and impertinent minx to use such terms of a man of honour, who will teach her to come here and corrupt the sons of gentlemen; and the valet a rascal who, as sure as my name is Géronte, shall hang before to-morrow's dawn.

IV   [*He goes out. Enter* SYLVESTRE *from the house.*

SYLVESTRE. Where on earth have you been? Do you know you have just been talking to your suitor's father?

ZERBINETTE. Yes. I've just found it out. And, what's more, I've unwittingly told him the whole story.

SYLVESTRE. Told him the whole story?

ZERBINETTE. Yes. I was so full of it, I was dying to tell it again. But it doesn't matter. So much the worse for him! I can't see that it makes any difference one way or the other.

SYLVESTRE. You can never keep your mouth shut. What a tongue you must have to go blurting out your private affairs like that!

ZERBINETTE. Oh, well, he would soon have heard it from someone else.

ARGANTE [*outside*]. Ho, Sylvestre!   V

SYLVESTRE. Go into the house. There's my master calling.

[ZERBINETTE *goes into the house. Enter* ARGANTE.

ARGANTE. So you are all in league to fool me, are you, you, Scapin, and my son; and you think I'll put up with it?

SYLVESTRE. God's truth, Sir, if Scapin has fooled you, it's nothing to do with me. I know nothing about it.

ARGANTE. I shall find you out, you rascal. I shall find you out. I don't intend to be made a fool of.

[*Enter* GÉRONTE.   VI

GÉRONTE. Ah, Seigneur Argante, a terrible thing has happened!

ARGANTE. A dreadful thing has happened to me too.

GÉRONTE. That rogue Scapin has cheated me out of five hundred ecus.

ARGANTE. That same rogue Scapin has cheated me out of two hundred pistoles.

GÉRONTE. And, not content with cheating me out of five hundred ecus, he has treated me in a way I am ashamed to speak of. But he shall pay for it.

ARGANTE. He shall certainly pay for the trick he has played me.

GÉRONTE. I mean to make an example of him.

SYLVESTRE [*aside*]. Please God I don't have any share in this!

GÉRONTE. But that's not all yet, Seigneur Argante. One misfortune is always followed by another. I was comforting myself to-day with the thought of having my beloved daughter with me again; and now my man tells me that she left Taranto a long time ago, and is thought to have gone down with the ship she sailed in.

ARGANTE. But why, if I may ask, did you keep her at Taranto, and deny yourself the pleasure of having her with you?

GÉRONTE. I had my reasons for that. Family considerations obliged me until now to keep my second marriage secret. But what is this?

VII　　　　[*Enter* NÉRINE.

NÉRINE [*throwing herself at* GÉRONTE'S *feet*]. Oh, Seigneur Pandolphe. . . .

GÉRONTE. Call me Géronte, and use that name no more. The reasons which obliged me to take it at Taranto exist no longer.

NÉRINE. Alas! It is this change of name that has made it so hard for us to find you here.

GÉRONTE. Where is my daughter and her mother?

NÉRINE. Your daughter, Sir, is here nearby. But, before you see her, I must beg your forgiveness for allowing her to marry. Being unable to find you, we were utterly destitute.

GÉRONTE. My daughter married?

NÉRINE. Yes, Sir.

GÉRONTE. And to whom?

NÉRINE. To a young man named Octave, son of a certain Seigneur Argante.

GÉRONTE. Heavens above!

ARGANTE. What a coincidence!

GÉRONTE. Take us to her at once.

NÉRINE. You have only to enter this house.

GÉRONTE. Lead the way, then. Come with me, come with me, Seigneur Argante.

　　　　[GÉRONTE, ARGANTE *and* NÉRINE *go into the house.*

SYLVESTRE. What an absolutely amazing discovery!

[*Enter* SCAPIN. VIII

SCAPIN. Hola, Sylvestre! How are our friends getting on?

SYLVESTRE. I have two bits of news for you. First, that Octave's business is comfortably settled. Our Hyacinthe turns out to be the daughter of Seigneur Géronte, and Fate has brought about the very thing the two fathers had planned. The other is that the two old men are threatening a dreadful revenge against you, particularly Seigneur Géronte.

SCAPIN. Oh, that's nothing to worry about. Threats have never done me any harm. They're like clouds sailing far above our heads.

SYLVESTRE. Well, look out for yourself. The sons will easily make it up with their fathers and leave you in the lurch.

SCAPIN. I'll soon find a way to pacify them, and. . . .

SYLVESTRE. Run. They're coming out now.

[SCAPIN *goes out quickly. Then, from the house, re-enter* IX
GÉRONTE, ARGANTE, HYACINTHE, ZERBINETTE
and NÉRINE.

GÉRONTE. Come, daughter, come home with me. My happiness had been complete if only your mother were with you.

ARGANTE. Here's Octave in the nick of time.

[*Enter* OCTAVE. X

Come, my son, come and rejoice with us over the happy business of your marriage. Heaven. . . .

OCTAVE. No, father; all your proposals of marriage will be useless. They have told you that I am married already, and. . . .

ARGANTE. Yes, but you don't know. . . .

OCTAVE. I know all I need to know.

ARGANTE. I want to tell you that the daughter of Seigneur Géronte. . .

OCTAVE. The daughter of Seigneur Géronte will never be anything to me.

GÉRONTE. It is she. . . .

OCTAVE. No, Sir. I am sorry, but I have quite made up my mind.

SYLVESTRE. Listen. . . .

OCTAVE. No. Be silent. I won't hear a word.

ARGANTE. Your wife. . . .

OCTAVE. No, father, I will rather die than leave my darling Hyacinthe. [*Going to stand beside her*]. Nothing you can say will move me. There she stands to whom my heart is given. I will love her all my life, and I will never have any other wife.

ARGANTE. Well, you've got her. What a silly fellow it is to keep harping on the same string!

HYACINTHE [*indicating* GÉRONTE]. Yes, Octave, there is my father found; and all our troubles are over.

GÉRONTE. Come home with me, all of you, and we can hear the whole story in comfort.

HYACINTHE [*indicating* ZERBINETTE]. Oh, father, don't let me be separated from this charming girl. You will love her when you know her better.

GÉRONTE. What, you expect me to take into my house a person with whom your brother is in love, and who has just roundly abused me to my face?

ZERBINETTE. I beg you'll forgive me, Sir; I wouldn't have said it if I'd known who you were. I only knew you by reputation.

GÉRONTE. How? What reputation?

HYACINTHE. Father, my brother's love for her is honourable, and I can vouch for her good character.

GÉRONTE. Here's a nice thing! You would have my son marry a vagabond girl from no one knows where?

[*Enter* LÉANDRE.　　　　　　　　　　　　　　　　XI

LÉANDRE. Father, you have no cause to complain that I love an unknown girl, without family or fortune. The gipsies have just told me that she was born in this town and of a good family. They stole her at the age of four. Here is a bracelet they have given me to help us find her parents.

ARGANTE. Let me see that bracelet. I lost my daughter at the age you mention.

GÉRONTE. Your daughter?

ARGANTE [*looking at the bracelet*]. Yes. It is she. I can see a likeness in her, which makes me sure of it.

HYACINTHE. Oh, Heavens! What a wonderful coincidence!

[*Enter* CARLE.　　　　　　　　　　　　　　　　XII

CARLE. Oh, Gentlemen, there has been a terrible accident.

GÉRONTE. What is it?

CARLE. Poor Scapin. . . .

GÉRONTE. A knave I mean to hang.

CARLE. Alas, Sir, you won't have the trouble. As he was walking beneath a scaffolding, a stonemason's hammer fell on his head and smashed his skull, laying bare all his brains. He is going fast, and he has begged us to bring him here to speak to you before he dies.

ARGANTE. Where is he?

CARLE. Here he is.

[SCAPIN *is brought in by two men, his head swathed in*　XIII
bandages, as if he had been injured].

SCAPIN. Ooh! ooh! Gentlemen, I am going to my last resting place. Ooh! I could not die without asking pardon of all those I have offended. Ooh! Yes, Gentlemen, before I breathe my last I earnestly beg you will forgive me all the wrong I have done you, in particular Seigneur Argante and Seigneur Géronte. Ooh! ooh!

ARGANTE. Very well, I forgive you. Die in peace.

SCAPIN [*to* GÉRONTE]. It is you I have offended most, Sir, by the beating that. . . .

GÉRONTE. Say no more about it. I forgive you too.

SCAPIN. It was an outrageous liberty for me to beat. . . .

GÉRONTE. It was nothing.

SCAPIN. It's an unspeakable grief to me in my last moments to think of the beating that. . . .

GÉRONTE. Be quiet!

SCAPIN. That unlucky beating that I. . . .

GÉRONTE. Be quiet, I tell you. It's forgotten.

SCAPIN. Oh, how generous you are! Do you really mean, Sir, that you forgive me that beating that I. . . .

GÉRONTE. Yes, yes. Don't mention it again, I forgive you everything. It's all over and done with.

SCAPIN. Ah, Sir, I feel better already, since you told me that.

GÉRONTE. Yes, but I only forgive you on condition that you die.

SCAPIN. What, Sir?

GÉRONTE. I take back my promise if you recover.

SCAPIN. Oh! Ooh! my weakness is stealing over me again.

ARGANTE. Seigneur Géronte, we are all so happy that, for our sakes, you must forgive him unconditionally.

GÉRONTE. Oh, very well.

ARGANTE. Come, let us all dine together to celebrate our good fortune.

SCAPIN. And carry *me* to a place at the end of the table, while I wait for death to overtake me.

EXPLANATORY NOTES

2 *a certain well-known proverb*: most editors suggest that Molière had in mind a saying often applied to actresses: 'she's only beautiful by candlelight'; but he may also be alluding to the proverb 'the game's not worth the candle'.

2 *'O tempora! O mores!'*: 'What times! What customs'; Cicero, *In Catalinam* I. i. 2 (Molière quotes this tag in French).

3 *Trivelino*: a clown of Italian comedy who acts the part of a judge in some plays.

7 *Aronce . . . Clélie . . . matter of course*: Molière's satire is directed here against those who made a cult of certain novels in vogue, notably Mlle de Scudéry's *Artamène ou le grand Cyrus* (10 vols., 1649–53) and her *Clélie* (10 vols., 1654–60), both of which were immensely long (*le grand Cyrus* has over 13,000 pages) and which tell of heroines whose suitors marry them (on the last page) after protracted and eventful courtships. The progress of the love affair is charted by a delicate and subtle analysis of the emotions which is allegorized in *Clélie* as an itinerary on a map (the 'Carte de Tendre'). It is easy to see how such a form of writing might give rise to inappropriate or excessive applications of such theories to real life: indeed, it seems as though the 'Carte de Tendre' itself was a codification of the rules of human intercourse imposed by Mlle de Scudéry on her friends.

8 *unknown worlds to them*: see above. These are allegorical places on the Carte de Tendre.

10 *Cirrus the Great*: see note to p. 7.

12 *petit coucher*: a royal ceremony (the King's retirement to bed) at which only his intimates and members of the highest nobility were allowed to be present.

13 *Amilcar*: a character in *Clélie*. See note to p. 7.

14 *Poetical Miscellany*: the *Recueil des plus beaux vers de ce temps* (1659) was the first of many collections of fashionable verse.

19 *Great Comedians*: the Grands Comédiens of the Hôtel de Bourgogne were Molière's main theatrical rivals in Paris. They were already well established there when he returned to the capital in 1658, and they specialized in tragedy. In his *Impromptu de Versailles* of 1663, Molière parodies their orotund acting manner.

20 *Perdrigeon*: the fashionable haberdasher of the day.

22 *a little pale*: Jodelet as a character part performed with his face masked with white flour.

23 *half-moon ... full moon*: a half-moon is a form of military fortification.

35 *Sardanapulus*: an Assyrian king, d. 876 BC, who was noted for his luxury, licentiousness and womanizing.

38 *Alexander*: Alexander the Great (356–323 BC), conqueror of Greece, Persia, Egypt, and parts of India.

61 *Father Christmas*: Molière's text has 'le moine bourru': a figure of dread or bogeyman, who, according to popular superstition, might be met in the streets in mid-winter, foretelling disaster.

193 *limping cur*: the actor Béjart, who played the part of La Flèche, became lame shortly before the first performance of the play.

205 *Gombaud and Macée*: a common genre subject taken from a novel in vogue in the early years of the seventeenth century (hence outmoded).

206 *Panurge*: a character in Rabelais's *Gargantua and Pantagruel* (see especially bk. III, ch. 2).

277 *Barbara ... Baralipton*: figures of scholastic logic or syllogisms as recorded in a medieval mnemonic, in which the vowels in each world stand for different sorts of proposition (universal, particular; positive, negative).

278 *A, E, I, O, U*: these vowels are of course to be pronounced as in French.

326 *lingua franca*: the language spoken in ports throughout the Mediterranean area.

American Literature

British and Irish Literature

Children's Literature

Classics and Ancient Literature

Colonial Literature

Eastern Literature

European Literature

Gothic Literature

History

Medieval Literature

Oxford English Drama

Poetry

Philosophy

Politics

Religion

The Oxford Shakespeare

A complete list of Oxford World's Classics, including Authors in Context, Oxford English Drama, and the Oxford Shakespeare, is available in the UK from the Marketing Services Department, Oxford University Press, Great Clarendon Street, Oxford OX2 6DP, or visit the website at www.oup.com/uk/worldsclassics.

In the USA, visit www.oup.com/us/owc for a complete title list.

Oxford World's Classics are available from all good bookshops. In case of difficulty, customers in the UK should contact Oxford University Press Bookshop, 116 High Street, Oxford OX1 4BR.